The Eighteenth Century
Confronts the
Gods

The Eighteenth Century Confronts the Gods

FRANK E. MANUEL

HARVARD UNIVERSITY PRESS

Cambridge, Massachusetts

1959

WITHDRAWN
UTSA LIBRARIES

© 1959 by the President and Fellows of Harvard College

Distributed in Great Britain by Oxford University Press, London

Publication of this book has been aided
by a grant from the Ford Foundation

Library of Congress Catalog Card Number 59–10318

Printed in the United States of America

In memoriam
SIMON RAWIDOWICZ

Preface

THIS BOOK deals with one of the oldest problems in the history of Western civilization — the nature of the gods. The idea for the study first occurred to me while reading Werner Jaeger's description of ancient rationalistic theory in *The Theology of the Early Greek Philosophers*. The affinity between Sophist and Enlightenment thought, to which Professor Jaeger there alludes in passing, challenged me. I set out to discover what had happened to the accumulated reflections on the origins of the gods by the eighteenth century, an age whose moral philosophy has occupied me for many years. The literary essays and scholarly treatises which were concerned with the pagan gods and their myths either directly or indirectly turned out to be voluminous, far more extensive than I had ever imagined. In time the theories, conjectures, and erudite exercises — orthodox and impious — which initially had appeared bewildering in their multiplicity and diversity grouped themselves into a finite number of patterns. These became the basis for the various chapters. Moreover, a historical sequence from one type of theory to another, at least a shift in emphasis, was discernible during the course of the century (a time period which for purposes of my problem begins roughly with Halley's comet in 1680 and runs through the French Revolution). The combination of an ideational and a chronological framework thus seemed eminently suited to the subject.

As a method of presentation an essay form which selects examples and suggests general lines of development but does not pretend to bibliographical exhaustiveness was deliberately chosen. There has been no attempt to duplicate the long lists of titles in the relevant sections of pioneer works like Otto Gruppe, *Geschichte*

der klassischen Mythologie und Religionsgeschichte, and Henri
Pinard de la Boullaye, *L'étude comparée des religions.* This effort
properly belongs to the history of ideas in the eighteenth century;
it is oriented neither toward the growth of classical scholarship nor
toward the development of the science of anthropology. And
though I have been interested in the iconography of the baroque,
I do not presume to invade the technical field of the art historian.

While the confrontation with the gods may not appear to be
pivotal in the traditional treatment of the major eighteenth-
century thinkers, it is my belief that in this inquiry, broadly
interpreted, the age reveals many of its deep-felt convictions as
well as its harrowing doubts. Eighteenth-century writers were
notoriously oblique; ideas of the gods often covered other concerns. Sometimes the question caught the age off guard; men told
more about themselves than they had intended. The *philosophes*
were always "unveiling" — scores of their works purport to "unveil" the primitive world, Antiquity, Christianity, the religious
Mysteries, Platonism, Nature. Now their turn too has come.

Research for this book was conducted originally in the Boston
area, in the libraries of Harvard University, the Boston Athe-
naeum, and the Boston Public Library, and to their staffs I owe
deep gratitude. A sabbatical leave from Brandeis University and a
Guggenheim Fellowship permitted me to consult the major
European collections. In Cambridge, England, the librarians of
Trinity and King's College were especially gracious in making
Newton's papers accessible. The British Museum in London, the
Bibliothèque Nationale, the Bibliothèque Mazarine, and the
Bibliothèque de l'Institut de France in Paris, the Bibliotheca
Nazionale Centrale Vittorio Emmanuele and the Biblioteca
Casanatense in Rome, the Biblioteca Nazionale Centrale in
Florence, the Biblioteca Nazionale in Naples, the Biblioteca
Nazionale Marciana in Venice, and the Österreichische National-
bibliothek in Vienna allowed me to fill lacunae when the works
were not available in America. Benedetto Croce's library in Naples
and the Zentralinstitut für Kunstgeschichte in Munich yielded
special items. For a number of months the library of the Pontificio
Istituto Biblico in Rome, with its excellently organized collection
on the history of religion, afforded me easy access to a wide variety

of sources. My eye was peeled for eighteenth-century images of the gods, and I occasionally found them in unlikely places: in an eighteenth-century engraving in the Jewish Museum in Prague; in John Adams' marginalia in his books in the Boston Public Library; in Newton's manuscripts in Cambridge; in Vico's annotations in copies of his works in Naples.

When eighteenth-century English translations of foreign languages exist I have tended to use them — with revisions — in order to preserve the flavor of the epoch. Other translations are my own, with one notable exception, the superb rendering into English of Vico's *Scienza Nuova* by Thomas G. Bergin and Max H. Fisch.

Colleagues both in America and abroad have been guides on specific points: I thank Fausto Nicolini, Dr. W. Mrazek, and Professors Giorgio de Santillana, Carlo Antoni, Leo Gershoy, Edward W. Fox, and Herbert Dieckmann for their assistance. I particularly remember a number of illuminating conversations on primitive religion with the late Paul Radin. Professors Crane Brinton and Claude Vigée read the manuscript, and I hope I have incorporated their perceptive suggestions. Professor David Berkowitz read the galleys and preserved me from numerous infelicities. Finally, I should like to mention the members of my seminar at Brandeis, who helped me to clarify my ideas: I have included facts first called to my attention by Mr. Harvey Fischtrom, Mr. Joseph S. Murphy, and Mr. Jonathan Schwartz.

The etching of the gods has already served as a frontispiece twice before, once for the idéologue of the Directorate Citoyen Charles Dupuis in 1795 and again for the Jesuit scholar Pinard de la Boullaye in 1922. May it preside over the fortunes of my work with no less favor.

Frank E. Manuel

Contents

CHAPTER VI

COUNTERATTACK FROM THE EAST

Illustrations

Introductory

"'Tis a Discourse of *Religion*, in a time when we have scarce any other Theme; 'tis grown so general a Mode, that even the Sword-men are now fiercer disputants than heretofore the lazier Gown-men were, while every Spark of noise enough, (sometimes the best of the Argument) shews his Wit and Learning on that subject. But since the stream runs that way, I believed it ridiculous to appear in good company drest like Mrs. *Abigail*, as (at this time) not to be arguing some points of Religion, tho never so *Mal à propo*. But least, by such an undertaking I should, as many do, but the more embarass the Mysteries of it, we shall treat here only of the *Pagan Religion*, and of the abominable Cheats of the Oracles and their Priests."

> — The Epistle Dedicatory, *The History of Oracles and the Cheats of the Pagan Priests*. In Two Parts. Made English. London, 1688.

*F*IFTEEN CENTURIES after the Church Fathers had valiantly routed the pagan deities and their philosophical apologists, Jupiter had returned in triumph to the realms of the most Christian kings of Europe. The château of Versailles was adorned with gracious images of the gods of Greece and Rome, while Christ and the saints were severely restricted to the chapel. Baroque frescoes depicting an alien pantheon, Christianized with the wand of allegory to be sure, decorated the ceilings of the great chambers in the new monastery at Melk and the magnificent royal library in Vienna. The coaches of aristocratic travelers and princes of the church were bedecked with voluptuous Venuses. Not a gilded mirror from the atelier of a Florentine artisan or a delicate piece of china from the manufactory of Josiah Wedgwood but displayed a coy little nymph or a cavorting satyr. In a Paris salon exposition of the 1750's mythological subjects outnumbered the sacred, and even the religious paintings were pagan in spirit. Jews, who for centuries had fiercely defended themselves against Christianity, were now occasionally tainted by pagan imagery. In a triumphal procession lavishly celebrating their re-entry into Prague after the lifting of the imperial ban, a rollicking Bacchus was pulled among the revelers.

When the nobility learned its letters the bards and philosophers of antiquity took precedence over the medieval Christian schoolmen. The poet in his similes invariably had recourse to the attributes of the pagan divinities. Translations from the classics were illustrated with lewd engravings of the gods. The new rendering of Ovid's *Métamorphoses* (1732) by the eminently respectable Abbé Banier of the Académie des Inscriptions et

3

Belles-Lettres, with figures by Bernard Picart, produced a perfect specimen of the art of bookmaking and satisfied a variety of tastes. In the theater, audiences wept with the heroes and heroines of a heathen world brought to the stage by Corneille and Racine. The opera house resounded with the melodies of Gluck's *Orpheus and Eurydice,* and the young prince of Mozart's *Zauberflöte* endured his trials to be initiated into the wisdom of Isis and Osiris. In outlining an ideal education for his daughter in a famous passage of *Le Neveu de Rameau,* Diderot included mythology as a respected and useful branch of learning, on a par with dancing.

With Christian symbols relegated to ecclesiastical performances, the men and women of the great families behaved, or so they fancied, like contemporaries of Augustus. In their debauches the Regent of France and his favorite cardinal revived the bacchanalia of the ancients. The literate urban gentleman and the wealthy bourgeois lived in imitation of the twelve greater divinities rather than Jesus and the Apostles. In their play the *philosophes* bestowed upon one another mythological nicknames: Claude-Adrien Helvétius was the son of Apollo, Jean-Philippe Rameau was Euclid-Orpheus, Argental and Antoine de Ferriol were Castor and Pollux, Madame du Châtelet was Vénus-Newton, a new syncretism, and Voltaire himself was Attis. Neoclassic canons of taste dominated the style of life, and if there were alien intrusions, violations of propriety and decorum, they came from "romantick" and not Christian sources. In the *honnête homme,* that uneasy compromise between the ideals of an other-worldly religion and Greco-Roman forms, the pagan had usurped the better part of man's fantasy.

The degree to which absorption with pagan artifacts was driving out the Christian word is exemplified in a long autobiographical passage in Dom Bernard de Montfaucon's *L'Antiquité expliquée et représentée en figures.* Some thirty years before, he recalled in 1719, his Benedictine superiors had instructed him to prepare an edition of the Greek Fathers, but he soon discovered that he could not annotate the revered texts without a thorough knowledge of paganism to help him elucidate their recondite classical allusions. He had therefore interrupted his labors to prepare himself by studying the whole corpus of classical literature. Soon he became completely immersed in the ancient world, its medals, statues, cameos, vases, and coins, the attributes of its gods and their protean shapes, and he published fifteen folio volumes on the explication of antiquity — while the Greek Fathers moldered.

The Abbé Noël Antoine Pluche, author of the *Histoire du ciel considéré selon les idées des poètes, des philosophes et de Moyse* (1739–41), one of the widely read vulgarizations of learning, was painfully aware of the iniquitous influence which the gods and goddesses of antiquity were exerting upon his contemporaries. The doctrine of association had penetrated his pious soul and had roused him to the religious perils which threatened the Christians of Europe, dallying among the pagans far more often than they contemplated the lives of the saints or worshiped at the feet of the Virgin and the holy martyrs. "Men pass away their youth among the gods. At their leaving the schools, they find them again on the stage, where they speak a language which requires no master, nor any application to be understood. All public shows repeat their adventures. You find them in your cantatas, songs, in the decorations of your apartments, gardens, and public squares. Engravings, pictures, poems, music, pleasant writings, learned dissertations, all in short conspire to show us under an honorable and pleasing outside, actions punished by the laws, and absurdities diametrically opposite to common sense. All these cares, and considerable expenses, aim not at persuading us of the reality of Jupiter's gallantries: but their intention is, under borrowed names, and the shelter of a mask, to fill our thoughts with pleasures, and indulge our passions." But how did the Abbé Pluche combat this wallowing of the minds of his generation "in a continual series of wanton sports?" [1] He too wrote a book on the explication of mythology.

Since the gods were ubiquitous there was a natural desire to know them more intimately. What did these divinities signify? How were the various figures to be identified? A body of learning had accumulated since the Renaissance which collated pagan myths from a variety of sources, explained their "meaning," and described the attributes of the gods. Some writings were rather technical. Compendia by Boccaccio, Gregorius Gyraldus, Cesare Ripa, and Natalis Comes had become indispensable works of reference for poets, orators, painters, architects, sculptors, and composers. In the 1780's the iconographic tradition was still maintained by Gravelot and Cochin's *Iconologie par figures ou Traité complet de la Science des Allégories en 350 figures.* There was also a steady outpouring of more popular mythological dictionaries in all languages for the education of laymen. Bell's *New Pantheon* (1790) was a typical English compilation. At the very height of the Revolution in 1793 Millin de Grandmaison sold a twelve-volume *Mythologie mise à la portée de tout le monde.* Of course interest in the gods of Greece and Rome was sometimes a mere pretext for pornographic illustration — the works of Pierre d'Hancarville on ancient gems for example, or the *Almanach érotique* (1787), subtitled *L'Amour à l'Olympe ou le Triomphe de Cupidon sur les dieux et les déesses.*

But though mythography was often intended to amuse and to appease the curiosity of gallants and their ladies, an important body of eighteenth-century thought on the nature of the gods was of a wholly different character. It was devoted to the explanation of ancient myth as a study of high seriousness. In these writings the "pagan gods" were not limited to the classical world of the eastern Mediterranean; paganism encompassed the deities of nations civilized and savage, ancient and modern, on all five continents. The science of mythology broke the bounds of classical antiquity and came to be related first to the investigation of primitive religion and soon to the fundamental psychic problem of the age, the very nature of religion itself. Indifference in matters of religion was rare. Paradoxically one might call the epoch of Voltaire and Hume the last religious century. Interpretations of myth and naturalistic theories of the birth of the gods were invariably dragged into the great trial of Christianity. The contestants summoned aboriginal man as the first witness to the truth or falsity of revealed religion. Even the more abstruse and esoteric researches into the origin of primitive religion and the meaning of myth disguised soul-searching inquiries into human nature.

There was a profusion of empirical data on world religions. As the sixteenth- and seventeenth-century compendia, works like Paolo Morigi's *Historia dell'origine di tutte le religioni che sin ad hora sono state* (1569), Purchas' *Pilgrimage* (1613), and Alexander Ross's *A View of all Religions in the World* (1653), became

outmoded, voluminous encyclopedias of religion enlisted popular
writers and talented engravers. The nine folios of the *Cérémonies
et coutumes religieuses de tous les peuples du monde* (1723–1743)
was perhaps the most lavish production in this field, but it had
competitors in English, Italian, and German. Throughout the
eighteenth century travel relations kept pouring in upon Europe,
as they had ever since the end of the Middle Ages, describing the
religious behavior and doctrines of civilized and primitive peoples
in all four corners of the earth. Sacred texts from the East were
translated and commented upon for the first time, cult objects
identified, exotic myths of both Indies narrated and elucidated.
The literary effusion depicting the varieties of religious experience
became a veritable cataract by mid-century. Formal expeditions to
Greece, Turkey, and Egypt were supported by academies for the
specific purpose of gathering the unpublished religious documents
of oriental heathens into royal libraries. Though a parochial debate had been dragging on since the late seventeenth century over
whether a nation of atheists could exist, nobody disagreed with
the proposition that the overwhelming number of societies had in
fact performed religious rites. A second question, the interpretation of the rituals and the explanation of their origins in human
nature, was, as Hume wrote in his classical understatement of the
problem, "exposed to some more difficulty."

Since naturalistic theories of the gods were first taught by the
pre-Socratics and the Sophists a wide diversity of schools of mythology and conjectures on the inception of religion had grown up
in Western society. Over the centuries the classical Christian doctrines had experienced changing fortunes, periods of exclusive
dominance and moments of total eclipse. Some of the more unorthodox systems had only recently been revived after a long
dormancy. The gods were born of fear with Democritus, Epicurus,
Lucretius, Spinoza, and Hobbes; the gods were born of gratitude
with Proclus; they were political inventions of statecraft with
Critias; heroes or rulers apotheosized with Euhemerus; allegories
of virtues and vices with Plato, the Stoics, the medieval commentators, the Renaissance Neoplatonists; embodiments of demons or
fallen angels with the Church Fathers. Or the myths were corruptions of sacred history, and sound seventeenth-century scholarship

with its etymological virtuosity could trace each god back to a
Hebrew patriarch or to the chance misreading of an obscure Biblical name.

During the course of the eighteenth century the voluminous
literary heritage from antiquity on the nature of the gods, in
authors like Herodotus, Cicero, Lucretius, Diodorus Siculus,
Plutarch, Lucian, Pausanias, Clement, Eusebius, was made even
more accessible to ordinary philosophical gentlemen who had
small Latin and less Greek by a steady outpouring of new translations from the classics and the Fathers. By 1700 it was not necessary to be very learned to enter the field of mythography and
weave a fantasy about the religion of the pagan postdiluvians,
though a Greek etymology, not to speak of a Hebrew one or
phrases from the Coptic and the Chaldean, lent great weight to
erudite fancies and appeared to ground them in the solid soil of
language. A Greek text was commonplace, a bombardment of rabbinic dicta in Hebrew more telling, but a Phoenician source carried the field. Eighteenth-century mythographers blandly lifted
ideas from the whole corpus of Greek and Latin and medieval
Judaic theory (Maimonides' *Avoda Zara* in Latin was a favorite)
with or without citations from authority as the spirit moved them.
Of course a learned Anglican bishop, or the great Newton, who
could get his folios printed without difficulty, was more profuse
with his baroque display of quotations from the ancients than a
hapless grubstreet Deist in his meager pamphlets, but their deriva-
tion was the same. Throughout the century the presses of Europe
kept pouring out recondite Latin dissertations on the myths and
practices of the pagan religions, based on compilations from the
classical corpus. Venice, Paris and Leipzig were centers of publication for this erudition by clerics and gentleman-scholars who usually spent themselves in one or two learned treatises. There was an
equally vast literature, primarily English and Dutch, on the idolatrous practices mentioned in the Bible. With the aid of rabbinic
sources a valiant effort was made to identify, describe, and catalogue the abominable rituals which were merely named in the
Hebrew text. The same passion for collecting which lay behind
the gathering of botanical specimens and culminated in Linnaeus
possessed the scholars who grouped the rituals and "superstitious"
practices of universal paganism.

Though a good part of this learning was devoid of broad concepts and was too casual and shallow to be of lasting worth, there was also a rich philosophical literature on the gods which was of central significance in Enlightenment thought. Of the major forms of ancient theory on the nature of the gods — the psychological, the Euhemerist-historical, the allegorical, and the demonological — the last virtually disappeared from eighteenth-century thought, since even the orthodox had ceased to consider demons efficient agents of human action. The witchcraft trials were late seventeenth-century phenomena. Father Jean François Baltus, who wrote an attack on Fontenelle's *Histoire des Oracles* from the vantage point of patristic demonology, breathed the last gasp of this doctrine under Louis XIV. Learned English divines, surrounded and harassed on all sides by infidel Deists, only rarely invoked the demons; they do not appear in the *mémoires* of the Académie des Inscriptions et Belles-Lettres — no one would have violated the canons of good taste.

Though the fortunes of allegorism were more complicated and its residual existence more protracted, the bulk of eighteenth-century thought on the origins of religion and the significance of myth was divided between the Euhemerist-historical and the psychological schools, the fundamental alternatives which still remain open to the analyst of religion, and these are the two traditions which figure most prominently in the present volume.

While the geographic bounds of this study are the continent of Europe, the major thinkers selected for illustration are French, English, Dutch, German, and Italian. Until the emergence of the Frenchifiers at the end of the century Spain was too traditionalist to participate in this hazardous inquiry, and when the problem was finally raised in the Royal Academy in Madrid the solution advanced was Euhemerist and stereotyped.[2] To the limited extent that clericalism in the Austrian heart of the Hapsburg Empire allowed for theory, the allegorist tradition, formalized and hardened by Jesuit masters, was dominant until the spiritual revolution of Joseph II. As a general rule the French, English, and Dutch thinkers constituted one intellectual world, from which the Italians and the Germans tended to be excluded. The waves of influence in the eighteenth century moved eastward across the Rhine and southward across the Alps. While the creative Germans in the far corner of the Baltic imbibed the voluminous outpourings of the western *philosophes,* their ideas were for the most part without recognition in England and France until the current was tumultuously reversed in the succeeding centuries. The two frontier societies of Europe, America and Russia, were still ill-prepared for serious original reflection on the nature of man and his gods. The echoes of the European debate in John Adams' marginalia and in his correspondence serve only as a scherzo.

Three of the greatest minds of the eighteenth century are central figures in this study — Newton, Vico, and Hume; others are on the periphery — Voltaire, Rousseau, and Diderot; the two giants of the Germanic world, Leibnitz and Kant, were virtually uninvolved, though Leibnitz did write notes in refutation of Toland, and Kant committed himself to a teleology of progress from the instinctual savage to the rational human of the future. Neither Rousseau, who simply accepted the historical primacy of polytheism in *Emile,* nor Voltaire, who wrote the trite *Dialogues d'Evhémère,* had anything novel to say on the subject. For the most part lesser men occupy the center of the stage, men closer not to the mass of the people but to the average educated intellectual of the age.

Throughout this work the idea of progress is related to the study of theories of mythology and primitive religion. Though the concept was fed from many sources, above all the steady accumulation of scientific knowledge, technological innovations, and industrial-commercial expansion throughout the globe, the discovery and elaboration of the character of primitive mentality is fundamental to rationalist progressism. One of the central themes of this book is the slow growth of the idea of a primitive mind and its relation to the contemporary; perhaps this was the most significant result of the investigation of the nature of myth and early religious experience. *Le rêve exotique,* romantic primitivism, the cult of the noble savage, was only one western European response to the barbaric world, not the predominant or the most enduring. The happier savages usually come from the warmer climates, and the Arcadian motifs increase with the exploration and conquest of the southern seas. There are gentle and sexually free Epicurean primitives and there are noble, brave, and self-possessed Stoic

primitives in eighteenth-century literature, but there are also terror-stricken savages who are neither happy nor strong. In seeking
for the origins of religion one important group of theorists tended
to select this latter type for illustration. Though for some the contemplation of childlike primitives was a regressive fantasy, for
others it was a challenge to action. The primitive was always a foil
for the man of reason, the official posture of the age.

Progress in the Turgot-Condorcet sense proclaimed the ban-
ishment of myth, the substitution of reason and its mathematical
language for the mythopoeic mind. The arrogant assumption of
superiority over the backward areas of the world which has characterized European thought and behavior in modern times   required a full-blown theory of the primitive to serve as a contrapuntal theme to the affirmation of triumphant Reason. This work
will demonstrate that such a doctrine did not await contemporary
scientific sociological and anthropological studies. The philosophical and intuitive expression of evolutionary concepts preceded their empirical demonstration.

The Turgot-Condorcet theory of progress was a rationalist
prophecy concerning the end of days, even as the eighteenth-
century conjectures, myths if you like, on the birth of the gods
were a substitute for Genesis. Together they formed one historical
world-view. If the eighteenth-century myth of origins ultimately
destroyed the ancient gods, pagan and Christian, *les progrès* became the new deities of the age, and the late eighteenth-century
definition of their attributes is in many respects canonical for
modern times. But the *philosophes* of mid-century were not converted to the new gods without suffering moments of critical scepticism. As they unveiled the benighted primitive, Bayle, Fontenelle, Vico, Hume, de Brosses, Boulanger, and Holbach amply
demonstrated their ambivalence toward the idea of progress. It
was not until the very end of the century in Condorcet that the
new heaven was finally accepted, virtually without a recrudescence
of doubt.

The nature of primitive mentality and its counterpart, the
meaning of rational progress, are not intelligible universes of discourse outside of a historical framework. Like the clouds of Ham-
let or the somewhat more stable inkblots, myths are such vague

and amorphous configurations that an epoch invariably tends to project itself into them. A progress, too, is a hope defined within the narrow limits of the obsessive desires of a specific age. The primitive mythic mind is lost forever; but every century has fantasies about its unknowable ancestors, and these are closer to our understanding. The long array of mythographers of the past twenty-five hundred years, from Democritus and Hecataeus of Miletus through Jung, all bear the distinctive physiognomies of their age. Present-day inquiries into the few remaining primitive societies have revealed the investigators more often than the savages. The contemporary who describes the primordial function of the myth in either a sociological or a psychic context often says more about his own attitude toward moral problems, toward progress, God and the devil, toward reason and the uses of the imagination than he does about the mind of aboriginal man.

This is a study of the eighteenth-century mind and sensibility, not an attempt to determine the nature of myth. The underlying questions raised by the Enlightenment are, however, enduring ones: Is there a unique primitive mentality differentiated from that of the rational, civilized man? If this is affirmed, what is the relationship between the man of reason and the man of the mythic world? Is he a respectworthy ancestor who will never visit the city of the future, or is he a monster ever threatening to return? Is he a contemporary, the human mob about us, poised to engulf the lone philosopher? Are there unique qualities in this mythic mind which the man of reason loses as the inevitable fate of growth and maturity, or should man rejoice in the imminent sloughing off of his prehistoric coils?

CHAPTER I

New Views of Pagan Religion

"I have often said that Paganism was nothing but a traffic or a banking operation between the gods and men. People attached themselves to the ceremonies of this religion in the hope of acquiring temporal goods and of turning away evils which might hurt either their persons or their harvest. These are the motives which stirred people to action. They went to the temples. They made offerings. The most crass avarice readily gave way before the desire for a profit which they hoped to gain. It was as if they were making loans at a high interest rate."
— Pierre Bayle, *Continuation des pensées diverses*, Rotterdam, 1705, II, 691.

1

Heathen Conformities

*T*HE REAPPRAISAL of paganism by Bayle and Fontenelle was refreshingly free from Renaissance allegorism, from the etymological obsessions of the seventeenth-century polyhistors, and from the turgid dissertations of German theological faculties, which laboriously traced the pagan myths to corruptions of Old Testament history. But Bayle and Fontenelle were not isolated innovators. They flourished in a ferment of intellectual influences and were as receptive to new ideas as they were facile and profuse in propagating their own reflections. Other scholars, literally scores of them — English, German, Dutch, and French — participated in devaluing the Renaissance vision of the piety of Greece and Rome and in bestowing corporeality on its ethereal inhabitants.

Unknowing supporters in this enterprise were the travel writers who had explored the dark continents of the world and the brave missionaries to the modern heathens — Abraham Roger, La Créquinière, Richard Blome, Joannes Schefferus, Arnoldus Montanus, Père Charles Le Gobien, Willem Bosman. Virtually any writing which shed light on "conformities" between Greco-Roman ritual and the religion of contemporaneous heathen societies, whether peoples living in a state of civility — the Chinese, the Hindus, the Persians — or savage Negroes and American Indians, helped fashion the new view of ancient paganism.

From the time of the first voyages of discovery, reports by European conquerors, explorers, commercial factors, and propagators of the true faith in its variant forms had included sections on the religion of savage natives. A traveler or a missionary

15

inquired into their cult practices with the same obsessive thoroughness that a modern anthropologist investigates their sexual habits. Though the purpose of these interrogations was primarily utilitarian in either a secular or a sacerdotal sense, it encouraged curious digressions, analogies with Christian practice or with what the writer remembered about heathen religions from his reading of the Old Testament and the classics. In Marc Lescarbot's *Histoire de la nouvelle France* (1609), a key work in fashioning the image of the American Indian for European society, the whole of the sixth book was devoted to conformities with the ancients, "particularly those who are in the same latitude." [1] To the business agents of the great companies native religious customs seemed important intelligence on the character of the inhabitants with whom they had to deal, and Greco-Roman illustrations were normal forms of communication with the educated directors in Amsterdam or London. The narratives of the Jesuit missionaries, far more active in the field at this period than the Protestants, were deliberately assembled in collections such as the *Lettres édifiantes* (1702) to instruct the newcomers in the art of conversion, and analogies to ancient pagan rites were made quite spontaneously to render heathen practices more comprehensible to Christian brothers who had been nurtured on the classical texts. It was virtually impossible to examine a strange savage religion without noting disparities and conformities with what one knew about ancient paganism.

By the second half of the seventeenth century learned treatises on Asian religions were enriched with a contrapuntal theme, a running commentary of comparisons with the rites of ancient Greeks, Romans, Egyptians, and Phoenicians. The Dutch missionary Abraham Roger had been a minister of the gospel in India for ten years, where he had been taught the secrets of Brahmanism, and his substantial volume on the origin and meaning of the bizarre ceremonials he had witnessed, *De open-deure tot het verborgen heydendom* (1651),[2] was written expressly to facilitate Protestant conversions. It was necessary to know the false doctrine Christians set out to vanquish and, like St. Paul himself in his debates with Greek pagans, to argue with the heathen in their own terms and thus slowly to win them over to the faith. But how could the good pastor Roger make other pious men in Europe comprehend the strange dogmas of the Brahmans without equating them with more familiar ideas? Frequent analogies to the Greeks and the Romans with which he embellished his text helped to elucidate Brahmanism, and acceptance of the tradition that Pythagoras and Plato had studied in India rendered identities in doctrine eminently plausible. Similarly when the learned Hebraist and Arabist Thomas Hyde published in Oxford in 1700 a massive presentation of the religion of the Zoroastrians, *Veterum Persarum et Parthorum et Medorum Religionis Historia,* he brought his dissertation nearer to his readers by demonstrating that fire worship was Greek and Roman as well as Persian.

In 1704 the gentleman-traveler La Créquinière wrote an account of a sojourn in India explicitly making the "agreement of the customs of the East Indies with those of the Jews and other ancient peoples" his central subject. He flattered himself that his was the "first essay of this kind," and that he had opened "a way for the knowledge of Antiquity." He categorically assured his readers that the study of the "Customs of the Indians is no ways useful in itself. That I thought myself oblig'd to make use of it, only to justify what is told us of the *Ancients,* and to explain it whenever an Occasion offers, and in a word that Antiquity was my only Aim." [3] As a consequence of his investigation La Créquinière became an anti-allegorist, imputing the false symbolizing of scholars to their ignorance of the actual facts of oriental custom. If they had ever examined the footprints of Antiquity left "among the simplest and plainest sort of People" they would not have resorted to symbolical interpretations of difficult passages in the classical theogonies. La Créquinière was commonsensical and matter-of-fact in his description of Indian religion, carefully noting the inadequacy of data from the coastal regions where native belief had been diluted with Christianity. He was intent upon proving that the ancient pagans were blind in matters of religion by painting for his readers a realistic picture of modern peoples living in the same abominable state of superstition. His observations of religious behavior in India led him to accept literally the Egyptian worship of beasts "and such as are the vilest among them, and even that which is most infamous in nature." [4] La Créquinière's little volume is full of stray insights into comparative religion: the universality of the serpent-cult, the similarity of teachings of metempsychosis in India and Greece, an identification of Laban's *teraphim* with the *penates,* the world-wide practice of lustration. But the man saw even more than equivalent rites. He sensed the frenzy of the Indian religious mystic, made analogy to the enthusiasm of the Hebrew prophets and pagan *Erinyes,* and, what is perhaps most significant, compared them all to children: "Nay, they seem to take a Pleasure in that which provokes their Fury, like Children, who love to hear sad and doleful Stories of Spirits, or Witches, altho' they make them afraid." [5] A psychology of infantile primitive mentality was already in the making.

Casual references to the conformities between the religion of the American Indians and the ancient Greeks in travel books like Richard Blome's *The present State of his Majestie's Isles and Territories in America* (1687) became commonplace in the second half of the seventeenth century. When the voyage literature had assumed great proportions and Dutch scholars prepared compendia of heathen religious practices — Godefridus Carolinus' comparative description of *Het hedendaagsche heidendom* (1661) in Asia, Africa, and Europe is a synthesis of more than fifty volumes — they invariably resorted to classical examples for the clarification of savage ritual. By the turn of the century the kinship between ancient and modern heathens had infiltrated theological controversy on the highest level; in Noël Alexandre's *Conformité des cérémonies chinoises avec l'idolatrie grecque et romaine* (1700) it served a Dominican diatribe against the spiritual compromises with Confucianism which had been permitted in the Jesuit conversion of the Chinese mandarins.

In the course of time the juxtaposing of ancient and modern cults gave birth to a new perception of Greco-Roman religion. With the accumulation of voyage literature and missionary relations and commercial reports the documents of the ancient religious world ceased to be mere book learning or source material for theological disputation among rival Christian sects which vilified each other as heathens. Pagan religion became a living

flesh-and-blood reality which was mirrored in contemporary barbarism. The development of this awareness was gradual; it required a number of generations before the two images, the
literary one of the classics and the existential one of the savage
or civilized heathen world, interpenetrated to such a degree that
men not only reported conformities but recognized them as common human experiences. A jump had to be made from a *dis-
putatio philologica* to a consciousness of historical reality. The
Jesuit Athanasius Kircher in the mid-seventeenth century had
studied voluminous reports on the heathen religions of Japan,
China, and Mexico in the archives of his order before he composed his monumental treatise on the ancient world, the *Oedipus
Aegyptiacus* (1652–1654), but a fixation on etymologies, allegories, and Egyptian diffusionism made him continue to treat
pagan religion as an exercise in learning, as had Gerard Vossius
in *De theologia gentili et physiologia Christiana sive de origine
ac progressu idololatriae* (1641) and Samuel Bochart in *Phaleg
et Chanaan* (1646) in the same generation. In the sixteenth
and early seventeenth centuries the subject of "idolatry" had
been touched upon peripherally in dissertations with seemingly
irrelevant titles, usually as a by-product of Protestant Biblical
exegesis or apologetics. After 1650 scholarly bookish critiques of
ancient paganism were undertaken more frequently as independent interpretive philosophical disquisitions. But not until the
last decades of the seventeenth century did the refashioned image
of Greco-Roman worship — coarse, crude, primitive, abhorrent,
at once fanatical and artificial — emerge as a historical experience of humanity. By the time Joseph François Lafitau, the
Jesuit missionary to the Iroquois, wrote his *Moeurs des sauvages
amériquains comparées aux moeurs des premiers temps* (1724),
the most famous and profusely documented book of heathen conformities, the two paganisms had been completely assimilated
with each other. The parallel always worked both ways: it infused
meaning into savage rites in the new world, and at the same
time it became the key to a reinterpretation of the spirit of the
ancients.

The growing late-seventeenth-century pejorative attitude toward paganism, the realization that the Greeks were primitives,

was concomitant to the literary quarrel between the ancients and the moderns, that many-faceted discussion which served to clear a path for the appearance of the idea of progress. The Dutch and *émigré* Huguenot scholars were denigrating pagan religion precisely during the years when the French moderns were undermining the superior genius of the ancients. A lowering of the image status of pagan religion was another proclamation of modernity, a counterpart to Charles Perrault's casting off the shackles of humility imposed by the classical literary archetypes. But with all its recognized broad implications the battle over the competitive merits of ancient and modern creative genius posed too narrowly the issues which troubled men's souls — it smelled of the literary critic's inkpot. The exposure of the true nature of ancient paganism and its equation with savage cults was a more powerful detonation; it had a way of breaking boundaries, crashing into problems as varied as the origins and history of devils and spirits, the content of primitive mentality, the validity of reason, the meaning of mythic expression, the psychology of religion.

Bayle and Fontenelle were the two great catalysts in this intellectual process, and they continued to be read for decades after the mountainous, dull, long-winded treatises on idolatry composed in a traditional vein by seventeenth-century clerics, pastors, and divines were forgotten.

2

The Grand Subterfuge

*T*HEORIZING about the nature of the gods, even other people's gods, has rarely if ever been an indifferent subject pursued out of pure scientific curiosity. The prickly issues it raised at the end of the seventeenth century had an immediate bearing upon the spiritual war of the age. In 1680 few dared to analyze religious emotion nakedly as an aspect of human nature, though the problem weighed upon men's minds. One grand subterfuge was a study of superstition as distinguished from true religion, a field in which Bayle and the English Deists labored with passion; and if a frontal attack on the existence of demons and spirits was still dangerous even in Holland — witness the tragic fate of the pastor Balthasar Bekker, author of *De Betoverde Weereld* (1691) — a writer could with impunity reveal the workings of the non-Christian religious mind. After 1700, as the philosophical movement gathered momentum, the inquiries became more brazen on both sides of the Channel, advancing in a progression from a scholarly natural history of pagan religion in Bayle's hands, to a natural history of superstition in general by English Deists like John Trenchard, to Hume's subtle natural history of religion *tout court,* and finally culminating in Holbach's clinical history of the sacred disease. But while the scope, style, and temper of the investigation underwent change from one generation to another, many of the syndromes of fanatical religious experience originally described by Bayle and Fontenelle in their treatment of ancient paganism reappeared with only slight variations in far broader frames of reference during the course of the succeeding century. The writings on the nature of

21

pagan religion in the period 1680 to 1710 had intellectual reverberations far beyond the reorientation of emotive attitudes toward the classical world.

For learned anticlericals the nature of paganism was most
favorable battle terrain. The erudite researchers into the beliefs,
rites, and theologies of the ancients always had one eye cocked
on orthodox Christianity. Whether a man wrote dissertations
on Greek oracles and Hebrew magic in ponderous Latin tomes
like the Anabaptist doctor of Haarlem, Antonius Van Dale, light
essays on myths like Fontenelle, a daring exposure of the impostures of diabolism, ancient pagan, contemporary savage, and
Christian, like Balthasar Bekker, or treatises on astronomic portents which strained to be popular, Bayle's device, the anti-
ecclesiastical implications were not lost on his readers. The late
seventeenth-century exposures of paganism and its survivals in
contemporary European society were invariably presented as
pious works of God, excising from Christianity the remnants of
false patristic traditions about idolatry so that the fabric of the
true religion might be strengthened. "No Men in the World are
more remote from any Atheistical Sentiments, more persuaded
of the Divinity of the Holy Writ, and more disposed to render
to God the Honour and Reverence due to him, than those, who
as I am, are opposed to the common Opinion of the Power and
Vertue of the Devil," [6] Balthasar Bekker vainly protested. But
in fact those who cried heresy accurately sensed the direction
of the main effort, for the routing of pagan spirits, demons, in-
cubi and succubi was an advance action preceding the central
attack on revealed religion.

In the studies on paganism the disparagement of Catholicism,
as distinct from the more general war on superstition, was
marked. The Reformation had lifted the immunity of Catholic
rites and beliefs, and by the 1680's if one were ensconced behind
the ramparts of English or Dutch Protestantism political con-
tingencies made it a patriotic act to equate pagan and papal
idolatry. In Holland, the world center of militant anti-Catholi-
cism, the scholarship of both Dutch Calvinists and Huguenots
was sparked by the anger which the religious persecutions and
political expansionism of Louis XIV had fanned to white heat.

Through the new "scientific" study of pagan rites and beliefs, the critical excerpting of descriptions in a wide range of sources —the classics, the Bible, the rabbis of the Talmud, and the Church Fathers — and the meticulous classification of types of ceremonials, it could be demonstrated that Catholic and heathen rites were identical and Rome was confounded. This was by no means a novel polemical technique, for the theological literature of the sixteenth and earlier seventeenth centuries was replete with such "conformities," particularly in Protestant treatises on idolatry. But toward the 1680's the theme was revived and accentuated as the scholars joined the fray with a sharp bite of antagonism against Popery. Throughout the eighteenth century it remained a standard Protestant weapon; its classical expression in the English-speaking world was probably Conyers Middleton's *A Letter from Rome, shewing an exact conformity between Popery and Paganism* (1729).

To make way for new interpretations of pagan religion dominant traditions had to be struck down. This work of demolition was undertaken with gusto by Pierre Bayle and Bernard Fontenelle and their cohorts. A few stray allegorists survived the onslaught and occasionally even a faltering demonologist raised his orthodox head, but they were rarely serious contenders in the world of mythology. Their day was done. Though they did not plan the assault together, Bayle and Fontenelle executed a double envelopment, the former overwhelming the symbolizers, the latter the demon-theorists. It was a smashing fight and in the fracas a goodly number of Christian bystanders were hurt.

3

The Derision of Allegory:
Pierre Bayle and his Contemporaries

*T*HE SON of an obscure French Protestant minister, Pierre
Bayle had in his youth gone through a series of religious somer-
saults and nominally ended up in the church into which he was
born. He was educated by the most rigorous logical discipli-
narians of the age, first the Jesuits of Toulouse and then the
Calvinist theologians of Geneva. An exile from his native Catholic
France in 1681, he was at first received in Rotterdam as a professor of philosophy and history, but later the consistory of the
Dutch Reformed Church dismissed him upon accusations of heresy
by his colleague and fellow-*émigré*, the redoubtable Huguenot
pastor Pierre Jurieu. Bayle's scholarship was prodigious, his memory phenomenal, his manner of writing that of a humanist
érudit of the sixteenth century. He lavishly adorned his work
with gems of learning from an inexhaustible storehouse and
composed intricate glosses which were plagiarized for more than
a century. A gentle man in his personal life, he was a hard polemi-
cist who demolished critics with the power of his logic. He manipulated a syllogism with virtuosity and involved his adversaries
in the coils of majors and minors. When necessary he smothered
an opponent with authorities, the grand names of Greek philosophy, Roman wisdom, and Christian saintliness. He loved nothing better than to pit one Church Father against another, a doctor
of the church against a widely-revered tradition, and perhaps
best of all a worthy against himself.

While he never overtly disavowed an article of faith of the

Calvinist Reformed Church, many a man who was drawn into his network of theological argument failed to extricate himself with belief in the dogmas of the Christian religion intact. His disputations were far from arid; the scholastic reasoning was spiced with anecdotes and histories, often obscene, garnered from the accounts of travelers among primitive peoples and contemporary peasant folklore as well as from the classical corpus and the Fathers. Reason and experience were forged into a machine which relentlessly destroyed all credence in the supernatural, the mysterious, the authoritative dogmatic, the traditional. Well into the nineteenth century men had to reckon with the Baylian doubt diffused through eight massive folios of collected works, the great source-books of impiety. If a reader digs into the footnotes of the *Dictionaire historique et critique* (1697) and remains on the alert for innuendoes he can, as Sainte-Beuve knew, find everything in Bayle, the whole of the eighteenth century wrestling valiantly with problems of faith, reason, nature, evil, right conduct, utility. Above all Bayle was a man of facts, a grand profusion of them — true, false, and dubious. His writing was "so full of things," said Stendhal.

For a quarter of a century, from the first edition of his reflections on the comet of 1680 through the *Réponse aux questions d'un provincial*, the last part of which was published the year of his death, the nature of pagan religion was a recurrent theme in Bayle's voluminous works, almost equivalent in mass to his Christian theological disputations. In de Marsy's *Analyse raisonnée de Bayle* a whole section was entitled "Système des payens sur l'origine des dieux."

Bayle approached his analysis of pagan cults well nourished on the varieties of religious experience throughout the world. The mid-seventeenth century had witnessed the revival of the fear theory on the origins of religion in the grand formulations of Hobbes and Spinoza, who were Bayle's immediate philosophical antecedents, and their impact upon his thinking was sharp and direct. Often when the writings of these great heretics proved to be wines too heady for later eighteenth-century *philosophes*, they were imbibed only after they had been watered by Bayle and Fontenelle. Bayle felt the full power of the *Tract-*

atus theologico-politicus (1670), which had boldly interpreted the Old Testament as documentation for a secular political history of the Jews; and though he was no Hebraist he was a thorough scholar of Richard Simon, one of the founders of "scientific" Biblical criticism. The increasing number of learned works on Eastern religions were accessible to him, and he kept abreast of the missionary reports from China, the translations of Mohammedan texts, and a reasonable sampling of the "voyages." He studied mythology in the Greek and Latin sources and was a repository of previous explanatory schemes in authors ancient and modern, pagan and Christian.

Of the traditional interpretations of Greco-Roman myth there was one school with which Bayle and his friends would brook no converse, Stoic and Neoplatonic "moralizing" of the gods, or for that matter any tropological or anagogical readings. The allegorists of antiquity had found inspired, philosophical, moral, marvelous wisdom in the simple, graphic, crude texts of early religions. The rabbis of Judaea and Philo of Alexandria had performed their feats on the canon of the Old Testament in order to combat anthropomorphism; the Church Fathers had adopted the method for the elucidation of the New Testament; and the Stoics and pagan apologists in a similar vein had spiritualized the myths of Hesiod and Homer. Though other ways were recognized, allegorism had remained the dominant mode of interpretation in the Middle Ages and the Renaissance, and well into the seventeenth century. By the eighteenth, however, the tide had turned completely. One of the striking expressions of the new scientific and material civilization of western Europe was an overwhelming tendency to become matter-of-fact, to eschew wonder, to reduce the fantastic to a commonsense narrative. There was a general movement to de-allegorize, to perceive the ordinary where previous generations had sought occult connotations. The world was obvious, the cloud of past obfuscations had lifted, things were to be seen and described as they were and as they should appear to reasonable people not possessed by romances or religious enthusiasm. With citation after citation from the ancient writers summoned as faithful contemporary witnesses, each a hammer blow, Bayle derided allegorism and insisted that the pagans themselves were completely convinced of the literal truth of every myth. The accounts of divine adulteries, rapes, lies, deceptions, robberies were not symbols of the moral conflict of virtues and vices leading to the final triumph of godliness. The pagans of antiquity believed in a commonsense way that these actions, so repugnant to Bayle's principles and conscience, actually took place precisely as described in the poetic tradition. In the king of the Olympians the pagan in the forum recognized no approximation of a universal spiritual being. Zeus was the ravisher of Ganymede and the constant betrayer of his wife Hera. The more evidence Bayle could accumulate about the lusts of the gods and goddesses, the degrading acts to which they were impelled by their passions, the greater his delight. Tales of divine incest and castration, heterosexual and homosexual rape, were spelled out and discoursed upon with mock solemnity. Bayle recreated a world of sex-mad divinities. While he insisted that in the pagan mind the traditions of divine adventures concerned authentic events, he expressed nothing but contempt for the unimaginative quality of the Greek mythic inventions, so sorely lacking in diversity if compared with modern novels. The major themes seemed to him repetitive and stereotyped — incest, cannibalism, rape, and murder.

The Baylian way with a myth can best be illustrated by his maltreatment of Adonis in the *Dictionaire*. After collecting the numerous literary versions of the relations between Venus and Adonis he critically analyzed their contradictions. Was the Adonis myth related to the agricultural cycle or the signs of the zodiac? Was Adonis identical with Tammuz or Osiris? What did the goring of Adonis by the boar really mean? Was it a symbolic expression of his emasculation? What significance should be attached to the bizarre detail that Venus buried her Adonis under a lettuce, which was supposed to render a man impotent? His own satirical conclusion reduced the myth of the tragic love of Venus and Adonis, which had become a great spiritual symbol, to an ordinary, rather ridiculous incident. "The source of all these stories might well be the report that Adonis, having eaten his fill of a certain lettuce that grows on the island of Cyprus, was killed by a boar. Those who will reflect on the place where the boar wounded him will without difficulty find the denouement to all this. Adonis having become impotent from eating too many of these lettuces, they made believe that he had received a mortal wound in the groin." [7] Who after reading this footnote could participate in the mystic longing of Venus?

The climax of Bayle's outright condemnation of the pagan spirit was his identification of Greek religion with the cults of the contemporary savage world, for which the ground had already been prepared in the voyage accounts. Drawing particularly upon the *Voyage de Guinée* (1705) [8] addressed to the directors of the General Company of the East Indies in Amsterdam by their "First Merchant" Willem Bosman, Bayle composed a long circumstantial parallel between the fetisheer and the Greek temple priest. Both adored their gods for utility's sake; both coaxed fat sacrifices out of their people to get the meat of the offerings for themselves; both intimidated their believers with the terrors of the next world. Bayle was determined to destroy the last vestiges of Renaissance allegorism by stamping upon the religions of Greece and Rome the ugly impress of the barbaric worship of cats, dogs, serpents, and sundry other low and disgusting objects. The ordinary Greeks, famed for their reason and genius, were on the same footing as African and Micronesian worshipers of fetishes. Like the tribal clients of the fetisheer they believed that graven images could succor them if they performed overt rites and ceremonials meticulously following the traditional arbitrary formulae. Greek religion was never for Bayle, as it was for some Christian apologists, a faltering step toward the true God, a prefiguration of Christian mysteries, or a distortion of primitive monotheism. Idolatry was a vulgar, stupid adoration of mere things, an affront to the dignity and rationality of man.

When Bayle established an analogy between fetishism and ancient paganism in the *Réponse aux questions d'un provincial,* Fontenelle had not yet published his comparison between primitive Greeks and American savages in the *Origine des fables,* but Balthasar Bekker's long digression on heathen religions in the first volume of *De Betoverde Weereld* had been in print for almost fifteen years and was well known among scholars. Bekker had written an embryonic treatise in comparative anthropology and had made a virtual cross-cultural index of religious practices in the ancient world and among five continents of the modern to demonstrate the ubiquity of an underlying primitive monotheism. Bayle's reflections, on the other hand, were directed toward proving the absurdity of all heathen religions. Willem Bosman himself, with a perfunctory apology, had occasionally compared Negro rites with pagan, popish, even Old Testament practices, but it was Bayle who gave this perception telling significance. The pagans of antiquity were primitives and materialists, as superstitious and subhuman as the naked barbarians of Guinea. Gone from Bayle is the high-flown Neoplatonic envelopment of the Greco-Roman world. In spirit his is a Protestant humanist rejection of the pagan Renaissance. Fifty years later his essay into comparative religion became the central thesis of de Brosses's revolutionary little work, *Du culte des dieux fétiches*.

In this deflation of the Renaissance image of paganism Bayle was supported by argument and evidence from diverse, sometimes improbable sources among his learned contemporaries. Though in controversy on points of theology Bayle had made an archenemy of Jean Le Clerc, the renowned editor of the *Bibliothèque universelle* and the *Bibliothèque choisie,* he nevertheless found in his adversary confirmation of his own militant anti-allegorism. A belated review of John Selden's *De Dis Syris Syntagmata* (1617) had afforded Le Clerc an opportunity to fire a volley against allegorical interpretations of classical myth. There was nothing in the ancient poets and mythographers which justified a presumption that they did not take the lives of the gods "à la lettre." [9] Selden, in the previous generation of scholarship, still venerating the classical world, had stood in awe of the giants of antiquity. Le Clerc, like Bayle, saw myths as mere literary expressions of barbarous peoples who, when they deified their kings, naively and unabashedly narrated their criminal acts because they had no concept of virtue. Le Clerc was fundamentally a Euhemerist who viewed myths as plain political history. His reasonable explanation for the original introduction of the allegorical method among the Stoics became a pointed weapon in the anti-allegorists' arsenal and was later used by Fontenelle, de Brosses, and many others. Allegorizing had been nothing more than a protective device of the late pagan philosophers to defend their gods from Jewish and Christian mockery. To cap his proof Le Clerc resorted to Father Clement, who had argued with consummate logic that if wise pagan geniuses rather than wicked demons had inspired the original myths in order to teach truth, they would not have garbed them in odious moral vestments which by example seduced the ignorant into crime and ultimately required allegorization. "I mean the parricides, the murders of children by their fathers, the impious relations of gods with their mothers, their sisters and their daughters, the shameful adulteries, the unnatural relations, the scandalous defilements, and a thousand other similar prohibited fornications." [10]

Though Bayle usually wrote about paganism as if it were mere popular superstition, he at times analyzed it as a religio-philosophical system, albeit a confused one. Pagan philosophers fared no better than the vulgar religion he despised and ridiculed. He had particular contempt for the theologies of Plato and Aristotle, no doubt because they had been conciliated with Christianity, and the Stoics who had attempted to allegorize the common religion. Epicurus alone was honored, the Bayle of antiquity who had dared to unmask the religious credulity of the Greeks. In this negative estimate of Greek philosophy Bayle was not alone. Heterodox Protestant pastors like the Arminian Matthieu Souverain were equally vehement in their attack on the "deprav'd Platonism" which had infiltrated Christianity. Le Platonisme dévoilé (1700) denounced the once revered doctrine as "absurd as the Theology of the Poets, and as unpolish'd as the Religion of the most superstitious vulgar." [11]

Pagan religion and the magic of charlatans throughout the ages were undifferentiated for Bayle. The evocation of the dead, the concoction of secret beverages, philters, potions, belief in the efficacy of talismans were stupidities by no means restricted to the common people, for emperors, even the sage Marcus Aurelius, and philosophers, even Pythagoras, practiced magical rites. Necromancy was the very heart of the public, state-authorized ceremonial religions of antiquity. The prescribed way in which each deity was invoked during solemn libations and sacrifices, the preparation of ritual offerings in accordance with ordained recipes were identical with the incantations of modern sorcery. In both, ceremonies had to be performed with meticulous exactitude lest any deviation turn the whole ritual against the suppliant. Bayle would not allow pagan rites to be spiritualized or made symbol; they were as repellent as the witches' brew. The mysteries which the Renaissance had revered as vehicles of occult wisdom, a tradition preserved by eighteenth-century Deists, were nothing but black magic. When his bulging chronicle of Greco-Roman rites was unrolled he dismissed them with a disdainful "Here is how magic and religion became confounded with each other." Ancient priests thought they could enslave the gods, command the sun and the moon. "What an affront to poor human reason!" [12] *En passant,* as Bayle strung out the catalogue of pagan inanities, he dropped, as if by accident, analogies to Christian Europe. Pagans believed in the myths of their gods as literally as a Catholic did in the Assumption and in the liquefaction of the blood of Saint Januarius; the trances of initiates in the pagan mysteries were not unlike the ecstasies of Christian religious mystics.

Bayle tried to discover the original error of paganism in its pristine materialism. To pagans the gods were real things composed of matter, creatures of a somewhat different consistency from men, more subtle perhaps, but essentially of the same substance as human beings, animals, or plants. This materialist predisposition of the pagan mind explained why the early Greeks could conceive of the transformation of a human into a tree or the birth of Aphrodite from the pudenda of Cronus without violence to their rationality, for divine and human metamorphoses were mere changes in forms of matter and there was fluidity of movement from the animal to the human to the divine worlds. "Common opinion of the pagans made the difference between gods and men one of mere degree." [13]

The core of Bayle's diatribe against paganism was a definition of its essential nature as ceremonial, formal, and ritualistic, entirely devoid of moral content. Here the Protestant spoke: "The pagans imputed the origins of the punishments which the gods visited upon them to the neglect of some superstition and not to the impurity of their lives, and therefore they believed that they had done enough if only they re-established the rite which had been forgotten." [14] Pagan religion had no bearing on right conduct, for it was purely mechanical and no sentiment accompanied acts of worship. Contrary to theories in the Critias tradition, Bayle found no evidence that pagan religion as a political instrument was ever useful in curbing secret malefaction, preserving tranquillity, and repressing sedition. Paganism as a religion had no utility at all for mankind.

Bitterness against the irrationality and immorality of paganism had been carried even further by Balthasar Bekker. The Amsterdam divine whose adamant denial of the potency of the devil in the historical world had brought about his destitution and excommunication drew strict logical consequences from his arraignment of pagan and contemporary Christian beliefs in spirits and demons. He turned to the educational system armed with Lockian psychology and traced the long-term evil consequences of erroneous impressions on tender childish brains. Among the most pernicious early "sensations" he singled out the myths of gods and goddesses, spirits and demons which were transmitted from Greek and Latin writings taught in schools. With a zeal almost Platonic Bekker would banish these image-provoking poets from Christian education and substitute mathematics and astronomy, disciplines which trained the mind and safeguarded it against false beliefs. Bayle never went quite so far in denunciation of the classical culture with which he was imbued, but the preservation of pagan works in rational Christian teaching created a problem, as it had in the first centuries of the Church.

Pierre Jurieu, the dour leader of the Huguenot *émigrés* and the inveterate enemy of Bayle, could hardly have been suspected of the unorthodox motives with which Bayle was charged when he too exercised his virtuosity on the favorite subject of Dutch scholarship, the classification and analysis of ancient pagan and Judaic rites and beliefs, under the characteristically long-winded title *Histoire critique des dogmes et des cultes bons et mauvais, qui ont été dans l'Eglise depuis Adam jusqu'au Jésus-Christ, où l'on trouve l'origine de toutes les Idolatries de l'ancien Paganisme, expliquées par rapport à celles des Juifs* (1704–05). There are passages in his work which anticipated Le Clerc in their vehement rejection of allegorism and paralleled Bayle in their revulsion against the spectacle of pagan religion. "Nothing in the world is more monstrous than pagan theology." [15] Jurieu defied anyone to discover sublime meaning in the genealogies of the gods, the tales of their concubinage, sodomies, rapes of young girls, drunkenness. The cult of Priapus was particularly odious to him and he rebutted with outrage that ingenious defense by Iamblichus which justified the practice as an outlet for the fury of concupiscence in man which would have been irritated and augmented if it had been suppressed.

But Jurieu was reluctant to acquiesce in the outright and total repudiation of Greco-Roman religion by men like Bayle and Bekker. The attack leveled against "pagano-papism" by orthodox Calvinists is distinct from the broader antipaganism of the Baylian rationalists. Since Jurieu upheld the doctrine of the innate idea of God, the total corruption of pagan mankind without exception which Bayle depicted was dangerous. Jurieu therefore in the Renaissance tradition allowed for the incorporation of enigmas of physical science and secrets of philosophy in some of the myths. In partial defense of allegory he quoted traditional examples of occult meaning, the Osiris myth as symbolic of the agricultural cycle and Saturn as the emblem of time which devours and consumes what it produces. To resolve his ambivalence toward paganism, his detestation of idolatry and yet his respect for ancient wisdom as the preservation of at least a glimmer of the idea of God, Jurieu had recourse to the same doctrine of the double truth then in vogue among blasphemous English Deists like Toland. Under this intellectual umbrella Jurieu sheltered a spiritualized pagan religion and a vulgar one too. A myth could at one and the same time relate the wicked adventures of a man deified and conceal sublime conceptions about nature. Pierre Jurieu refused to identify the Jupiter who was the creator of all things, the Roman philosophers' god, with the vicious Jupiter, King of Crete, central protagonist of the myths of popular pagan religion — for which Bayle was quick to pounce upon him. All orthodoxy, Protestant and Catholic alike, sensed as if instinctively that there was something inimical to priesthood, to established religion itself, in the vehemence of the Baylian strictures against paganism, and drew back.

4

Bayle's Psychology of Paganism

*T*HE MASTERPIECE of Bayle's formidable irony was the paradox for which he became notorious throughout Europe, that atheism was preferred to pagan idolatry by God. Having embarked upon this course he was pulled into ever deeper waters. He denied the common Christian tradition that nations of atheists could not exist and flouted the orthodox proposition that an idea of God or divinity was in all men. A *Journal des Sçavans* report of a deaf young man of Chartres who, after regaining the power of hearing, evinced no knowledge of a God despite the fact that he had been performing religious ceremonials all his life, bolstered Bayle's argument against innateness, as it would La Mettrie's atheism half a century later. Bayle combed the travel literature for accounts of atheist savages, in order to demolish the argument, set forth in the *Institutes* and revived by Jacques Bernard, that the general consensus of nations was a witness to the existence of a divinity. If majority voting were a demonstration, he warned, contemporary idolators would easily bear away the palm of victory. At times he intimated that the original savage state might have been atheist, not even idolatrous. And he followed his evidence on the existence of atheist savage nations with the astounding report that those primitives who were without religion, far from being bestial and vicious, were benign and mild toward one another — dramatic proof that religion had nothing to do with right conduct.

Bayle was a great sceptic and brilliant destructive critic. When he came to elaborating positive hypotheses on the natural origins of pagan religion he was derivative. For the most part he accepted with slight variations both the Epicurean fear-theory and the Euhemerist apotheosis of dead heroes. Antinoüs, the favorite whom Hadrian divinized into a star and who continued to be worshiped even after the death of the Emperor, was for Bayle a good verifiable historical instance of straightforward Euhemerism. The casual hints that some myths and ceremonies were related to magical fertility rites and Bayle's dalliance with the sexual symbolism of myths now arrest our attention because of the later flowering of these theories. Throughout most of his writing, however, the reasoning ran along classical lines. His imagery for the fear-theory betrays its Lucretian source. When men saw an eclipse or a comet they at once feared for the future, recognizing this as a portent of divine indignation. Thunder filled men with great terror because in their ignorance of rational causes they could only interpret the horrendous sounds as indications of a god's wrath. "Primus in orbe Deos fecit timor," he quoted from Petronius.[16] Perhaps there is a somewhat new emphasis in Bayle's conception that after primitive men had been frightened by cataclysms, a general anxiety gradually pervaded their whole existence which made them apprehensive of any novelty, however trivial, but the seed of even this idea can be found in *De rerum natura.*

Bayle did not subscribe to the imposture theory of religion pure and simple, either in its priestly or in its political versions. Man had psychological characteristics — this is the emphasis — which made him susceptible to the artifices of priests or, as Bayle playfully turned the argument in his reflections on comets where he affected the theological position of a doctor of the Sorbonne, to the machinations of demons. "I shall only note that the Demons had no great difficulty in persuading men that mystery and prodigies abounded everywhere. For it must be admitted to the shame of our species that it has a natural penchant in this direction. *Facile erat vincere non repugnantes.* And apparently the soil was so favorable for this sort of fruit that it would have produced them abundantly even if it had not been cultivated." [17] Bayle paraded the patristic demonological theory of idolatry in so perverse a manner that it became more patently ridiculous with each new application. Political and clerical abuse under paganism consisted in taking undue advantage of pre-existing human frailties. The primary weakness of man leading him to magical religions is his overriding anxiety about the future, which renders him an easy prey to augurers, astrologers, fortune-tellers, necromancers, and other purveyors of fraud, the men wicked enough to exploit his terrors. This is an elaboration of the Hobbesian idea of the omnipresence of the fear of death as the psychic foundation both of the state and of religion. The travel literature which depicted the Negro savage panic-stricken by every natural catastrophe, rushing to his fetish for salvation, had infused the ancient fear-theory with the vigor of graphic empirical evidence. Timorous man, unenlightened by reason, thus had a natural propensity to superstition even before the intrusion of impostors and before the "malady" of seeing omens in prodigies had struck deep roots. Common psychological traits had only aggravated the disease: as men retained the memory of evil more readily than the recollection of good, when "evil portents" were accidentally fulfilled they created a lasting impression; a single prophecy that materialized made a deeper imprint than twenty which failed. Other dominant passions in conjunction with fear on which the pagan charlatans operated were human pride and vanity, and here the fakers were particularly effective, worming their way into the confidence of princes by making them believe that heroes would neither be born nor die without creating a stir in the heavens in the form of a comet or an eclipse. Politicians themselves eventually became adept in manipulating auguries either to fill their subjects with confidence or to intimidate them. At the end of the seventeenth century fear and pride as the two primal sources for religious belief was good literary psychology.

Bayle's analysis of the psychopathology of religious experience was probably his most illuminating contribution. Fraud, though accepted as an element in paganism, was neither the sole nor the primary explanation for the religious extravagances of ancient Orphics and Bacchants, the most irrational manifestations of Greek and Roman religion. The same symptoms which Bayle discovered in pagan demoniacs he recognized in modern enthusiasts, and what he diagnosed as illness in contemporary religion helped him to clarify ancient religious mania. The demoniacs cured by Christian priests in formal ceremonies for which special manuals of exorcism were composed were not prima facie impostors, though there were numerous recorded instances in which possession was simulated by wily peasants. Most of the wretches were rather victims of disease. The human imagination could become so excited that the patients actually suffered the anguish they described. Religious mystics and demoniacs exhibited symptoms identical to those of madness, as Bayle showed in case histories from Catholic nunneries. Among visionaries the senses which communicated with the external world were cut off by more powerful internal affects. A religious mania was like a dream. In sleep too the mind proliferated fantasies in response to inner stimulation by the memory of weird legends and grotesque myths. The tales of spirits, sorcerers, and demons heard by children left a "profound trace on their brain" which could be irritated into a hallucination. "If a lively attention to these objects, accompanied by fear, arouses the imagination, be certain that the action of the animal spirits on this trace will be stronger than the action of light on the optic nerve. The imagination will then be stronger than sight and will depict its objects as present, so that even while awake, one will believe that one sees something that is not before one's eyes, but is apparent only to the inner senses. Consider for a moment what happens during dreams. The most reasonable heads have extravagant dreams and they fashion more bizarre chimeras than madmen whom one locks up in asylums. The objects of the dreams appear as if they were present to the external senses; one believes that one sees fauns and satyrs, hears a tree speak or a river. Whence all this? From the fact that the action of the senses is interrupted and the imagination dominates. The same thing can happen to those who are not asleep if, by the effect of some fear or some powerful internal emotion, the acts of the imagination have greater power than those of sight and hearing."[18]

Bayle's appreciation of the plausibility of pagan temple cures and the attested efficacy of Christian relics is in the same spirit. Both priestly corps were able to inspire psychological "confidence" in their patients, even as a doctor who succeeded in freeing a sick man from the fear of death. The animal economy was such that this "confidence," however achieved, was useful in emancipating a man from the terrors which were the strongest impediment to his convalescence. Unfortunately the same sacerdotal agents who administered benign psychological remedies were also capable of poisoning the minds of their victims. While psychic forces were potent in their effect on the mass of people, only reason was ultimately good.

Bayle's preoccupation with religious pathology was not unique. The resurgence of witchcraft trials in the seventeenth century had been accompanied by a flood of books on demonology, both for and against the devils, written by lawyers, doctors, ministers, and gentlemen scholars. Bekker's work, which perhaps out of discretion Bayle virtually neglected in his writings, was the center of the controversy at the turn of the century. There were three ways of dealing with the possessed. For a great number of writers, impressed by the testimony of the Bible, of the ancient classics, of the Church Fathers, of travelers in the Americas and the Indies, as well as eyewitnesses of demoniac convulsions, the empirical evidence on the side of the existence of demons seemed overwhelming. For disbelievers there were the alternatives of considering the demoniacs either impostors or mentally ill. When Fontenelle's exposure of oracles was published in 1686, Bayle referred to it with elegant praise; he had reviewed Antonius Van Dale's original work with relish as the opening article of the first issue of his *Nouvelles de la République des Lettres* in March 1684, testimony of his basic agreement with the opinion that pagan oracles were artifices whose psychological tricks and mechanical devices could be revealed. Bayle joined with Van Dale and Fontenelle in supporting a naturalistic interpretation for the cessation of pagan oracles. The "demons" in Apollo's temple at Daphne suspended their operations not in terror of the words of Christ emanating from a nearby church but because the pagan priests wanted no Christian eyes spying out their deceptions. Bayle and Fontenelle were secret allies who did not need to correspond to abet each other. But while Van Dale and Fontenelle tended in the direction of the imposture thesis, exposing mechanics, Bayle and Bekker seemed more partial to a medical interpretation of the whole experience — the original weakness was in man himself.

Pagan religion was thus for Bayle magical, venal, and irrational.

It played on and exploited primary human passions, fear and anxiety and pride. It had no conception of a higher spiritual nature and was a general materialism. Pagan idolatry was still the religion of the greatest number of human beings in the world, but it was not demonstrated that it was universal, and where the gods were not known men were as honest as in the heart of idolatry — or Christianity. The existence of a primitve monotheism which had degenerated into idolatry through error or demoniac wiles was unprovable. And Greco-Roman religion was no simulacrum of Christian monotheism despite the Jupiter figure. Those who wanted to grasp the essence of paganism had only to read the travel records about contemporary savages or examine the evidence on European sorcery, magic, and superstition, both among peasants and their lords, most of which had survived in Christianity from pagan antiquity without change — except of course insofar as basic articles of faith were concerned, he added cautiously. Idolatry was an offspring of the meeting of weakness and malice. The weakness, expressed in credulity, terror, vanity, hallucinations, should be cured either by demonstrations or by a doctor of souls; the malice, the fraud, should be exposed relentlessly, though men must remain mindful of the dangers of sedition.

That the prejudices of paganism had passed relatively unchanged into Christian Europe was a Baylian observation of great moment, which later was taken up first by Hume in his famous essay, where the survival of polytheism in the bosom of Christianity was one of the central threads of the argument, and then, with self-conscious satisfaction, by the Holbachians. In his *Pensées* Bayle communicated a sense of the extraordinary pertinacity of irrational beliefs once they had established themselves in a society. By depicting the transition from paganism to Christianity as a fluid phenomenon, not marked by a sharp break, he propagated a historical view of religious syncretism of whose full implications he himself may not have been aware. This merging of one religious world into the other was not limited to the vulgar; Bayle made the troublesome observation that the early Church Fathers who had once been Platonists preserved the "spirit of this sect" even after their conversion.

The analogy between Greek religion, savage fetishism, and contemporary popular superstition, the crucial idea of this period which Bayle shared with a number of his fellows in the republic of letters, became more fecund in Fontenelle. Bayle still used the travel literature mostly as argument for the debunking of paganism, and only rarely indicated that he was conscious of a primitive mentality. Fundamentally he had no conception of evolutionary development. When he quoted the same tripartite division of historical time from Varro which Vico later adopted as the underlying schema of his *Scienza Nuova,* he made nothing of it beyond identifying the mythical period as the age when paganism first established itself in Greece. Bayle did not distinguish among benighted, superstitious people whether in the Guinea bush, in the sanctuary at Delphi, in a Protestant village quaking with tales of sorcery, or on a Catholic pilgrimage to a miracle-working relic. For him the essential cleavage was between the superstitious mind and the enlightened mind, a timeless divide.

The morality of Bayle's realistic portrayal of the pagan world, of his transvaluation of paganism, is Epicuréan in a spiritualized Gassendi sense. The pagan philosopher whom centuries of Christian thought had denounced as the incarnation of atheist evil and depravity was rehabilitated as the great humane teacher of mankind. Let man finally rid his society of the remnants of paganism and savagery — which are identical — and accept the rule of reason, eradicating superstition. Bayle was no more sanguine than Hume, who derived from him directly, about any wholesale conversion of the people to the true laws of rational will, which were as absolute as the laws of syllogistic reasoning, for only a few rare minds, after instruction, had the strength to overcome the passions. Historical evidence led to scepticism, and yet Bayle fought as if he believed in the triumph of reason. The optimist-pessimist ambivalence of the eighteenth century, the bitter smile of Voltaire, is already on Bayle's lips. Would the Christians of the enlightened age be more rational and moral than the Greeks and the Romans?

5

The Discovery of Primitive Mentality:
Bernard Fontenelle

*F*ONTENELLE, BAYLE'S Catholic counterpart in Paris, was a man of a different stripe. The worldly nephew of the great Corneille lived for a solid century, 1657 to 1757, and in his last days witnessed the full triumph of the philosophical movement which he had nourished in the eighties and nineties with a succession of delightfully snide works on apparently innocent subjects as recondite as pagan oracles and life in Borneo. Fontenelle was a man from the provinces who conquered the capital and ruled over the French academies. In elegant obituaries he eulogized the lifework of scores of scientific colleagues whom he had the stamina to survive, and he wrote on science and literature for the ladies and gentlemen of the court. Though he had a measure of disdain for the dull learned treatises on ancient religion which emanated from Holland, he was not above utilizing them when they were cleansed of their pedantry and made presentable to the gallants. He became an ideal personality image for the French *philosophes,* the man of both worlds, science and belles-lettres, the prototype for d'Alembert and Condorcet. During the last years of Louis XIV Fontenelle faced his moment of danger, when the King's fanatical confessor, Le Tellier, aroused the orthodox to the grave heretical implications of his writings on paganism, and he narrowly escaped the Bastille, but throughout most of his long life he basked in the glory of the most gracious and sophisticated society in the grandest court in the world.

While he was in many respects less profound and surely less

burdened with learning than Bayle, his forays were often more adventuresome. In linking the concept of a primitive mentality to the idea of progress Fontenelle was a seminal thinker. He was not a systematizer and he failed to construct a full-blown theory, but in two pithy and brilliant essays, one on the origins of myth, the other on the mechanics of oracles, he expressed in embryonic form a conception of primitive mankind and the nature of pagan religion which held sway in European thought until the early nineteenth century and was integrated into positivist French sociology. Traces of his argument are discernible in Turgot; a recent work on Saint-Simon should have mentioned him as a direct source; both Auguste Comte and Lévy-Bruhl paid homage to the originality of his perceptions. His influence on English thought is no less marked: many themes in Hume's essay on the history of natural religion derive from Fontenelle; in *Myth, Ritual, and Religion* Andrew Lang praised the novelty of his anthropological hypotheses.

Fontenelle discovered a primitive mentality by aligning observations on the early Greeks, derived from the poets, particularly Homer, on American savages, drawn from travel literature, and on simple peasants and children. Reflections on the psyche of early man and his myth-making capacity that were merely hinted at or buried under scholarly references in Bayle were spelled out with Cartesian clarity in Fontenelle. The comparison of the early Greeks with contemporary American savages had crystallized in his mind as early as 1680, though it was not committed to writing until sometime between 1691 and 1699, and was not published until the 1724 edition of his works. By this time the idea of relating ancient and modern paganism was common European intellectual currency. Its most influential formulation for the eighteenth century, Lafitau's work, also appeared in that year, and the first *Scienza Nuova* by Giambattista Vico is dated 1725.

In the *Origine des fables* [19] Fontenelle used relatively few examples of the "astonishing conformity" between Pelasgians and American Indians: the muddy lakes where the Indians sent the souls of those who had been wicked, and the banks of the River Styx; the American belief that rain was poured on earth when a young maiden's pitcher was broken in play by her brother, and the Greek water nymphs; the Inca myth that "Manco Guyna Capac," son of the sun, through his eloquence had enticed men out of the forests where they had lived like beasts and had taught them rational laws, and the Orpheus myth, he too a son of the sun. The Greeks had once been as savage as Indians; witness the fact that both peoples when they emerged from barbarism were led to adopt the same solar imagery for their great civilizers. Initially the Greeks had been endowed with intellects no more rational than the Indians', and if the Americans had been left to themselves they would have developed a capacity to think equal to that of the Greeks — a preposterous idea in the age of Louis XIV. Progress was a long autonomous rationalizing process to which all nations, however diverse, were subject. No peoples were born reasonable, not even the wise Greeks and the noble Romans; in fact it was difficult for a modern to fathom the depths of primitive human ignorance and barbarism by studying contemporary Iroquois and Laplanders, because the savages depicted in travel literature already represented a degree of civilization over the first men.

At the very outset of his essay Fontenelle took the momentous leap — he psychologized myth, treating it as a profound revelation of the mind of man. Bizarre manifestations like mythology had most to teach about essential human nature. Since myths were tales told by aborigines on an even lower level of civilization than American Indians, they were the closest approximations to the thinking of original man, which was similar in certain limited respects to enlightened contemporary mentality, yet different, distinct in its mode of expression. Fontenelle's primitive was a fantast, and at the same time he had the vanity common to all men. A natural tendency to exaggerate, to imagine rather than to observe with plausible accuracy, rendered everything about him marvelous. In the pursuit of wonderment he had a compulsion to drive himself to the utmost limits of extravagance, never content with the mere embellishment of an event. Transmission through the ages had only multiplied and embroidered the earlier fancies. Tales of natural prodigies, recounted from father to son, had been distorted to the point where hardly a jot of the original falsification of the first narrator, himself addicted to hyperbole, had survived. The earliest myths of the gods were thus neither secret wisdom nor priestly fabrication. They were the unintentional errors, the faulty perceptions of infantile reason, of ignorant barbarians akin to peasant dolts and fibbing children. The grain of fact in myth was no longer discoverable, and details in the vast conglomerate of mythology were not to be investigated too seriously or subjected to minute analysis, advice which Fontenelle's Euhemerist colleagues of the Académie des Inscriptions rejected.

In the *Digression sur les anciens et les modernes*,[20] an amplification of the underlying conception of the *Origine des fables*, Fontenelle revived the Augustinian analogy between the history of mankind and the development of the child to maturity, and envisioned the historical process as the gradual elimination of puerile myth and its replacement by adult mathematical-physical reasoning. Fontenelle defined primitive mentality, but he did not admire it; this was a stage of human consciousness which mankind was fortunate enough to have outgrown. In comparing the ancients, the savages, the peasants, and the children, Fontenelle allowed them the attributes of humanity, even a rudimentary capacity to reason, but he regarded them as incapable of exercising those higher powers of abstraction so remarkably concentrated among members of the French academies. For every event, Fontenelle believed, the primitive, like the peasant, demanded a concrete specific cause. This curious creature could be termed a philosopher and his myths defined as systems. But the Descartes of remote antiquity, so poor in accumulated facts, had only one fundamental source for explanations, his immediate concrete experience of the limited familiar world. Hence whenever he was driven to search out causes he resorted to the known to explain the unknown. This tendency of men to project into nature their own experience was an eternal psychic rule. Where men of the more enlightened age read weights, springs, and levers into natural phenomena, primitives projected what they knew from their own simple lives and emotive reactions. We shall encounter this principle of psychological projection again in Vico, whose notes on the 1730 edition of the *Scienza Nuova* establish it as the primary axiom of human nature. As an antidote to an excessive pan-Vichianism, one could defend the idea that Fontenelle was the

prior influence in north European thought. Any effect on Vico,
however, is doubtful, since he knew little French and refers to one
of Fontenelle's theses only to refute it.

Fontenelle's psychology of primitives was a prolegomenon to
his theory of the origin of the gods. When men first became aware
of the powerful agitations of nature — he followed the Democri-
tan and Epicurean fear-theory — they had to conjure up creatures
great enough to produce such overwhelming effects; as they knew
no images other than the ordinary human ones, their gods
and goddesses became magnified anthropomorphic projections.
"Those beings had to be made like men. What other shape could
they have had?" [21] Like their human progenitors they were cruel
and ignorant, manifestations of mere physical power. The gods
were in a continual state of violent conflict with one another because the forces which men saw in nature clashed. When in the
Iliad Mars was wounded by Diomedes, the stuck god could only
bellow with a force ten thousand times louder than a man's,
proof that amplification of human strength was the limit of the
pagan religious imagination. Fontenelle would have none of the
ancient theory, or of its modern counterparts, that derived the
idea of God from a rational contemplation of the natural order
of the universe, because a primitive in the infancy of reason was
utterly incapable of admiring or even perceiving a divine plan.
Throughout the century this argument against an early cognition
of the harmony of nature will endure in refuting both Deist and
orthodox hypotheses on primitive monotheism, and Hume will
accept it as a cardinal principle of *The Natural History of Religion.*

"The pagans have always copied their divinities after themselves." [22] The origins of the dictum can be found in antiquity,
but Fontenelle's essay developed it with a new historical principle.
For he conceived not of a static, but of a progressive paganism, a
bold stroke which served to reconcile conflicting ancient literary
evidence on the nature of the gods. The first humans were brutal
and they created the bellicose, uncouth gods of Homer; when men
became wiser and more just, the gods reflected their changing
character. In Cicero's day they were virtually philosophers because philosophers had participated in fashioning them. Throughout the eighteenth century an appreciation of the ungentleman-

like qualities of the Homeric personalities is evidence of the new comprehension of the primitive; and while Fontenelle cannot be said to have "discovered the true Homer," Vico's great achievement, he did understand the barbaric character both of the epic heroes and of their gods.

Fontenelle rejected a climatological explanation for myths, which already had a few partisans around 1700. Myth-making was a common experience of all early peoples throughout the world, and not solely the attribute of the "lively imagination of the orientals." The same process would be repeated if men inhabited the poles. Fontenelle is in the autonomous-development school of which Vico became the most ardent exponent. In eighteenth-century theories on the beginnings of culture the innovators were antidiffusionists, in reaction against those etymologists of the seventeenth whose stock-in-trade was the illustration of lines of transmission through the establishment of linguistic similarities on the flimsiest of evidence. Those who held for the autonomous invention of culture, myth, and religion granted that some details were transferred, but they contended that fundamentally myth-making was a stage in the history of reason common to all peoples. Fontenelle, and later Vico, Boulanger, de Brosses, Hume, and Herder would be in accord, for their very conception of a universal human nature made it possible for them to dispense with the cumbersome migration of the gods hypothesized in the previous century.

Fontenelle's facile eclectic streak appears in the unraveling of the last stages in the history of mythology. Later Mediterranean myths were traceable to the natural corruptions of language and the faulty translation of names and ideas from the Phoenician and the Egyptian into Greek. As man's mythopoeic nature yielded to reason the sources of myth dried up, but the myths themselves, once having been committed to writing, were preserved by national pride since they described a people's version of the origin of things. In the end, symbolic interpretations were grafted onto these ancient myths and they were made to teach virtue. Thus Fontenelle did not completely dismiss allegorism; he merely restricted it to a late adaptation of myths which had had their beginnings in the distant past in a completely different world of thought and feeling.

6

The Imposture Thesis Resumed

FONTENELLE'S INTEREST in religion as a source of power for latter-day pagan politicians and their priestly corps matured into an exposure of the artifices of pagan religious charlatanry, an ancient theme for which Lucian of Samosata's satire against the false prophet Alexander was the classical model. Fontenelle — and in this area he parallels Bayle — also ventured into the hazardous terrain of the psychology of superstition. Here the Gassendi Epicureans had preceded him. Fontenelle's analysis of the duped is more nuanced if less noble in diction than the one powerful fixed idea immortalized in Lucretius' masterpiece.

He was not committed to a single theory of the establishment of pagan religion. After an initial amorphous stage during which myths were invented by primitives, organized religion usually appeared as a political instrument. The worship of the gods was proclaimed by sages and legislators who shrouded their announcement in mysteries. There were also more spontaneous deifications when the people in a surge of gratitude apotheosized a hero who had been their benefactor. Fontenelle introduced only slight variations in the theories of Critias and Euhemerus. Though he allowed for some primitive seed of religious emotion based upon an erroneous evaluation of causes — his theory of myths — religious institutions were the premeditated imposture of the more cunning among men, who capitalized on the natural superstitious proclivities of their fellows.

Pagan myth was error, but spontaneous error. Fontenelle attacked the oracles of antiquity in a different temper. Here he recognized deliberate and conscious deceit; these were the workings of politicians, not primitive foolish mythic imaginings. In exposing pagan oracles Fontenelle was treading upon far more dangerous controversial ground than in his psychological explanation of the nature of primitive myth.

In 1686 this gifted philosophical popularizer sold in Paris with the royal privilege an elegant little volume entitled *Histoire des oracles*. It was an avowed adaptation of the heavy, turgid *De Oraculis veterum Ethnicorum dissertationes duae*, published in Amsterdam by Dr. Van Dale a few years earlier (1683). Van Dale's original work on pagan oracles and an equally weighty companion volume anatomizing Jewish superstitions and magical rites as if they were biological specimens were in the ponderous style of Dutch humanist scholarship. The basic text of the second work, the *Dissertationes de origine ac progressu idololatriae et superstitionum* (1696), was Latin, intercalated with long citations in Greek, Hebrew, and Aramaic, and if Van Dale sometimes relented and translated into Latin an original Hebrew source, a Midrash or a quotation from Maimonides, many of his arguments hinged upon a knowledge of the Oriental languages. Acquaintance with the Rabbinic tradition, with Bible commentators like Onkelos, and the more important medieval Jewish philosophers — particularly the *More Nebuchim* — was taken for granted in the Dutch and German learning of this period. Though the difficulties of scholarship confined the use of Van Dale's writings to the more bookish members of the republic of letters, the implications of his works were intrinsically far more heretical to Catholic and Protestant orthodoxy than Fontenelle's piquant essay. Van Dale had written not only on pagan oracles; he had brazenly dissected Judaism in an exhaustive classification of the various types of magic and superstition mentioned in the Biblical and Talmudic texts, and he had equated them with similar Greco-Roman beliefs and practices. Van Dale became a focus of controversy in his own right; he was sharply criticized by Georgius Moebius,[23] one of the more erudite orthodox German scholars whose special field of study he had invaded, and he was drawn upon with approval and defended by Bayle and Bekker and Toland, but he would probably have been forgotten had he not been noticed by one of the most elegant writers of France.

Fontenelle took such liberties with Van Dale's text that the Dutch doctor was unhappy about the adaptation. The light touch of irony, the judicious suppression of prolix examples, the insertion of amusing asides, and the total rearrangement of the material into a logical structure transformed the treatises into a delightful essay which won immediate success and was reprinted seven times during the course of the next century. The French literary man who had revamped Van Dale to entertain the ladies and gentlemen of his society, as well as to propagate scientific truth about the practices of historical paganism, wisely refrained from replying to the broadside attack on his work when it was formally denounced as heretical by Père Baltus in 1707, twenty years after its first publication.[24] Jean Le Clerc in Holland answered for him, and the ensuing polemic, European in scope, turned into a major battle in the war against superstition. Strangely enough, the original publication of the Fontenelle essay in 1686 may have been officially welcomed as an antidote to the violence of an uncontrolled outburst of prosecutions for witchcraft. For the eighteenth century this none too subtle diatribe against religious chicanery remained the source-book on the history of paganism.

The problem of oracles resurrected by Fontenelle — how they operated, when and why they ceased to function — was on its face hardly a burning issue fifteen hundred years after Plutarch had raised the subject. But Fontenelle had the temerity to contradict the Church Fathers on two traditions which they had evolved during the early centuries of Christianity. Demons, working through human agency, had been generally credited by the church with devising and maintaining these abominable oracles. The idea was sanctioned by Augustine and was the normal way of accounting for the fact that pagans, even the philosophers among them, were persuaded to false beliefs. A complementary patristic doctrine taught that the coming of Christ and the power of the true word had finally silenced the oracles. The Church Fathers had not subscribed exclusively to the doctrine of the demoniac origin of pagan religion, for elements of Euhemerism, Stoic allegorism, and even the Sophist fear-theory found their way into patristic literature; but whatever other ideas intruded, over the centuries Christianity had become fundamentally committed to the intervention of concrete demons as cunning misleaders of pagan man. In late medieval painting demons in lieu of idols were frequently depicted standing on antique columns, an iconographic embodiment of the theory.

There was no innocence in Fontenelle's history of oracles; nothing which touched the origins, mechanics, ritual, and beliefs of any religion was treated without premeditation during this revolutionary period in the spiritual consciousness of Europe. As long as demons were behind the magical and seductive prophecies of oracles and the true God was the source of Christianity the two religious worlds could be kept sharply distinct from each other, one the empire of Satan and the other the beneficiary of revelation. But if a writer drew back the veil of Isis and produced detailed rationalistic, scientific, matter-of-fact, and above all human explanations of the apparently miraculous performances of pagan priests and augurers, including psychological motivations for both the heathen dupes and their sacerdotal deceivers, his exposure was a dangerous threat to all established religious institutions which attested miracles and exorcized demons. Throughout the eighteenth century no discussion of pagan or exotic religion ever lost its heretical overtones, however fervid the philosophers' protests that they were only combatting the false gods of the gentiles and were not impugning the established truth of Christianity. When the Holbachian atheists appeared in mid-century they found no difficulty in translating the works of French sceptics and English Deists into virulent anti-Christian tirades. An unmasking of paganism was a prelude to Holbach's *L'Enfer détruit* (1769). Allegorizing pagan beliefs in the Stoic manner was a far more salutary exercise in the eyes of established religion than revealing them as impostures.

Fontenelle was a wary man, with no passion for martyrdom, and he was writing a year after the revocation of the Edict of Nantes. The *Histoire des oracles* has been called "prudent and perfidious." His precautions included a preface to the effect that he was primarily a translator and adapter of Van Dale's work, which did not imply total acceptance; he carefully excised the Protestant Van Dale's anecdotes about contemporary Catholic demonology; he cited a work by Père Thomassin for somewhat farfetched support; excluded the general problem of magic from his analysis; and admitted that demons might well exist, though he wished to restrict their empire. But despite these circumscriptions of his central proposition, knowing readers still could understand that whenever he bared the machinery of pagan oracles, he was hinting at behind-the-scenes manipulation in all miraculous events.

With an air of piety Fontenelle charged that the demonological theory, for all its patristic authority, had shown undue leniency towards idolatry by exculpating the pagan priests of any evil intention or imposture. The pagans could now plead that they were victims of powerful demons who animated their statues and thus left them helpless. Having rendered lip service to true religion Fontenelle proceeded to the heart of his thesis, a skillful presentation, with the aid of classical and patristic sources laboriously collected by Van Dale, of the operational code of pagan priestcraft. His ideas parallel those of Bayle, but what the professor spread through many folios was here concentrated in one succinct essay on the psychology of religious deception. "We who are men, do we not know to what extent other men can be impostors or dupes?" [25] The sites of the oracles as at Delphi were, Fontenelle showed, selected with a view to arousing wonderment and terror, fear and hope. He dwelt on the height of the ceiling in the caverns and crypts and the pleasant odors which announced the presence of the god. Drugs, perfumes, intoxicating vapors, potions, impregnated skins for coverlets, strange sounds and weird sights, massages, nocturnal baths, fasts — all were in the priestly bag of tricks. "How many machines could operate in this darkness?" [26] The new age which was delighted by mechanical chessplayers instinctively mechanized the pagan artifices. An adept was emotionally prepared by the surroundings, which generated fear and uneasiness, to accept any message from the god. On a par with these ministrations was a highly organized network of information in the great centers of population and at the site of the oracle. The priests knew what was being asked before the suppliant arrived; through agents they were kept acquainted with the problems which burdened the minds of prominent devotees who came to solicit oracular advice. At religious sanctuaries, whose inhabitants lived on the trade of visitors, the obedience of the people to the instructions of the priests was strengthened by interest. As Lucian had said, the hangers-on of temples and oracles literally subsisted on myths and miracles. If preparations were incomplete the day was declared unpropitious for oracular pronouncements. The secrecy in which mysteries were enveloped was really a security measure to conceal the cheats of the priests. The final closing down of oracles was to be imputed not to the glorious sign of Jesus but to a variety of historical causes, among them the exposure of the priestly craft by philosophers, the slow growth of reason, and the political triumph of the Christians.

In many passages Fontenelle's doubt about the existence of any profound pagan faith approached Bayle's view of idolatry as mere external ritual without internal conviction. Pagans, wrote Fontenelle, practiced merely to deliver themselves from the uneasiness which failure to perform prescribed ceremonials might have generated. Was he not thinking of Parisian pagans, too? The philosophical reappraisal of myth and pagan religion, in the general depreciatory tone of Bekker, Le Clerc, and Van Dale, raised many of the same vexatious questions for his world-outlook that it had for Pierre Bayle. Like Bayle he had a sense of the extraordinary tenacity of error once it had taken root in mankind. The imagination was conceived of as a virtually separate compartment of the soul, relatively inaccessible to reason. Often ideas which had been disproved by the rational faculties took refuge and remained embedded in the imagination: witness the longevity of the Greek myths; for even though Christian Europeans no longer believed in them rationally as the pagans had, the same myths still delighted them in painting and poetry. "Nothing proves better that imagination and reason hardly have converse with each other and things of which reason is completely disabused lose none of their attractions for the imagination." [27] Fontenelle, of the first generation of the Enlightenment, was never without doubts in his theory of progress; it took a century to achieve Condorcet's clamorous optimism.

The very possibility of an undying mythic mind and the lack of assurance in the enduring triumph of rationality remained a source of misgivings to Fontenelle despite his confidence in the exhaustion of error, in the accumulative value of knowledge and of the sheer addition of experiences, which was voiced in the *Digression sur les anciens et les modernes*. Hence his preoccupation with myth, his need — more profound than either the exhibition of fashionable anticlericalism or the affirmation of modernity — to comprehend the true nature of paganism. Fontenelle tolled the bell for the Age of Reason: "All men resemble one another so strongly that there is not a people whose stupidities should fail to make us tremble."[28] Bayle's great erudition had hardly muffled the echo of the same doubt: "But we must remember that there is no absurdity from which the human mind is immune." [29] The realities of historical paganism were a dire warning to mankind.

CHAPTER II

The English Deists

"Natural Religion was easy first and plain,
Tales made it Mystery, Offrings made it Gain
Sacrifices and Shows were at length prepar'd
The Priests ate Roast-meat and the People
star'd."

— John Toland, *Letters to Serena* (1704).

1

Primitive Monotheism Republished

*P*RIMITIVE MONOTHEISM, the orthodox theory among both Catholics and Protestants, was assimilated into the system of natural religion evolved by the followers of Lord Herbert of Cherbury, though the heterodox glosses they insinuated were far from palatable either to the highly ritualistic or to the enthusiastic branches of Christianity. The Deist view of the origin of religion was propagated by a wide variety of writers, many of them bitterly inimical to one another, ranging from the rambunctious pantheist John Toland through respectable Anglican cathedral deans with a penchant for rationality in religion. The ideas were by no means exclusively English. Respectable abbés like Charles Le Batteux could subscribe to a Deist-like adaptation of the dogma of primitive monotheism colored by the eighteenth-century philosophical spirit and still remain in the Académie des Inscriptions et Belles-Lettres. Voltaire had imported the doctrine into France along with the rest of the Deist philosophy and later defended it against the Holbachian atheists in *Dieu et les hommes par le docteur Obern* (1769), which by order of the Parlement was consumed in the same flames as the *Système de la nature*. Diderot found primitive monotheism wholly acceptable, at least in the mood of the *Essai sur le mérite et la vertu* (1745) and *De la suffisance de la religion naturelle* (1747). German professors of Göttingen like Johann Mosheim had a natural affinity for the religious theory of their fellow subjects of the Hanoverian dynasty, though they would never have identified themselves as Deists. The Germans of the *Aufklärung* who reduced religion to morality — Gotthold Ephraim Lessing and Moses Mendelssohn, Starck

57

and Meiners — were in the same school, demystifying all religions, identifying their common rationality, equating the *lex rationis* and the *lex naturae* with revelation. But despite the profuse continental imitations Deism retained a predominantly English flavor, and its treatment of nonrationalist religious manifestations was unique, and somewhat parochial.

The English Deists were especially favored by the political circumstances of the period immediately following the Glorious Revolution. The new monarchy wanted neither fanatic Puritans nor miracle-making Papists about — it looked to an orderly, sober church establishment. The line of tolerance was still drawn at atheism or at a denial of the divinity of Christ, but for the most part this was an open society in which religious controversy was permitted in high places. The intellectual temper was in many respects freer than later in the century. Deism in England had its poverty-stricken, vain, boisterous, hapless, uncontrollable pamphleteers, but it also enjoyed prestige and power in the realm, for among its adepts were great lords and noble gentlemen, Shaftesbury, Bolingbroke, Anthony Collins, Blount. Only in England had the separation of church and state proceeded so far that disputants could engage in open theological debate without jeopardizing their personal liberty, interpret Biblical texts loosely, and discuss miracles and the psychology of religion with impunity. Englishmen did not need to expose the impostures of pagan oracles as a subterfuge when their real target was ritualistic Judaism and Christianity. There were occasional threats from the attorney-general and a measure of self-censorship among publishers, but there was no Bastille.

The major problems confronting a Deist in the reconstruction of a world history of religion had already been faced by the orthodox. How explain the bewildering variety of religious experience, which the voyage literature and translations from the Chinese, Indian, Persian, and Vedic sacred writings had thrust into the forefront of European consciousness? How account for the startling conformities among heathens ancient and modern and the even more disturbing fact that pagan rituals and beliefs showed marked resemblances to the Judaic and Christian revelations and ceremonial practices? Why had God allowed mon-

strous perversions of His pure Being to exist in the world? By
1700 a body of traditional solutions had been accumulated in
Christendom which satisfied the pious. Savage cult objects and
rituals which had counterparts in Christianity were, after mo-
mentary dismay, neatly enlisted as proofs of true religion. The
barbaric rite was a remnant of the primitive monotheism of
Adam, a corruption which still preserved enough of the authentic
revelation to resemble the original; or it was a prefiguration of
the truth which was to be announced, crude in form, but a foretelling, like the words of the Old Testament prophets and the
utterances of the sibyls; or it was an early usage which God, out
of condescension, because it was harmless and amenable to a
Christian interpretation, allowed to be metamorphosed into a
sacrament. Maimonides had used the same conception to justify
the continuation of paganlike sacrifices under Mosaic law. Conformities among savage idolatries themselves were easy to explain
through the patristic demonological doctrine. The same demons
were operative in all paganisms; these seducers of mankind were
incapable of novelty and were repetitive. The noncreative demons, the apes of God, could only imitate and corrupt with slight
variations the one true religious tradition which had a continuous
history from Adam through Christ.

The eighteenth-century Deists rejected the demonology, the
condescension, and the prefiguration as crude anthropomor-
phisms, and set out in search of fresh naturalistic interpretations,
though many of the older religious motifs are still discernible
beneath the new vestments.

The belief that there was some common denominator in all religious manifestations had been growing among Europeans since
the discoveries of the New World. What Calvin in the *Institutes*
recognized as a glimmer of truth in the darkness of paganism became the Deist natural religion embodied in different forms and
shapes. Ralph Cudworth's *True Intellectual System of the Universe* (1678) expressed enlightened English Protestant theory
in his day. "Having treated largely concerning the Two most
eminent Polytheists among the ancient Pagans, Zoroaster and
Orpheus, and clearly proved that they asserted One Supreme
Deity; we shall in the next place observe, that the Egyptians

themselves also, notwithstanding their Multifarious *Polytheisms* and Idolatry, had an acknowledgement, amongst them, of one Supreme, and Universal Numen." [1] Primitive Christianity, the unadorned teachings of Christ, was the essence of religion in all times and places, universally admitted. When the seventeenth-century Jesuits allowed ancient Chinese formulae such as "Adore the Heavens" to remain in the temples of their new converts they were unwittingly bolstering a form of universal Deism, and the Dominicans were quick to warn the Papacy of this latitudinarian danger. If the Jesuits could presume that the Chinese mandarins had reached the halfway mark toward Christianity, why should Greek and Roman philosophical authors, whose profound moral sentiments were the education of Europe, be denied a knowledge of one God? The ancient pagans could offer no resistance to their ex post facto conversion to Deist Christianity. What the Jesuits did for the Chinese, the philosophical divines of the Anglican Church accomplished for the more worthy philosophers among the Greeks, the Romans, and the Egyptians. The prospect was opened up for these religious English humanists that some day in another sphere they might have converse in the groves of Academe with Cicero, Seneca, and Plutarch, perhaps even with Socrates himself.

Most Deists were far more interested in proving that man was naturally a religious animal than in exalting the special character of Christian revelation. The religious debate had been transferred to another level: there was no longer a question of showing the superiority of Christianity over Judaism and Mohammedanism or the truth of a particular Christian sect, but of defending religion itself against the libertine argument that it was not necessary to man. Even for orthodox Catholics it had become more important to demonstrate that the most benighted savage, that a wild foundling discovered crawling in the woods, had a natural inkling of God than to win a battle over theological niceties. Inevitably, in the course of the facile conversion of American savages, Chinese mandarins, and Greek polytheists to primitive monotheism, the traditionalist Christians bent their dogma more than a little in the direction of Deist conceptions whose name they would have abhorred.

Despite John Locke's famous refutation of the innate idea of God in the *Essay Concerning Humane Understanding* (1690), even those Deists who accepted his general epistemology clung to the notion that man was created with a religious spark in his bosom, an inborn sentiment which was in content virtually equivalent to the moral principles of a Christian English Deist circa 1700. Original man was a benign creature, ever prone as an instinctive impulse of his being to love his brethren and to worship the Deity who created the world. The quintessential nature of man, constant in his devotion to God, beneficent and pious, was identical throughout time. In his effusions of kindness and gratitude to God for the bountiful nature which sustained him he acted spontaneously, but he was also a rational creature who comprehended the natural order and the philosophical justification for his sentiments. Arguments from design fortified his primitive monotheism. This tender man, loving and reasonable, religious and sociable, needed no positive law to guide him and required no sacerdotal establishments to prescribe forms of worship, since adoration was a natural emanation of his being. "The most antient Egyptians, Persians, and Romans, the first Patriarchs of the Hebrews, with several other Nations and Sects," wrote John Toland in the *Letters to Serena* (1704), "had no sacred Images or Statues, no peculiar Places or costly Fashions of Worship; the plain Easiness of their Religion being most agreeable to the Simplicity of the Divine Nature, an indifference of Place and Time were the best expressions of infinite Power and Omnipresence." [2] Ritual was superfluous and artificial — some Deists said mechanical. When allowed free expression, natural religion manifested itself in simple, intimate, joyful praise, accompanied by symbolic gifts. This Deist idyll was a composite of images from classical Arcadia and the Garden of Eden before the Fall, crowned with the idea of innate reasonableness.

But the contradictions between this ideal of natural religion and the ugly realities of religious experience familiar to the most casual observer of world history cried out for conciliation. What had happened to defile the purity of natural religion? How did mankind fall from the rational precepts and natural sentiments related to primitive monotheism into the abyss of the more vulgar

positive religions? Man had the mind to conceive of a Supreme
Being; he knew through his natural benevolence the basic moral
precepts of love toward fellow men and thankfulness toward
God. What then had corrupted him? The eruption of idolatrous
behavior sometime in remote antiquity — the precise date was
in controversy — was readily recognized by the Fathers as a
symptom of evil and original sin, but the rationalist Deists could
not resort to such supernatural explanations. In tracing the history of religious decline from pure primitive monotheism, the
Deists were constrained to invent a commonsense rationale for
the growth of the multifarious burdensome superstitious ceremonials of all organized priesthoods, among the heathen, savage
and civil, in Judaism, and in Christianity; to offer historical or
at least psychological causes for the abominable rituals that were
a disgrace to human dignity, for anthropomorphic idolatry and
brute-worship; and to explain the pollution of what was originally
the adoration of a benign God with bloody sacrifices of animals
and fellow men.

As a way out of their quandary the Deists had recourse to general reflections on human nature which rendered the naive, bland
portrait of early man more complex, more "interesting," as
Nietzsche would say. True, man was created with innate religious
virtues, but he was born also with natural frailty. Wherever the
orthodox said sin, the Deists substituted feebleness and disease.
Wherever the Puritans had thundered depravity, the Deists dole-
fully described error, a failure of the mechanism of true perception, a disorder of the senses, a confusion in the brain. Human
reason, though it could grasp the truth, was weak; it could not
hold it firmly; other aspects of man's nature — his imagination,
his concupiscence — led him astray, so that he was lost as in a
labyrinth of uncontrolled passions. The doctrine of frailty assumed alternative forms. One posited human debility as equal in
all times and places, thus preserving the predominant Deist ahistorical temper. A less frequent variant allowed that there had
been a measure of change in mankind, that in the first ages human
reason had been peculiarly susceptible to distortions, since like a
child's brain the fibres were then very tender, a theory which led
the Deists into the progressist camp where they did not ordinarily

belong, for they had to conceive of a strengthening or modifica-
tion of the rational tissues in time. A third possibility was perhaps
the most commonly accepted of all; it entailed not one fall, one
momentous degeneration, but a whole series of injuries to the
reason of man, followed by periodic natural recuperation after the
ministrations of great spiritual leaders who were, so to speak,
the doctors of humanity, who from time to time set men's erring
intellects aright with the fresh elucidation of the truths of primitive monotheism and natural religion. These religious guides had
appeared at intervals in various parts of the world, and as the
readings of the sacred texts of Jews, Mohammedans, Persians,
Indians, and Chinese attested, they always preached the same
gospel, albeit in diverse forms. Differences among the holy writings of East and West could be brushed aside as superficial local
variations responsive to climatic conditions. Beneath the apparent confusion of creeds the same uniform religious principles
which had never been altered since Creation endured.

Since most English Deists were also Christians, they were willing
to allow for one exception in this history of religious reaffirmation
— the revelation of Jesus, superior in its formulation of truth to
all other teachings throughout the world. Over the precise quality
of the uniqueness of the Christian dispensation violent theological
controversy raged, and there was a whole spectrum of variegated
opinion from the natural religion of respected Anglican bishops
to Collins the "free-thinker." For some Deists the Christ was still
a divine revelation *sui generis;* for others his preachments merely
differed in their degree of excellence from what had been received among the Hindus, the Chinese, the American savages.
"Christianity as Ancient as the World," Tindal announced. For
his followers Christ's message did not differ in essence from the
natural knowledge of God with which Adam had been endowed;
it was a republication of the truth, not a new discovery; it was
the most perfect of the versions, not an entirely novel revelation
to mankind. It was not always clear whether in the future there
would be further editions of natural religion or whether the
teachings of Jesus would stand for all time as the most complete.
Certainly many English Deists conceived of themselves as re-
storers of primitive Christianity.

The true God of the Deists was never a god of fear and trembling, of punishment and damnation. Though Herbert of Cherbury's Deism included immortality among the five principles of religion, the previews of the hereafter were conspicuously lacking in scenes of fire and brimstone. In positive priestly religions, pagan as well as Christian, the idea of a rational God had been grossly distorted into a monstrous image of vengeance, gloating over human suffering, demanding victims. Deism, which was the original primitive monotheism, had been perverted. Into the same ignominious company should be thrust a savage American devil-worship, a Greek Zeus with his thunderbolts, a Chinese monster-god, and a Christian fanatic's god of eternal hellfire.

2

The Twofold Philosophy

$\mathcal{Q}$UA HISTORIANS of ancient pagan religion many of these good Deists were driven by their insight into human weakness to propound the "twofold philosophy," a doctrine which serves to identify them beyond their common preaching of sweet reasonableness and natural religion. The formula of the double truth had been lying about in the classical corpus and needed only to be adapted and embroidered with historical evidence to resolve the apparent internal contradictions of pagan, Judaic, and even Christian practice recorded in the religious annals of mankind. At no time in human history, the theory asserted, among no people, had the belief in primitive monotheism been totally eradicated, despite the universal prevalence of idolatries and bestial popular rites. What had happened was that one group of men in a society, usually the stronger in some sense, often an organized corps, had monopolized the monotheist doctrine, transforming it into a mystery which they veiled from the people. The initiatory ceremonies of all ancient cults preserved the truths of natural religion in a secret hieroglyphic and symbolic language.

In one form or another the double-truth doctrine was entertained by episcopal worthies like Warburton, avowed pantheists like Toland, cautious philosophical skeptics like Hume, grand Deist lords like Bolingbroke, abbés like Le Batteux, scholarly authors who specialized in the mystery cults like Sainte-Croix, that most outrageous materialist Dr. La Mettrie, the most popular orthodox scientific writer, Abbé Pluche, the revolutionary atheist Charles Dupuis. Wherever a sounding is made one comes upon the idea that there were always two pagan religions: gross polytheism, with human sacrifices, brute-worship, even cabbage-worship, for the masses; secret monotheism, a religion of virtue, love, adoration of the First Cause, for an elite. The eighteenth-century writers were obviously projecting their own religious problems and solutions back into antiquity. These elegant aristocrats of England, university men from Scotland, worldly *philosophes* in Paris, the capital of the universe, materialist doctors in Frederick II's court knew that religious ceremonials, rites, and the power of organized clergies were not necessary for their own understanding of science and nature and the rational First Cause; and yet beyond the gates of their academies and salons was a howling mob, attracted by nothing but childish superstitions, which followed the fanatic dissenters, the Methodist preachers, the miracles of the Abbé de Pâris, adored the painted dolls in Neapolitan churches and worshipped saints like idols. It was this realization which informed David Hume's *Natural History of Religion*. His contemporaries the papist idolators and the fanatical believers in the Jansenist miracles were no different from the most vulgar primitive polytheists. There had been men of sense in antiquity, Socrates, Epicurus, Lucretius, and there was a handful of men in his own day capable of spiritual abstractions, Hume himself and his moralist friends, his antecedents Shaftesbury and Bayle and Bolingbroke. There were two religions in every society, one for the men of reason and one for the fanatics, one for those who comprehended the marvelous order of the world and one for those who still relied on gods for every event, the ignorant men full of terrors which they allayed with ludicrous rituals.

The Humean doctrine had been preached fifty years earlier by John Toland, a magnificent stylist whose pungent writings in Latin and translations from the English dominated the continental debate for more than a century. For his equals, the philosophers, he wrote a service to be performed behind closed doors, *Praise to the All*. Hymns were to be chanted to free inquiry, to knowledge and truth, but only after the servants had left the banquet as in antiquity. The common herd could not understand the mysteries, neither in ancient times nor in modern. "We shall be in Safety," he wrote in the *Pantheisticon, sive formula celebrandae sodalitatis Socraticae* (1720), "if we separate ourselves from the Multi-

tude; for the Multitude is a Proof of what is worst."[3] The mass
was credulous, and since the Deists had joined ranks in a war
against credulity they were often involved in a war against the
people. The wise men of all time, hierophants of the mystery
religions, formed a sort of esoteric brotherhood which throughout
the ages had taught the same pantheism and identical Pythagorean astronomy — "or to speak with the Moderns the Coperni-
can" — all equally incomprehensible to the mob. The ancient
mysteries were a necessary barrier before the ignorant, creating a
pathos of distance to preserve truth, "inasmuch as all Philosophy
is divided by the Pantheists, as well as other antient Sages, into
External, or popular and depraved; and Internal, or pure and
genuine." [4] The theory was not new in England. Ralph Cudworth
had in 1678 already described the simultaneous existence among
the Egyptians, the Persians, and the Indians of a "Vulgar and
Fabulous Theory and an Arcane and Recondite Theology," but
Toland made a program of action out of the doctrine.

Toland looked upon the people as children to be humored,
and unwittingly contributed to the literature which assimilated
the infantile, the primitive, the mad, and the superstitious.
"Wherefore the Pantheists, Persons of the strictest Moderation,
behave Towards frantic, foolish, and stubborn Men, as fond
Nurses do towards their babbling Minions, who imbibe from
them the pleasing Infatuation of imagining themselves Kings and
Queens, that they are only Papa and Mama's Pets, and that there
are none so pretty and so finy as they. Those who flatter not
Infants in these Trifles are odious and disagreeable to them." [5]
In militant Deists like Toland the fear of the mob sometimes
acquired a passionate tone. The ancient founders of mysteries
had rightly secreted their truths from the blind masses; in fact the
wise elite in all ages would probably have to subscribe to the
double-truth doctrine, allowing the common people to wallow
in their superstitious corruptions of primitive monotheism while
the select few communicated their natural truths to one another.
Toland's pessimism, though not generally normative for Deist
philosophy, was a current of thought which ran deep in some
segments of this school. In his bitter pamphlets he denounced a
condition of ecclesiastical society which forced him, a free

Christian, to avail himself of a heathen practice, but there was no choice.

Warburton, the bishop with a mace spiked with learning which he wildly heaved about him against the Tolands and the Tindals, somehow found himself plucking from their doctrinal vineyards. This "rather knock-kneed giant of theology," in one of the most confused yet remarkably influential works of the great religious controversy, ended up by demonstrating to any commonsense reader not "the divine legation of Moses" but the twofold philosophy. In the Egyptian mysteries the priests taught monotheism, future rewards and punishments. Only the ignorant peasants enmeshed in error and trapped by the deceits of their masters had come to believe that the hieroglyphic images were actual gods when in reality they were only word-paintings. The Abbé Pluche received this doctrine from across the Channel and embellished it in his own inimitable scientific manner, but the heart of the matter was the same: there was one religion for the stupid Egyptians and another for those favored few initiated into the mysteries.

These eighteenth-century admirers and imitators of the ancients envisaged themselves as the legatees of secret truth, pantheist, deist, or atheist, but like the wise men of old they were sworn to preserve this truth only for those prepared to receive it. While the philosophers were permitted absolute freedom for their speculations the multitude would have to be directed by the orthodox religious establishment. In part this ancient theory of the double truth was revived for the personal security of *philosophes,* but this was not the only motive: they really believed the common people to be incapable of behaving in a moral manner without the dread sanctions of religion. Among French Deists like Voltaire the idea persisted to the eve of the Revolution. Not until the Holbachians argued that the secular sovereign could dispense with the church as a prop of the social order did the double-truth doctrine become superfluous in anticlerical thought. It was the hangman and not the priest who deterred the common people from committing crimes against property.

One branch of Deist thought, exemplified by Trenchard, while it recognized the doctrine of the double truth as a historical real-

ity in most ancient theocracies, was uneasy about this bifurcation
of humanity. A great evil had been perpetrated by the purveyors
of the twofold philosophy, perhaps the greatest iniquity of all
time. The truth of natural religion and primitive monotheism
had been shrouded from the mass of the people and preserved in
secret not by benign philosophers but by wicked men in pursuit
of power. Politicians or a priestly corps were endowed with intelligence and a shrewd scheming capacity, while the people were
left in their ignorance and stupidity. Bishop Warburton out of a
sense of solidarity with the priesthood of Egypt laid the original
corruption of mankind to politicians — these later seduced the
priests. Condorcet, in the classical version of this theory in the
Esquisse d'un tableau historique des progrès de l'esprit humain,
after it had been usurped by the revolutionary atheists, imputed
the initial plot to priests acting with complete self-consciousness.
Variations on this theme are numerous: in Abbé Pluche's history
the people fell into the error of idolatry naturally and the priests
could do nothing to rescue them; in other versions the priests
sinned by tolerating the frailty of the masses. Only a minority of
theorists, Condorcet among them, carried the double-truth doctrine to the point where the sacerdotal plotters, ensconced in their
citadel of exclusive knowledge, became so lazy and routinized
that they were themselves enveloped by the vapors of darkness
which they had originally generated.

Deists of a more tender persuasion denied wicked or evil intent
on the part of the original founders of the mysteries; either their
symbols were necessary forms of pictorial language used by ancient
teachers in oriental lands that had a natural addiction to imagistic
figures, or they were a means of communication among all primitive humans not yet accustomed to rationalist modes of expression. Through error, that convenient eighteenth-century catchall,
the meaning of the original primitive monotheist allegories had
been forgotten, sometimes by the very priestly corps who had first
devised them.

3

A Psychopathology of Enthusiasm

*T*HE ORDINARY Deist analysis of the degeneration of natural religion was often a monotonous reworking of a few classical themes. In the end it affirmed primitive monotheism as arbitrarily as did the orthodox dogma. In their psychopathology of religious experience, however, those Deist writers who recognized the insufficiency and essential poverty of the imposture theory introduced real novelty into eighteenth-century thought.

The study of psychology had been significantly stimulated by the seventeenth-century outbreaks of demonism and witch hunting. The trials were often long inquiries in which rational men brought up in the law participated and the judges showed a decent respect for testimony. Doctors were summoned to examine patients who were possessed by demons, and both ecclesiastical and secular authorities were on the lookout for pious frauds, the rascally peasants who came to the church to be exorcised with the prospect of profit when they turned out to be the objects of a miraculous cure by the local priest. The weight of the empirical evidence was overwhelmingly in favor of the existence of demons. In the seventeenth century a new scientific attitude had penetrated even the study of demonology and it was possible to couple an honest belief in demons with circumstantial detailed medical descriptions of the uniform characteristics of demoniacs, for it seemed that even the devil had to obey the natural laws of his profession. The words pathology and physiology crept into the dissertations of faithful believers in the devil, in works like Joannes Casparus Westphal's *Pathologia Daemoniaca, id est Observationes et Meditationes Physiologico-Magico-Medicae circa Dae-*

70

monomanias (1707). It was equally scientific that the opponents of the devil, the good English Deists, should use the data assembled in works on the possessed as symptoms of plain insanity and then extend their perceptions to all similar forms of religious extravagance, pagan and Christian. In lieu of demons a mechanistic psychology with great emphasis upon the diverse effects of environmental conditions upon the senses was made to account for most of the strange religious phenomena reported in antiquity as well as in the marvelous episodes of modern times.

Paradoxical as it may seem, the initiation of the study of individual and mass psychology was rooted not in any abstract scientific curiosity about the nature of man, but in a religious purpose of great moment. English psychology was born the newest handmaiden of true religion. The Quaker illuminations and the Puritan fanaticism, the Anabaptist ravings and the convulsionaries, the miracle-making Jansenists and the witchcraft accusations had led the sober rational Deists to identify such manifestations a priori with disease and madness. This was in one respect a polemical device, not unknown in our own contemporary intellectual controversies, to explode millenarian visions by declaring them projections of a sick body and a deranged mind, hence not witnesses of God. Any religious experience other than the rational perception of the coordinated workings of the mechanical universe under a Creator was for these Deists uniformly a symptom of disease like the ague or epilepsy. A "normal" or "natural" healthy psychic state was conceived as necessary not so much for worldly happiness as for a comprehension of the true God. Psychology was thus the consequence of a need for an objective criterion to evaluate aberrant religious experience, an ancient problem which had once shaken the body politic of Israel, the differentiation between the true and the false prophet. The modern enthusiast was false because he was in "distemper" and his knowledge of God was polluted. A German echo of this kind of thinking, in a more pious garb, can be found later in the century in Johann Lorenz von Mosheim's *Philosophisch-theologische Abhandlung von den moralischen Krankheiten des menschlichen Geschlechts* (1771).

The two little-known English Deists, John Trenchard and Thomas Gordon, wrote at a crucial intermediary moment in the development of the psychology of religion. They came in the wake of the pioneer revolutionary Dutch and French works, the exposures of the Greco-Roman and Hebrew religious artifices and superstitions by Van Dale and Fontenelle, Bekker's exile of devils from the world and their enchainment in Hell, a stream of medical investigations of demoniacs, and above all Bayle's eclectic assimilation both of priestly imposture and psychopathological behavior as plausible explanations for the strange manifestations of credulity ancient and modern. Trenchard and Gordon were steeped in earlier English analyses of religious enthusiasm, in Burton's famous *Anatomy of Melancholy* and in Shaftesbury's *Characteristicks*. At times their works, which have a journalistic character, were virtual paraphrases of more eminent predecessors, but no other writings of the period were as candid in their factual description of religious experience and as forceful in their free and easy use of a vigorous English diction reminiscent of the polemics of the Revolution, or as acute in their diagnosis of the psychic origins of religious mysticism. Trenchard's *Natural History of Superstition* — the scientific title is noteworthy — dated 1709, has never been reprinted and is a great rarity. When Trenchard collaborated with Thomas Gordon in the publication of the *Independent Whig* in 1720 his old arguments were presented in an even more vehement style and amplified with new themes. This series of essays on politics and religion, which lived up to its title, was an extraordinary success, saw many re-editions, and even made its way across the Atlantic. Though it is not cited in his writings, David Hume probably perused it; at least many of his observations on the psychology of religion parallel its reasoning. The Bishop of Mann condemned this "most pestilent book" in a bull, despite the honest Deism of its authors and their adoration of Christ. If the original text was no more sacrilegious than the run of Deist literature of the Tindal variety, its later fortunes on the continent seem to justify the Bishop's censure, for it was translated by the atheist Holbach and appropriated by the "great Synagogue." The wicked Baron also pretended that *La Contagion sacrée* was a translation of the *Natural History of Superstition,* but it was really introduced only in one or two sections and should not bear the onus for Holbach's outright blasphemy.[6]

Religious ideas like those which Conyers Middleton, the respectable librarian of Trinity College, paraded publicly in the first decades of the eighteenth century would have been considered terrible heresies in France. In its very first number on January 20, 1720, the *Independent Whig* highlighted the differences in the temper of the two societies, rejoicing in English spiritual liberty. True there were freethinking abbés in Paris, but they did not hold the public position of a Tillotson. Bishop Warburton, in England a "bigot" who used his ecclesiastical powers to intimidate libertines, was on the continent a *philosophe* whose early writings were widely admired. But as the century wore on, English treatises on theological subjects tended to become more conservative, stereotyped, and orthodox. The wild days of Toland and Collins were soon over, and Hume avoided publication of his famous dialogue during his lifetime. In France in the meantime the radical temper had possessed society. With the triumph of the philosophical sect in the sixties all manner of flagrant violations of moderate opinion were perpetrated, not with the royal patent, to be sure, but nevertheless with general knowledge and amid widespread literary comment. It was during this period that the robust early-eighteenth-century English Deists, pretty much passé in their own country, were introduced into France, where they no longer served the cause of the pure love of a benign God and a gentle Jesus, but the most outrageous atheism, which mocked Adam, Abraham, Christ, and the pagan gods in the same licentious tone.

The *Independent Whig* and the little essay on superstition which preceded it were still written in the earthy language of seventeenth-century Puritan sermons, though their subject was the contempt of hellfire. The ideas were far less elegantly expressed than in their later version in Hume, who wrote with Cicero, Horace, and Lucretius peering over his shoulder and guiding his hand. This was rough journalism, and even Holbach thinned out many passages of the original text to conform to the taste of his genteel French atheists. The early-eighteenth-century English Deists wrote the way Diderot sometimes talked. "Sometimes you are to scarify your Backside for the Healing of your Soul," wrote the *Independent Whig* on October 5, 1720, "and reconcile yourself to Heaven by the Dint of Lashings which will sometimes serve for another *Purpose;* and so a Scourge made of Broom, is made the Scourge of God." Trenchard and Gordon were fighting popery, priests, their English imitators in the Anglican Church, enthusiastic Protestant sectarians of every variety. Theirs was not a mild gentlemanly unitarianism. It was Deism militant, a ferocious, rampant, sarcastic, battling, idol-breaking, priest-hating, fanatic-loathing crusade. But it was far from devoid of analytic elements; the rhetoric always contained a hard rationalist kernel.

For these Deists religious experience was plainly divisible into two categories, the true and the false. A belief in a rational Creator and in the gospel of Christ preaching love was the totality of the true religion, even more abbreviated than Herbert of Cherbury's. All other religious manifestations were false, and these were the subject of Trenchard's first inquiry in 1709 into the origins and etiology of superstition, not a minor concern since it comprised the cult practices and creeds of most human beings throughout all time. Half a century before the publication of Hume's magisterial essay, *The Natural History of Superstition* posed fundamental questions related to the psychology of religious emotion. Why were men possessed by "panick fears," prone to superstition? Why did they have bizarre religious feelings and perform unnatural acts in the name of God? How could rational men be so readily deceived by priestly frauds? How was it possible for them to believe in myths of abominable gods as if they were realities? How could a religious mystic credit his hallucinations? For answers Trenchard turned to a study of human nature, "to examine into the frame and constitution of our own Bodies, and search into the causes of our Passions and Infirmities." [7] There he discovered why the mind, for all its perfection, had been misled and betrayed into superstition, why despite the wondrous natural order of the world and the excellence of the human mechanism it had been possible for priests to perpetrate sacerdotal deceits and for enthusiasts to see visions.

Trenchard first offered a secular physiological equivalent of original sin. There was in fact "something innate in our Constitutions" which made us susceptible to these delusions. Man, governed by the postulates of Lockian sensationalism, sought to avoid pain, or what he imagined might hurt him. Above all, he was preoccupied with that greatest pain, death, and what transpired in the hereafter. Since man was both inquisitive and a cause-seeker, as Fontenelle had already defined him, he was driven by a passionate desire to know the identity and intentions of his potential pain-inflicter, but unfortunately the cause of things was hidden, and in his anxious bewilderment he accepted either the word of authority or whatever his imagination concocted at random. This same theme can be discovered earlier in a crude form in John Toland and later, expressed with subtlety, in Nicolas Fréret's *Lettre de Thrasybule à Leucippe,* which the Baron d'Holbach published.[8] The prospect of death had led men to the invention of the pagan gods and the myriad arts of divination, which Trenchard catalogued in a Joycelike passage clearly lifted from Balthasar Bekker, *De Betoverde Weereld:* "To these Weaknesses and our own, and Frauds of others, we owe the Heathen Gods and Goddesses, Oracles and Prophets, Nimphs and Satyrs, Fawns and Tritons, Furies and Demons, most of the Stories of Conjurers and Witches, Spirits and Apparitions, Fairies and Hobgoblins, the Doctrine of Prognosticks, the numerous ways of Divination, viz. Oniromancy, Sideromancy, Tephranomancy, Botonomancy, Crommyomancy, Cleromancy, Aeromancy, Onomatomancy, Arithomancy, Geomancy, Alectryomancy, Cephalomancy, Axinomancy, Coscinomancy, Hydromancy, Onychomancy, Dactylomancy, Christallomancy, Cataptromancy, Gastromancy, Lecanomancy, Alphitomancy, Chiromancy, Orneomancy, and Necromancy, Horoscopy, Astrology and Augury, Metoposcopy and Palmistry, the fear of Eclipses, Comets, Meteors, Earthquakes, Inundations, and any uncommon Appearances, though never so much depending upon Natural and Necessary Causes, nor are there wanting People otherwise of good understanding, who are affected with the falling of a Salt-Seller, crossing of a Hare, croaking of a Raven, howling of Dogs, screaching of Owls, the motion of Worms in a Bedsteed, mistaken for Death-Watches, and other senseless and trifling accidents." [9]

During the ceremonials of divination the clients actually saw visions which appeased their hunger for a knowledge of their fate, and they really believed that they had visited heaven and hell. Trenchard took directly out of Pierre Bayle a hypothesis explaining the psychophysiological operations of the delusion. Under given circumstances, often artificially arranged, inner stimuli in the body aroused visions which were not contradicted by the senses that normally recorded impressions from the outside. The key to hallucinations was thus the blockage of communication with the real world, "when the Organs of Sense (which are the Avenues and Doors to let in external objects) are shut and locked up."[10] Loss of contact occurred under a wide variety of circumstances: during sleep, in states of delirium, in madness, in ordinary physical sickness, in melancholy, in states of exclusive concentration on single objects, under the shock of environmental conditions that terrified or deceived. These situations all had in common the fact that the internally generated images "reign without any Rival" and are continually "striking strongly upon, and affecting the Brain, Spirits, or Organ where the imaginative faculty resides."[11] This adaptation of Lockian epistemology adequately explained the "inward light" of the visionaries cut off from the outward senses, the only "conduits of knowledge." Any hallucination was then believed as reality. The victims "embrace their own Clouds and Foggs for Deities"; some may see "beatifick visions," others "Divels with instruments of Fear and Horrour." Melancholy and "hypocondriack men" might have specific delusions, like Reverend Peling who believed himself pregnant. A man might think he was a glass, a bottle, a god, the Messiah, the Pope, a dog, cat, or wolf. He might imagine, as did John Beaumont, author of *An Historical, Physiological and Theological Treatise of Spirits, Apparitions, Witchcrafts and other Magical Practises . . . With a Refutation of Dr. Bekker's World Bewitch'd; and other Authors that have opposed the Belief of them* (1705), that he had conversations with spirits, and record them. "Many instances of this kind are to be found in Burton's Melancholy, and more to be seen in Bedlam." [12] Trenchard was well acquainted with the contemporary literature of psychopathological experience; his innovation was to identify these delusions with any "non-rationalist" religious perception and to assign to them all a unifom physiological cause. Monastic spiritual excercises and their physical accompaniments such as fasting, whipping, and seclusion were merely mechanical devices which induced psychic states akin to those generated by bodily illness and ordinary mental derangement. True religion exhilarated the spirit, but those monks who enjoyed reputations for exceptional piety had invariably been melancholic recluses. These men were sick, for it was unnatural to sequester oneself. Their physical organs were disturbed and consequently their visions both waking and asleep, far from being revelations of true religion, were nothing but the symptoms of disease.

Trenchard's conception of the interrelations between body and soul, while derivative from seventeenth-century psychology and well known to Spinoza, was set forth in terms that would have been completely comprehensible toward the end of the century to Dr. Cabanis the *idéologue,* reflecting on the reciprocal influences of the physical and the spiritual (with the substitution of *la Nature* for Divine Wisdom, of course): "It's evident the Divine Wisdom hath so formed and united our Souls and Bodies that they mutually act upon one another, insomuch that there is no action of the Mind that does not cause a correspondent one in the Body; nor no motion of the Body that does not produce a suitable affection in the Mind.[13] In this Deist rehabilitation of the flesh the body, no longer conceived of as the evil tyrant of the mind, had a parallel being and its elementary requirements could not be denied without immediate deleterious morbid reactions in the spirit. When a monk castigated the flesh he generated spiritual illness, insanity.

For Trenchard, the phantasms of the religionist were not merely the concern of a lone fanatic, because such hallucinations were readily communicable to great masses of people. In literary images which were an admixture of Epicurean and Newtonian physics — not as preposterous a combination as one might imagine — adapted to human bodies, Trenchard devised a physical theory to account for the rapid spread of religious mania. "Both Mind and Body are visibly affected with the actions of other beings, and of one another, and wherever we move we are surrounded with Bodies, all of which in some degree operate upon us. . . . Besides everything in Nature is in constant Motion, and perpetually emitting Effluviums and minute Particles of its Substance, which operate upon, and strike other Bodies." [14] "Effluvia" rather than witchcraft might naturalistically account for the convulsive fits of children in the proximity of old hags. "And the poisonous and melancholy Vapours streaming from an Enthusiast, cause Distraction and Raving as well as the Bite of a Mad Dog." In an effort to explain the spread of religious enthusiasm and sympathies Trenchard tried musical analogies. "When two violins are tuned alike if you strike upon one, the other sounds." [15] George Keith in his famous exposure, *The Magick of Quakerism* (1707), had studied the sensitivity which the brethren had perfected in recognizing each other's "effluvia," and many of Trenchard's reflections are based on his analysis of their experience.

Lord Shaftesbury was simultaneously teaching the same doctrine as Trenchard. In the *Soliloquy: or Advice to an Author,* first printed in 1710, he raised psychology to an eminence above all other science and knowledge, because its norms were determinant in distinguishing between true and false religion. The "Study of Human Affection . . . has not its Name, as other Philosophys, from the mere Subtlety and Nicety of the Speculation; but by way of Excellence, from its being superior to all other Speculations; from its presiding over all other Sciences and Occupations; teaching the measure of each, and assigning the just Value of everything in Life. By this Science Religion itself is judged, *Spirits* are search'd, Prophecys prov'd, Miracles distinguish'd: the sole Measure and Standard being taken from moral Rectitude, and from the Discernment of what is sound and just in the Affections." [16] This aristocratic, introspective invalid psychologized all religious emotion in the *Characteristicks,* one of the most influential treatises of the age. Shaftesbury, who was Bayle's friend during his long stay in Holland, had no doubt discussed psychopathic religious experiences with him, but the problem of influence should not be resolved mechanically; Bayle wrote few passages which equal Shaftesbury's abnormal psychology of religion. A Whig in politics, like Trenchard and Gordon, he ridiculed the religious enthusiasts of all nations, Jews, Greeks, Catholics, Puritans, French Protestants. In passages of superb acumen he described the fanatic who was profoundly convinced of the divine source of his inspiration, the prophetic seer, the wild-eyed possessed one, transformed in an instant into the bigot, the perse-

cutor, the inquisitor. Many of the clumsily phrased psychological
reflections of La Mettrie and d'Holbach on the relationship between fanaticism and cruelty were anticipated in these elegant
lordly essays written in a classical style that still betrays the school-
boy who could converse in the Latin of Horace.

Men had projected their own foul moods into their gods. A
religion born of fear and excitation was impure because it derived from a psychological malaise, was the thesis of the *Letter
concerning Enthusiasm*. "We can never be fit to contemplate anything above us, when we are in no condition to look into ourselves,
and calmly examine the temper of our own mind and passions.
For then it is we see wrath, and fury, and revenge, and terrors in
the Deity: when we are full of disturbances and fears within, and
have, by sufferance and anxiety, lost so much of the natural calm
and easiness of our temper." [17] The embittered dissenter created
a vicious and jealous God; men in good humor would never attribute vengefulness and terrible punishments to Him. Nature
bore men no malice and they should not impute to the Deity the
defects, the imperfections, and the passions which existed only in
themselves. Benign Deists like Shaftesbury, for whom true Christianity was a religion of humanity, tried to establish sordid psychological origins for the terrible Christian prophecies of universal
destruction and of awful retribution on sinners in the next world.
Such ravings sprang from sour natures and were incompatible
with the image of a God of love. The religious enthusiast had to
be cured — and either wit or mockery were the remedies, never
persecution. But why these outbursts of "distemper"? Shaftesbury's reply was an analogy naively physiological. "There are certain humours in mankind which of necessity must have vent. The
human mind and body are both of them naturally subject to com-
motions: and as there are strange ferments in the blood, which
in many bodies occasion of extraordinary discharge; so in reason,
too, there are heterogeneous particles which must be thrown off
by fermentation." [18]

The descriptions of mass delusion and popular religious mania
in the *Letter concerning Enthusiasm* were in the spirit of *The
Natural History of Superstition*. The idea of a sacred contagion
was adorned with the same Lucretian "scientificisms" in which

Trenchard delighted. "And in this state their very looks are infectious. The fury flies from face to face; and the disease is no sooner seen than caught. They who in a better situation of mind have beheld a multitude under the power of this passion, have owned that they saw in the countenances of man something more ghastly and terrible than at other times is expressed on the most passionate occasions. . . . And thus is Religion also Pannick; when Enthusiasm of any kind gets up; as oft on melancholy occasions, it will do. For Vapors naturally rise; and in bad times especially, when the Spirits of Men are low, as either in publick Calamitys, or during the Unwholesomeness of Air or Diet, or when convulsions happen in Nature, Storms, Earthquakes, or other Amazing Prodigys." [19]

After the *Independent Whig* submitted organized religious institutions, ancient and modern, to rational analysis it discovered that the same techniques of deceit had been practiced in all ages. There had always been dupes, ordinary people subject to a variety of passions which in their ignorance and state of emotional excitability they attributed to supernatural powers; and above them had hovered the canny impostors, men who had made shrewd observations on the psychological infirmities of mankind in order to exploit them. "There is not a living Creature in the Universe, which has not some innate Weakness, or original Imbecility coeval to its Being: that is, some Inclinations or Disgusts, some peculiar Desires or Fears which render it easy Prey to other animals, who, from their constitutional Sagacity or Experience, know how to take Advantage of this Infirmity. . . . The peculiar Foible of Mankind, is Superstition, or an intrinsick and pannick Fear of invisible and unknown Beings." [20] Knowledge of the "sympathetic emotions" and the spontaneous human reactions of wonderment had historically been the major psychic weapons in the arsenal of imposture. The wily ones had learned how these feelings could be artificially stimulated in others, they discovered the "secret of hitting luckily upon this Foible and native imbecility of Mankind," and once possessed of this power they could manipulate the dupes as they pleased.

Since pathological religious phenomena were diseases, they were virtually the same in modern times as in antiquity. The

Quakers were like an "Infamous Sect in Old Rome," the Pythian prophetess, the sibyls, the *Alumbrados* in Spain. In one passage of the *Natural History,* patently Burtonian, Trenchard had identified the enthusiast as a psychological type naturally prone to the disease, and he gave him a name, the *Atra-bilis* or melancholy man characterized by "Inquietude and Alienation of the Mind, Grief, Anxiety, Dejection, Absurd Thoughts, Anxious and Pannick Fears, and a desire for Solitude." [21] In another he likened religious enthusiasm to inebriation. His dramatic description of the violent aggressiveness and maniacal destructiveness of this melancholy, self-tortured, diseased fanatic should be familiar to modern psychologists. "Aversion, Pride and Fury in the shape of Zeal, like a mighty Storm ruffles his Mind into Beating Billows, and Boisterous Fluctuations: At last he is all in a Rage, and no Church Buckets to quench his Fiery Religion, Religion and the Glory of God drives him on: The Holy Enthusiastick longs to Feast and Riot upon humane Sacrifices, turn Cities and Nations into Shambles, and destroy with Fire and Sword such who dare thwart his Frenzy and all the while like another Nero, Plays upon his Harpe, and sings Te Deum at the Conflagration." [22]

The Deist psychopathology of enthusiasm becomes directly relevant to our inquiry into the nature of primitive mentality and the genesis of religion later in the century. While the Deists themselves remained steadfast in their doctrine of original monotheism, their empirical analysis of existing religious fanaticism, a degeneration of truth into a "Rout of Ceremonies," was adapted to another historical context once the rationalist evolutionary idea of progress was formulated. In defining the emotional situation of the primitive worshipers of cruel, savage gods, eighteenth-century atheists, above all the Holbachians, merely transposed to aboriginal man the ugly characteristics of the contemporary fanatic personality which Shaftesbury and Trenchard had anatomized. "Pannick fear," which the Deist doctors of souls had diagnosed clinically among their possessed fellows, was assimilated to the ancient fear-theory of the origins of religion. The terror-stricken savage and the pagan of antiquity who spawned religions were both psychically ill. They were victims of *la contagion sacrée.*

CHAPTER III

The Euhemerists and Isaac Newton

". . . Saturn's Conduct towards his Father
Uranus had killed him with Grief, as he himself died by Reason of his Son *Jupiter's* Be-
haviour towards him; or, if you please to take
the very ingenious Conjecture of Mr. le Clerc,
the Meaning of it is, that Saturn had debauched
most of his Father's Council. . . . What makes
the Conjecture of this Author very probable is,
that the word which *Hesiod* uses to denote the
fatal Amputation which I have mentionned,
may equally signify *Concilium* or *Pudenda*."
— Abbé Antoine Banier, *The Mythology
and Fables of the Ancients,* English
translation, London, 1740, II, 181.

1

Chiron the Centaur's Sphere

THE DISCOVERY of Sir Isaac Newton among the mythographers, a Saul among the prophets, may astound those who know him only as a physical scientist. Though any subject he touched upon bore his unique imprint, Newton's historical method was characteristic of a substantial body of eighteenth-century thought. If his writings on ancient chronology and mythology are considered along with those of his contemporaries Nicolas Fréret, Abbé Antoine Banier, Abbé Etienne Fourmont, William Whiston, Humphrey Prideaux, Samuel Shuckford, Bishop William Warburton, and their lesser colleagues, a school of learning which has usually been dismissed as a mere curiosity of literature can serve as one of the best illustrations of prevalent eighteenth-century thinking on prehistory. Newton's uncritical fixation on a handful of early astronomic texts, his capricious rejection of some traditional narratives, and his assimilation of Euhemerism in its most vulgar form are not aberrations, chinks in the intellectual armor of the greatest genius of modern times. In these theories, depressing symptoms of normality, he most closely approached the commonplace. The Euhemerist-historical doctrines of Newton and the members of the Académie des Inscriptions et Belles-Lettres were by all odds the most popular if insipid eighteenth-century theories of mythology. The Euhemerist historicizers of myth were slavishly dependent upon the compilations of seventeenth-century etymological scholarship. In this quagmire they raised their pretentious structures, and the new psychology of religion developed by Bayle, Fontenelle, and the English Deists left no impress upon them.

In the 1720's rumor spread among the antiquarians of Paris that the aged Newton, already crowned with the laurels of immortality, had descended from the heavens where he had divined the laws of movement of the planets and had deigned to study mythology and the revolutions of states and empires. The learned abbés of the Académie des Inscriptions et Belles-Lettres and their secular colleagues were all agog because it was reported that the conqueror of the physical universe had devised a system of chronology founded upon novel principles which disrupted the traditional concordance of ancient sacred and profane history. The chronologists were at first delighted, or that at least is the academician Bougainville's later testimony, to welcome Newton into their company, as he sought new triumphs in a savage land where the common herd saw only rocks and thorny bushes. Mathematics in his hands seemed a universal instrument capable of resolving all problems. Why should he not free history from its alloy of mythological fictions?

Word had it that the Signor Abate Conte Antonio Conti, a Venetian nobleman, one of those brilliant picaresque figures of the eighteenth-century intellectual world, a poetaster, a tragedian, a translator of Racine and Pope, a dabbler in the sciences, a dilettante who intrigued with equal adroitness among princesses and natural philosophers in England, France, Germany, and Italy, was in actual possession of an abstract of Newton's chronology which contained the whole system in brief. The Abbé Conti, as he was known throughout Europe, had acquired a copy of the text in England from Caroline of Ansbach, Princess of Wales, who kept the original manuscript among her most treasured possessions. Newton had been persuaded to prepare the abstract when during a conversation on education with the Princess he intimated that for many years he had been working on an ancient history with a new plan, though his papers, dating back to Cambridge days, were faulty and in disorder. Sir Isaac granted Conti's request to have a transcript made, with the admonition that it must be kept private. Though he habitually enveloped his writings with secrecy and mystification, he was often deceived about the discretion with which they were handled in England. A number of copies of the abstract had been made without his knowledge, at least three of which are extant, one in King's College Library, Cambridge, its first page decorated with a foliated border and an illuminated initial, two in the British Museum suffixed by polemical appendices from unknown disputants.[1]

While the Abbé Conti in Paris did not surrender the manuscript to a printer he certainly talked freely about its contents and paraded his intimacy with Newton in the aristocratic and scholarly salons which he frequented. He whetted the appetite of many *érudits;* the text itself he showed only to favorites, among them the Jesuit Father Etienne Souciet, an authority on ancient chronology. The abstract was really nothing more than a chronological index to ancient history, about twenty pages in length, and scholars were left to guess the theoretical basis of the revolutionary system from passing hints. Through the intermediary of scientists in Newton's circle with whom he had established amicable relations during his sojourn in England, Abbé Conti sought clarification of moot points, but he met with a wall of silence. Newton had previously warned him that he would not reply to objections. There seems to have been only one exception to the rule. Abbé Souciet's learned queries prepared in 1720 were shown to Newton by John Keill, the Oxford astronomer, himself involved in controversies on the early revolutions of the planet, who received by word of mouth the intelligence that the Conti manuscript was an abstract of a much longer work, "and he hath not set down the proofs"; in another laconic pronouncement Newton casually quoted from memory his source for redating the Argonautic expedition, whose crucial significance for the whole new system of chronology the perspicacious Father Souciet had sensed at once. Keill transmitted the great Newton's oracular answer to Brook Taylor, former secretary of the Royal Society then in Paris, who in turn communicated it to Father Souciet.

The Keill letter released the astronomic key to the mystery of the new chronology even before its publication: the principle of the retrogression of the equinoctial points. "According to his best remembrance he [Newton] found that the ancients had recorded that at the time of the Argonauts Chiron had found the equinoctial points to be in the middle or 15th degree of the constellation Aries. In Meton's time it was found to be in the 8th and in Hipparchus' in the 4th degree of that constellation. Hipparchus reckoned the recession to one degree every seventy-two years and by that means if we compute we shall find the time of the Argonautical expedition to have fallen out at the time Sir Isaac puts it." [2] The Jesuit chronologist was by no means satisfied with this response to his inquiries but he maintained "la religion du secret" and published nothing on the subject, though he at once set to work in private to undermine the Newtonian system and to raise his own in its place.

By 1724 the garrulous Abbé Conti could restrain himself no longer and he began passing the text about indiscriminately to learned men. M. de Pouilly of the Académie des Inscriptions et Belles-Lettres allowed his colleague Nicolas Fréret, a scholar of antiquities then at the height of his powers, to copy and translate the manuscript he had been loaned by Abbé Conti. When Fréret, who had command of Greek, Latin, Hebrew, and Arabic and could dispute the etymologies of Samuel Bochart and other polyhistors of the previous century, analyzed Newton's text he was aghast. The abstract had fixed the Argonautic expedition at 936 B.C., had cut four to five hundred years off the traditional record of Greek history, telescoping events in an unprecedented manner, and had then slashed even greater chunks of time from the antiquity of the other ancient kingdoms. More than twenty-five years later Jean-Pierre de Bougainville was still apologizing uneasily for the next step taken by his predecessor in the permanent secretaryship of the Academy — the unauthorized publication of the abstract, with a critique. "At the prospect of a revolution about to change the face or at least the perspective of the historical world it was natural, shall we say it was correct, that M. Fréret should become alarmed and that he should move to the frontier to reconnoiter the terrain." [3]

Fréret remains one of the most enigmatic figures of eighteenth-century scholarship. He had been an intimate of the Count de Boulainvilliers, an aristocrat-scholar of the older generation who was early impressed with his astounding erudition and introduced him to the notorious freethinking circle of the Duke de Noailles. Ancient chronology and the history of religion were frequent topics of serious inquiry in the private "academy" of this group, where they could express themselves freely without fear of censorship. The Count, one of the leading secret propagators of heretical ideas in the early part of the century, had himself written a heterodox *Abrégé d'histoire universelle* (c. 1700) for the education of his children which has survived in manuscript copies in the Mazarine and the Bibliothèque Nationale. His protégé the young Fréret was no sober academician. At his reception into the Académie des Inscriptions et Belles-Lettres as an *élève* on November 13, 1714, he delivered a *Discours sur l'origine des Français* so defiant of accepted opinion that it was denounced by an indignant senior member and earned him a sojourn in the Bastille, where he is said to have devoured Bayle's dictionary in its entirety. After his liberation he became more circumspect, assiduously pursued traditional historical studies, and was ultimately raised to the secretaryship of the Academy. Clandestine manuscripts circulated under his name, however, among them the *Lettre de Thrasybule à Leucippe,* one of the subtlest antireligious diatribes of the age. Though the mid-nineteenth-century secretary of the Academy, Baron Walckenaer, indignantly contested the imputation of authorship to Fréret, his name has been associated with Boulainvilliers, Lévesque de Burigny, and the author of *Le Militaire Philosophe* as a purveyor of impiety, a predecessor of the Holbachians. In the Newton controversy Fréret wore his official mask, that of the meticulous scholar, the defender of tradition, the French Catholic academician prepared to pinpoint Newton's scientific errors and Protestant prejudices.

A glimpse at the deliberations behind the closed doors of the Académie des Inscriptions et Belles-Lettres, whose minutes are preserved in a manuscript *Registre* in the Institut de France, will help explain the havoc raised by the publication of Newton's abstract, which in a few meager pages covered history from creation through Alexander. In the world of antiquities this body held a position equivalent to that of the Royal Society of London in physical science, and the intrusion of Newton aroused resentment as well as curiosity. In their secret sessions the twenty-odd members of the Academy engaged for the most part in the presentation of limited specific problems of textual interpretation in the theogonies and mythology of the classical corpus, or in the description of particular pagan and Jewish religious rites, when they were not preparing inscriptions for new medals celebrating royal birthdays and military triumphs. Precisely at the time when the abstract of Newton's universal system was being printed Fréret, their most brilliant if contentious member, was reading dissertations on the chronology of the kings of Lydia; Abbé Banier was discussing a passage in Xenophon; Abbé Gédoyn was analyzing terminology in Pausanias; Elie Blanchard, a few paragraphs in Sextus Empiricus. On occasion a freakish contribution was made, such as Abbé Fontenu's study of changes in body size during night and day, not legitimately in the province of the Academy but tolerated. The private debates were vehement; during the session when the introduction of horseback-riding into Greece was under discussion — Fréret was one of the contenders — the president of the *séance,* Gros de Boze, was unable to tranquilize his excited scholars and had to resort to the reading of the history of the Academy in order to silence them.

Fréret's papers delivered at intervals between February 15 and March 17, 1724, are of special interest because this was the period when Cavelier, the Parisian printer, first contemplated the issuance of the abstract. Their subject was unwontedly philosophical for the Academy, *Réflexions générales sur l'étude de l'ancienne histoire et sur le degré de certitude des diférentes preuves historiques,* and though Newton's name was not mentioned they seem clearly aimed at the historical method of the new chronology. A man of cultivated intellect and keen perception, Fréret died before archaeology revised and gave new life to man's view of antiquity. His death in 1749 occurred at the very moment when the excavations at Herculaneum were being made known in northern Europe. Restricted as he was to mythological sources for his reconstruction of the remote past, he posed before the Academy the essential problem of the reliability of this kind of evidence. His language reflected the spirit of pure reason, and many a passage is so far in advance of his contemporaries in its appreciation of fact and of scientific accuracy that it calls to mind Dr. Cabanis's famous treatise on the degree of certainty attainable in medicine, published on the eve of the Revolution. Fréret's position lay midway between the uncritical chronologists and polyhistors of the seventeenth century, who blindly accepted every shred of literary evidence at face value if only it bolstered one of their favorite schemes, and the Pyrrhonism which had become associated with Pierre Bayle and was represented in the Academy by de Pouilly. Having reviewed the works of Scaliger, Petau, Ussher, Marsham, Pezron, and Dodwell, the chronologists who thought they had decisively fixed the dates of major events in the ancient history of Assyria, Egypt, Phoenicia, Babylonia, and Greece, Fréret found their method corrupt because of their failure to distinguish not only between the true and the false but between the more and the less probable. History, dependent as it was upon literary sources, could never achieve the exactitude of the mathematical sciences, which had begun to dominate all forms of knowledge because of their widespread prestige; rather it was necessary to establish the "differences in the various kinds of certainty appropriate to each science and to each matter, for there is not one but it has its own *dialectique*," [4] a most sophisticated conception for the period. The old chronologists constructed arbitrary hypotheses after only a "light and superficial inspection of a few of the fragments which remain." In drawing upon sources they accepted whatever fit their purpose and discarded the rest, violating the basic principle of criticism that "testimony is indivisible." Fréret was particularly sharp in his treatment of John Marsham, who had become possessed of an inordinate passion for system. The parallel with Newton, who had misused texts with equal brashness and was also addicted to a system, is transparent.

On the other hand Fréret would not reject literary evidence merely because it was by definition polluted with error and exaggeration. Though contemporary eyewitness accounts were subject to hyperbole, they were not for that reason dismissed outright. Like a good man of his age he would strip the ancient narratives of the fantastic and the absurd, but he would not thrust them aside merely because of their admixture of superstition. Though the myth of Alexander's divine ancestry was no longer given credence, educated men did not therefore deny all other details of his biography. In Euhemerist fashion Fréret was brought in this paper (he later changed his mind) to accept most of the mythic heroes of Greece as historical personages when divested of the marvelous. Theseus, like Alexander, had once existed, only he was not the son of Neptune. The rationalist spirit of his eminent colleague Fontenelle as expressed in the recently published *Origine des fables* seems to pervade Fréret's critical evaluation of mythology. The duty of the historian was to "examine everything, to weigh the various degrees of probability, to cast aside the false, and to assign to each fact the degree of truth or of probability which belongs to it." [5]

Newton had steadfastly refused to admit the credibility of any literary historians before Herodotus; hence his fundamental reliance upon "astronomic" evidence in the *Abstract of Chronology*. Fréret saw no basis for their exclusion. The ancient historians of Egypt, Assyria, and Greece wrote in the presence of monuments more antique still and their contemporaries had been able to control the accuracy of their assertions. If in Fréret's day there were Greek inscriptions over two thousand years old why should monuments not have existed at the time of Pisistratus that were a thousand years old? Like modern monks, temple priests kept records of sacrifices and other important events which provided source materials for later historians. The chronology of the ancient writers was therefore established on solid ground. Fréret ridiculed the intrusion of the *théorie des combinaisons* into history and morals; a work by Newton's intimate friend John Craig, the *Theologiae Christianae Principia Mathematica* (1699), which abounded in complex algebraic equations to demonstrate the truths of Christianity and to fix the end of the world at 1500 years thence, was chosen to illustrate and mock the new fad.

In the numerous dissertations he read before the Academy, Fréret often failed to practice the lofty critical principles he had outlined, and he was not always averse to the discovery in the poets of references to astronomic and geological events, which he too presumed to date with the aid of the new science, but his *Réflexions* of 1724 was a manifesto of common sense after a century of foggy etymologists and monist systematizers. Though buried in the *Mémoires* of the Academy and rarely noticed, the piece is a brilliant examination of the problems of historical method and historical scepticism, and of the validity of using mythology as a source. At a time when sober men in French academic circles were moving away from voluminous, comprehensive theories, Newton's work seemed to be another fanciful elaboration of a single principle.

When the pirated edition of the abstract appeared in 1725 it was attached as a supplement to a French version of the seven volumes of Dean Humphrey Prideaux's *History of the Jews and Neighbouring Nations, from the Declension of the Kingdom of Israel and Judah to the time of Christ*. This was a most unfortunate union, for though the Dean had corresponded with Newton on ancient calendars and there is a British Museum manuscript setting forth Newton's opinions on the subject to the Bishop of Worcester which passed through his hands, Prideaux in the preface to the first London edition of his work in 1715 had declared Archbishop Ussher's to be "the greatest and most perfect work of Chronology that hath been published." The two chronologies did not mesh; they flagrantly contradicted each other.

Fréret's remarks appended anonymously to the translation of the *Abstract* were on the whole deferential. He pleaded before the public that final judgment be reserved until the appearance of Newton's complete system. For the first time in print allusion was made to Father Souciet's criticisms, which had been bruited about, and Fréret aligned himself on his side. He questioned two of Newton's fundamental propositions, the advancement of the date of the Argonautic expedition to 936 B.C. and the contention of the great mathematician that the ancients erroneously reckoned royal reigns as averaging three to a century when the empirical evidence proved that kings lasted on their thrones an average of only eighteen to twenty years. Fréret upheld the antiquity of the Egyptians and their discovery of the arts and sciences on Biblical grounds. It seemed inconsistent for Newton to brush aside the testimony of Egyptian priests on the beginnings of their culture and yet to accept uncritically the mythic traditions of the Greek poets, certainly less reliable sources. Doubt was cast on Newton's identification of Sesostris and Osiris. Fréret politely praised Newton's ingenuity, then detracted from the purported novelty of many of his findings by noting the priority of John Marsham and his friend Count de Boulainvilliers.

When word of this illegitimate French publication reached Newton, the aged scientist was outraged. In high dudgeon he prepared a defense of his system in a paper to the Royal Society, seven separate drafts of which exist, testimony to his deep involvement. He created an international scandal. As with his major scientific discoveries, Newton was reluctant to publish, but once the plunge was taken he was acutely sensitive to criticism and passionate in defense of his position. From the presidency of the most august scientific body in the world he denounced the pirated edition and uncovered a plot in which Abbé Conti was the master mind, Fréret his agent, and Cavelier the printer a mere tool.

Newton's comments on the "Observator" Fréret, not mentioned by name though known to everyone in Paris, were superior and magisterial in tone. The French critic had completely misunderstood Newton's dating of the Argonautic expedition. He had presumptuously undertaken to refute a work whose very principles he did not comprehend. Though it was true that in his Cambridge period, Newton confessed, he had occupied himself agreeably with history and chronology when he was fatigued by other studies, he had never intended to prepare a work on the subject as the "Observator" had announced.

Fréret was treated mildly in comparison with the formal public denunciation of Abbé Conti. This man was a false scientist, an intriguer who under the pretense of mediating the quarrel with Leibnitz had tried to entice Newton into further disputations on universal gravitation, the Sensorium of God, on time, space, the perfection of the universe. Newton disdainfully concluded with the hope that he would no longer be troubled by Conti's scientific communications, no more than by perpetual motion. While the paper inserted in the Philosophical Transactions of the Royal Society for 1725 was rational and pointed it was irascible, not at all in harmony with the image of majestic calm which was the official portrait of Newton toward the end of his life.

Conti had the last word. He published a French translation of Newton's communication along with a rejoinder, *Réponse aux Observations sur la chronologie de M. Newton avec une lettre de*

M. l'Abbé Conti au sujet de ladite réponse. Newton had erred
when he claimed that Conti's was the only copy of the abstract;
he knew of the existence of three or four others. The promise of
secrecy did not preclude criticism, and he had tried in vain to
discover the basis for Newton's identification of Sesostris and
Osiris. He openly admitted discussion of the system and Father
Souciet's attempts to receive further clarification. Newton might
have avoided the whole affair had he deigned to transmit in
writing the reply he had just printed. Conti's excuses for his
breach of confidence were rather lame. Was it not patent that a
work of which there were several other copies would sooner or
later be presented in print? Was that a crime which merited a
public reproach? "Anyone but Mr. Newton would have been delighted by the favorable idea which I had formed of the merit
of his work and my eagerness to make it known that he was as
enlightened in history and criticism as he was profound in Mathematics and in Philosophy." Turning the tables he maliciously
reminded his readers that Newton himself published without
permission a letter by Leibnitz which Conti had shown him. As
for the accusation that he was a perfidious friend, Conti called
to witness a whole galaxy of French learned men and aristocrats
in whose presence he had defended the Newtonian system.

The Venetian noble who had been insulted before the whole
of Europe could not allow the charges to stand without a counter-
thrust. "It is astonishing that Mr. Newton, who in Philosophy is
willing only to reason on facts, abandons this method in the judgment of human actions. If he persists in his accusations *is he not
obliged,* according to his own principle, to prove them, *at the
risk of becoming* guilty of calumny? Now how will he demonstrate, as he would a geometric curve . . . my masquerade of
friendship, my clandestine intervention and the other chimeras
with which it has suited him to embellish the opinion he has
formed of me?" Abbé Conti gave vent to a full measure of aristocratic scorn for the commoner, for he was above the pettiness of
scientific controversy. "I apply myself to study neither to make a
fortune nor to acquire a great name. I study as I travel, that is to
say, for my pleasure." In experimental philosophy and mathematics he had no great involvement, hence Newton's opinion

could not touch him. "I like this sort of study very much but it does not at all agitate me. At bottom I do not hold it in any greater esteem than the quadrille or hunting. It all comes to the same when one examines the matter dispassionately. And moreover I am of the opinion that if one should make exception of fifteen or twenty problems useful to the arts and practices of society, all the rest will perhaps one day be as much an object of contempt as certain scholastic problems." [6] With this flippant denigration of science he avenged himself on its most celebrated genius.

After the Abbé Conti's death the editor of his papers described amicable conversations with Newton in 1715 on ancient history and religion, during which the fundamental principles of the new chronology had been received by word of mouth. He suggested direct intent on the part of the French scholars to smoke Newton out and force him into a defense of his system by publishing the *Abstract*. Newton's was the intemperate reply of an old bigot, touched in the head by the "Prophets of London," seeing visions. "In Paris they generally took Conti's side." [7]

Once Fréret had published the text Father Souciet considered himself absolved of the vow of secrecy. His five mammoth dissertations against the little *Abstract of Chronology* published in 1726 were an avalanche of astronomical, literary, and numismatic evidence presented with logical precision which did not leave a Newtonian date unassailed. The later dissertations had been written after Newton's outburst, and Father Souciet joined the fray in sympathy with his friend and protector Abbé Conti. "Good God!" he exclaimed in a most unecclesiastical apostrophe, "How little these gentlemen make use of their Philosophy! Or what a strange Philosophy theirs must be." [8] Defending Conti's integrity and dedicating his work to him, he taunted the Englishman: "But why all this mystery? Does Newton want to repeat with some new Leibnitz the scene that was enacted over the infinitesimal calculus?" [9] His conclusion was complacent: "Mr. Newton's Chronology cannot stand, . . . he has made an error of about 530 years and . . . mine on the contrary is correct." [10]

When John Conduitt, the husband of Newton's niece, heard of the Souciet assault he was so afraid of further upsetting the aged scientist with the prospect of another international polemic

that he had the main points summarized by a friend, excising
the more contentious animadversions. Much to Conduitt's sur-
prise, when Newton later read the text in full he seemed not at
all perturbed, but his opinions remained unaltered; the Jesuit
was simply wrong. The scientific war in which eighteenth-century scholars reveled was on and it continued intermittently for
more than fifty years — theologians, historians (even the great
Gibbon in his youth), astronomers, and amateur scholars all
joined the contest. The battle array was by no means exclusively
national, even though there were echoes of the clash between
English Newtonians and French Cartesians.

The fight had hardly gathered momentum when its principal
contender died and was buried with honors such as had not yet
been bestowed upon any European scientist. To the astute
Fontenelle fell the task of reading his eulogy before the French
Académie des Sciences, which had honored Newton with mem-
bership. Primed with memoranda from John Conduitt, Fontenelle delivered a classical panegyric, but he could not avoid reference to the *Abstract* which had involved a colleague of Fréret's
eminence in the "little *académie*." With consummate skill he
managed to turn the piracy and critique of the *Abstract* into a
compliment to the great deceased. "Does not their very eagerness
do honor to Mr. Newton? They quickly seized the chance for the
glory of having such an adversary." [11] If Fréret sinned in allowing
the *Abstract* to be issued without permission, strange historical
vengeance was wrought upon his memory later in the century
when the wicked Baron d'Holbach, without leave, printed scur-
rilous atheist pamphlets as the posthumous works of the renowned permanent secretary of the Académie des Inscriptions
et Belles-Lettres.

Abbé Conti, pursuing the quarrel with relentless tenacity even
after Newton's death, soon discovered a rival Italian system on
the early history of mankind to pit against his enemy. Its author
was the obscure Giambattista Vico. With pathetic gratitude the
unrecognized Neapolitan reproduced favorable letters from Conti
in the introduction to the 1730 edition of the *Scienza Nuova*.
Abbé Conti had sent extracts of the work to Father Souciet in
Paris; he had encouraged the impecunious Vico to rearrange his

materials and to issue a new version in larger type; above all he praised the originality of his ideas which even the English would be "obliged" to concede.

Newton had been greatly wounded by the foreign criticism of the *Abstract*. The Right Reverend Zachary Pearce, Lord Bishop of Rochester, described him sitting in dimmed chambers — his eyes could no longer endure the sun upon which he had gazed for so many years seeking to penetrate its mystery — working day and night on manuscript drafts of chronology which had been piling up for decades. There is ample corroboration of Newton's preoccupation with the system in his last year, for most of his reported conversations center about ancient history and the beginning of things. On Christmas Day 1725 he showed his friend Stuckeley a copy of his drawing of the plan of Solomon's Temple which became the basis of the fifth chapter in the *Chronology*.

After Newton's death, when the executors began to examine and appraise his voluminous manuscripts, they were generally unimpressed with what they found. Thomas Pellet wrote on Newton's *Commonplace Book*, "Not fit to print," and the *Chronology* might have been consigned to like obscurity had it not been for William Whiston's prodding and not disinterested insistence that it be brought out. Whiston had for years stored up rancor against his former patron and he was chafing at the bit, anxious for a chance to demolish the system. It was finally published in 1728 as *The Chronology of Ancient Kingdoms Amended* with a dedication to the Queen by Conduitt, a bit of florid prose which had benefited from the revision of none other than Alexander Pope himself.

As a result of the Keill letter and Newton's paper to the Royal Society, even before the publication of the full *Chronology* his general procedures in arriving at 936 B.C. for the voyage of the Argonauts had been publicly established. Father Souciet and Nicolas Fréret had correctly surmised his method. Accepting Chiron the Centaur and the Argonauts as historical personages in the prevailing Euhemerist manner, Newton had constructed an elaborate scientific hypothesis to date their heroic expedition.

Newton was an avid reader of the ante-Nicene Fathers and he frequently quoted from them. Numerous sections in the *Stromata*

of Clement of Alexandria, one of Newton's favorites, are devoted
to the demonstration that Greek philosophy and culture were
derived from Hebrew sources. In Clement Newton found two
words that became the cornerstone of the new system of chronology, which on astronomic evidence alone squeezed Greek history into the first millennium and exalted the Hebrews for their
greater antiquity, thus at once humbling the heathen and vindi-
cating the diffusionist thesis of the Fathers. In Book I Clement
had mentioned in passing an anonymous Greek *Titanomachia*,
in which Chiron the Centaur was described as the first who "led
the race of mortals to righteousness by teaching them the solemnity of the oath and propitiatory sacrifices and σχήματα 'Ολύμπου." [12]
These crucial last words Newton translated as *Asterisms* and in-
ferred from them that Chiron had been the first to make a celestial sphere. From the same poetic source he adduced that
Chiron's daughter Hippo had learned from her father practical
astronomy which she in turn taught to her husband Aeolus. A passage in Diogenes Laertius indicated that Musaeus, one of the
Argonauts, had drawn a sphere. According to Suidas' *Lexicon*
there was a tradition on the island of Corcyra that Nausicaa the
daughter of Alcinous also had invented one, which led Newton
to conjecture on the basis of Apollodorus' account of the return
of the Argonauts "that it's most probable" they had taught her
astronomy when they stopped by on their way home. However
diverse the ancient sources, for Newton they all pointed to the
historic fact that the good ship Argo had the first sphere, on
which Chiron had marked the constellations. The more common
Argonautic traditions had usually portrayed Chiron as a physi-
cian, but it was generally accepted that he was Jason's tutor and
counselor, and Newton was only stretching a point in designating
him the father of astronomy.

The problem remained how to discover where the solstices
were placed on Chiron's sphere at the period when the Argonauts used it to guide them through perilous seas. If these could
be established comparison might be made with the position of
the solstices on later spheres whose dates of observation were
known, and the enigma of ancient chronology resolved. Conveniently in the third volume of the 1703 edition of Petau's

De doctrina temporum (1630) there was reproduced and translated into Latin the famous polemical work of the astronomer Hipparchus of the second century, *Ad Arati et Eudoxi Phaenomena enarrationum libri tres,* which quoted descriptions by Eudoxus of a sphere of the ancients that "placed the Solstices and Equinoxes in the middles of the Constellations of Aries, Cancer, Chelae, and Capricorn." The same text of Hipparchus also criticized the didactic astronomic poem by Aratus in which, according to Newton, all the constellations named in the primitive sphere "relate to the Argonauts and their contemporaries and to persons one or two generations older and nothing later than that Expedition was delineated there originally." [13] From these astronomic fragments Newton leaped to the conclusion that the Eudoxus "sphere of the ancients" was precisely the one referred to by the unknown author of the *Titanomachia* preserved in Clement. Since Newton knew where the cardinal points on the sphere were in 1689 A.D. and where they were in Chiron's day and since the equinox retrogressed fifty seconds in one year and one degree in seventy-two years, the Argonautic expedition had to be set at about 2625 years before the Glorious Revolution; further corrections fixed it definitely at 936 B.C., forty-three years after the death of Solomon. During the 1720's Newton's French critics dutifully accepted the association of the Eudoxus "sphere of the ancients" with the Argonauts and directed the main barrage of their criticism against Newton's interpretation of the details in Hipparchus. They seemed intent upon vanquishing him on his own battleground, readings of astronomy, not ancient tradition.

Dr. Edmund Halley, the Astronomer Royal, who after Newton's death felt called upon to defend his friend, the late President of the Royal Society, from French calumny, in a paper in the *Philosophical Transactions* for 1727 cautiously avoided committing himself on the general validity of the new theory of chronology. "And first I observe that P. Souciet readily allows what seems to be the most exceptionable part of the whole System, viz. that Chiron the Centaur fixt the Colures in the ancient Sphere of fixt Stars, in the same places as Hipparchus tells us that they had been supposed by Eudoxus many Centuries of years after Chiron. . . . This, undoubtedly, was the Position of the Colure of the

Vernal Equinox many centuries before Eudoxus; but whether as old as Chiron, and the Argonautick Expedition, I shall not undertake at this time to enquire." [14] But if one adopted Newton's premise that on Chiron's sphere, as described by Eudoxus, the colures were placed 7° 36′ from the first star of Aries, then, extrapolating backward from the position as defined in the astronomic tables for 1690 A.D., the Argonautic expedition had to be dated 934 B.C. and Newton's calculations were correct. *En passant* Dr. Halley took Father Souciet down a peg and advised him in his next edition to inform himself in the "Sphericks." With consummate sobriety Dr. Halley found the dispute to be "chiefly over what part of the Back of Aries the Colure past: the Words of Hipparchus, as from Eudoxus, are simply, that it past over the Back, without saying over what Star, or over what part of the Back it past." [15] To add to the confusion, Newton's description of the solstices which appeared in the final edition of the *Chronology* differed from his contention in the Royal Society paper, where he had attacked Fréret for misconstruing him. Such verbal variants, which involved centuries of ancient chronology, multiplied the scholarly quibbling over the precise location of the solstices on Chiron's sphere for five decades and produced a voluminous literature.

Only late in the controversy was the simple point made that the whole new system of chronology was founded upon Newton's reading of Clement's quotation of two words in the *Titanomachia* of a lost Greek poet. First Père Hardouin, then Fréret ventured the reflection that there was no evidence at all that the ancient sphere referred to by Eudoxus was the one drawn by Chiron who, to make matters worse, was well on in years at the time of the Argonautic expedition and no doubt suffered from poor eyesight so that his view of the fixed stars must have been impaired. But even if one should adopt the tradition, Fréret pleaded in his *Défense de la chronologie fondée sur les monumens de l'histoire ancienne, contre le système de M. Newton*, first published in 1758, "does one have to conclude from it that the sphere of Eudoxus was that of the first inventor of Greek astronomy? Is it not probable that this first sphere, very crude and faulty as the first essays of the human spirit always are in the sciences, had been later refashioned and that it was this sphere corrected several centuries after the time of Chiron which Eudoxus used?" [16]

This was the heart of the matter. There was a subsidiary wrangle over the average duration of royal reigns, but most of the learning which poured forth against the *Chronology* either revolved around the reading of the Eudoxus fragment in Hipparchus or marshaled literary evidence to confute various dates in Newton's new calendar. On both sides of the controversy there were remarkable exercises in Euhemerist madness.

Though Newton was at first a terrifying meteor in the world of Euhemerist chronologists because of the extraordinary authority with which he could speak about the revolutions of the heavens, in the end he was something of a fizzle when the rather amateurish manner in which he manipulated classical texts was exposed by the antiquarians.

Newton's histories now appear far more outlandish than they did to contemporaries, for whom chronology and mythography were the very core of studies of antiquity. To the early eighteenth-century scholar, who had no archaeological findings to sustain him except perhaps the Arundelian Marbles, who could not even identify in general terms the pieces of ancient sculpture which had been casually left about or had been accidentally unearthed, the meaning and interpretation of the vast body of myths and the genealogies of pagan gods was a central historical problem. The facility with which Newton transformed heroes and demigods and the great twelve themselves into datable personages takes us aback, but this was standard procedure in learned Europe. We are startled by the directness with which Newton made Ceres a woman whose daughter had been kidnaped and who was divinized for introducing the cultivation of wheat into Italy. And when, in his zeal to elucidate the astronomic lore of the Greeks at the time of the Argonautic expedition, he metamorphoses even the engaging Nausicaa, daughter of Alcinous, into a female astronomer it is our impulse to call a halt. But this technique did not seem extravagant to Newton's contemporaries, though more workmanlike practitioners of the art like Fréret and the Abbé Banier, whose lifelong preoccupation was the study of myth and ancient history, treated some of Newton's glib constructions with a measure of contempt.

2

Variations on Euhemerus

*I*N PAGAN ANTIQUITY Euhemerus had the reputation of an impious philosopher because of his atheist novel describing the discovery on a remote island in the Indian Ocean of a stele setting forth the circumstances of the human birth of the major gods and the manner of their deification. The Church Fathers utilized Euhemerus in their polemics against the pagan apologists, to disprove the existence of the gods from the mouth of the Greek who pretended to have seen evidence engraved in stone that these deities were originally humans who had divinized themselves. Therefore despite the charges of atheism, the theory of Euhemerus was permissible in orthodox Christian Europe alongside the Stoic allegorical tradition and the demonological doctrine.

If the term Euhemerist were severely restricted to those theories which ascribed the origins of pagan religion in every instance to a historical apotheosis of a king or hero, it would apply to very few eighteenth-century writers. Virtually all mythographers attached to the process of deification complex corollaries, and hardly any of them committed himself to ancient Euhemerism as the sole explanation for every pagan deity. Similarly, few would have contended that every myth without exception was explicable as the distortion of a historic incident in the life of a royal or heroic personage who was later divinized. Euhemerists of the narrow persuasion are truly rare — Newton and Bishop Cumberland approached this rigid position as closely as any contemporaries. But if Euhemerism is broadened to include those who recognized in most pagan myths the elaboration of ancient political and other historic events of great moment, then the concept would encom-

pass the majority of mythographers and chronologists who flourished in the first half of the eighteenth century — Banier, Fréret,
Le Clerc, Foucher, Warburton, Fourmont, Pluche, Shuckford.

Euhemerus struck a responsive note among theorists in the age
of enlightened despotism. Ancient Euhemerism had often been
related to Critias' conception of the gods as divine policemen introduced by shrewd tyrants in order to assure obedience to the
laws in public and in private, both when secular power sanctions
were manifest and when they were not, as in secret crime. The
eighteenth century had a natural affinity for Sophist theory and
the view that a state religion was a necessary political institution.
Atheist radicals as notorious as Dr. La Mettrie were quite willing
to accept a religious establishment as an adjunct of the state for
the maintenance of a civilized order which might otherwise
founder. What more reasonable justification for ancient religious
practice to eighteenth-century *philosophes* and philosophical
bishops than the supposition that a wise tyrant or a wily one, an
enlightened despot of antiquity, had divinized himself as an act
of policy. Euhemerist conceptions penetrated the image of the
Roi Soleil.

The Euhemerus novel was the first Greek prose work ever
translated into Latin, by Ennius, some indication of its ancient
popularity, but no text was discovered in the Renaissance and it
was preserved only in a few meager quotations in the writers of
the Hellenistic and Roman periods. With time the doctrine had
assimilated many cognate ideas and had become a fluid concept
as shapeless as the body of myth itself. Euhemerism was skillfully
embroidered with variations derived from what contemporary
observers surmised about the nature of man and society, or
learned from the classics. In eighteenth-century Euhemerism the
heroes transfigured reflected the ideal types of the age: they were
men who had introduced the useful arts, to whom the people felt
instinctive gratitude; they were military leaders who warded off
foreign enemies; they were lawgivers and distributors of justice,
promulgators of codes, again monarchs like Frederick II and
Maria Theresa and Catherine. Diderot later developed the idea
of immortality in the remembrance of mankind as the future reward for those geniuses who had bestowed great benefits upon

humanity and alleviated its sufferings. What more natural than for ancient peoples, still unenlightened and superstitious but motivated by similar sentiments, to apotheosize their geniuses, their heroes, their Prometheus, Ceres, and Bacchus, their Hephaestus, Apollo, and Aesculapius, the men and women who had brought them fire, wheat, wine, tools, music, medicine.

Fundamental to most Euhemerism remained the idea that in their origins the gods had their existence on earth, that they were ordinary human beings, and that the myths were commemorations of their acts in this world. Since the initial design of the myth was a historical event, however luminous and ethereal its ultimate divine fabric, a host of provocative antiquarian problems confronted the eighteenth-century Euhemerist. The notion that the god was a hero, a man, and the myth an incident from his life experience challenged the mythographer to employ the arts of criticism and the new philological knowledge accumulated by *érudits* in order to discover the kernel of historical reality that had been obscured by legendary accretions. Mythography came to be conceived as a historical science using linguistic and soon astronomic data, following the method of hypothesis and verification precisely as did the other sciences. It was the art of separating truth from nonsense, fiction from fact, superstition from actual occurrence, a respectable scientific practice in which men of reason delighted. The mythic tradition itself, in its multifarious transformations through the ages, became a subject of separate historical inquiry. The problems of establishing "connections," a comparative chronology among empires, and the routes of human migration signalized by the mythic movement of the gods were solved by English rectors and French abbés and German professors working independently but with the same stout pens. No myth but the Abbé Banier could see through to describe its political content, no event in Hesiod but Shuckford could date. The temper of these writers was completely unphilosophical, unmetaphysical; out of the mythic morass they brought to western society reasonable historical narratives.

But few eighteenth-century mythographers, though they generally accepted the central theme of Euhemerus that gods were originally heroes or kings, and though his fragments were studied

in *Mémoires* of the Academy, would have called themselves
Euhemerists. Impious overtones clung to the name even in the
Christian world, despite the fact that Euhemerus had been quoted
with approval by the Fathers. In France the two leading contemporary mythographers of the Académie des Inscriptions et Belles-
Lettres, Abbé Banier and Nicolas Fréret, who were by any obvious
interpretation of their writings in the Euhemerist-historical tradition, would have rejected the label for a number of reasons, only
one of which derived from their repugnance to an atheist philosopher. These antiquarians prided themselves on not being adepts
of any single system of mythography; the myths were so diverse
that no exclusive method of explication was applicable to all of
them. Banier recognized that some myths taught moral lessons in
allegorical form, others were philosophical, still others rehearsed
geological and astronomic cataclysms, and some were disguised
records of political events. Those passages in which he wittily
demonstrated that each mythographer with a system had in the
past read his own professional bias, scientific or allegorical, into
myths, were taken over verbatim by Diderot in the *Encyclopédie*
and later by the atheist editors of the *Encyclopédie méthodique,*
who were in sympathy with his commonsensical antisystematic
spirit. But despite Banier's urbane protestations of eclecticism
and candid avowal that to him some myths were plain nonsense
and meant nothing, the bulk of the writing in his most famous
work, *La Mythologie et les fables expliquées par l'histoire* (1738–
1740), remained ordinary Euhemerism, and most of his mythological interpretations made kings out of the gods in the traditional genealogies, awarded them specific territorial jurisdictions
in the eastern Mediterranean, and identified each adventure as a
political action. "My Design in this Work," he wrote in the introduction, "is to prove, that notwithstanding all the Ornaments
which accompany Fables, yet it is no difficult matter to see that
they contain a Part of the History of primitive Times; and that
neither the Allegory nor Moral were the primary Intention of
those who invented them, an Opinion I am so far from having
altered that my late Studies do but establish me in it more. Not
as if there were not some particular Fictions, where it would be
in vain to look for any Footsteps of History; but in general all of

them almost have some relation to it, or are connected with events that are supported by the best Authority of Antiquity." [17] The whole mythic world was transformed into a society where readily comprehensible events transpired in ancient kingdoms that bore a remarkable resemblance to small eighteenth-century duchies. The most bloodcurdling Greek tales of parricide and infanticide were reduced to normal, commonplace intrigues, revolutions, disputes between kings and princes. The readings were not universalized, as in moral allegorist interpretations, but particularized. Out of Ovid the Abbé Banier managed to draw facts for a most detailed and circumstantial political history of the ancient world, and there were no documents to contradict him. When some myths were refractory, such as the vivid description of castration in Hesiod's *Theogony*, the good Abbé succeeded with the aid of etymology in twisting the *pudenda* into *concilium* and thus rendering the whole tale quite acceptable to polite society — it was a palace cabal. Philo could not tolerate a vulgar anthropomorphism in the Bible; an eighteenth-century abbé who lived on his classical erudition could not accept indecencies in the Greek poets.

It was in the subtlety and frank eclecticism of his argument that Banier differed from Isaac Newton. Whereas Newton, still in the seventeenth-century tradition of Euhemerism, flatly maintained in the *Chronology of Ancient Kingdoms Amended* that idolatry had its principal origins in the deification of heroes, the Abbé could exhibit sixteen different possible sources and motives for the beginnings of pagan religion, all rational, utilitarian, and for the most part political. Newton's old-fashioned Euhemerism was too confining for so imaginative and flexible a historian as Banier. The Abbé, who considered his writing a part of polite literature, did not bother about the new physical science and the dating of ancient events through astronomy; in the last analysis, however, most of Banier's renderings of the political history of early Greece, Egypt, Assyria, and Phoenicia were in complete accord with the Euhemerist school of myth interpretation.

Fréret, by far the most sophisticated mythologist of the first half of the eighteenth century, also vaunted his eclecticism: there were some philosophical and scientific myths and some political ones. He disliked the simplicist Euhemerism of his contemporaries and at least in theory subscribed to a far broader historical view of the meaning of mythology. Instead of regarding myths as ordinary political occurrences, mostly dynastic history, which was the popular form of Euhemerism, Fréret particularly in his later years extended the horizon of his interpretations to the point where they became the history of culture. He was less interested in identifying in the myth the family squabbles of a divinized king than a history of the arts and the sciences, the migration of peoples, the diffusion of religions from one Mediterranean area to another. The grand truths of sociological history were found concealed in the major myths.

Fréret's method purported to be rigorously scientific; he did not, like his seventeenth-century predecessors, accept the first version of a myth that came to hand, but sifted out the common elements in different texts, those which appeared most reasonable, where the weight of evidence was preponderant. In writing a dissertation on a hero he would garner all possible references to his myth from the whole classical corpus with its bewildering, contradictory versions in Homer, Hesiod, Pindar, the dramatists. After the figures in the myth had been translated back into common everyday-life objects he would construct a hypothesis, which was usually a description of events of cultural history, and he would be satisfied that his "conjecture" had been proved when it fit most or almost all forms of the myth, inconsistencies having been either conciliated or dropped out of sight. Newton's naive Euhemerism was an easy target for this refined mind. Pagan religion could not have had its first beginnings in the apotheosis of heroes, his reading of Newton, since the very act of deification implied some prior awareness of a supernatural force or being. Fréret was especially acute in criticizing contemporary English Euhemerism as a prejudiced theory deliberately espoused by militant Protestants because of the presumed similarity between the deification of pagan heroes and the adoration of Catholic saints, and he accused Newton of this bias. The theme of pagano-papism was an old one, introduced with the Reformation, and there is a substantial measure of truth in Fréret's charge. Newton had no compunctions about referring to Euhemerus by name, as he does in the manuscript fragment *The Original of Monarchies,* now in King's

College Library, but he would doubtless have been annoyed by Fréret's emphasis on the atheism of the ancient mythographer, the barb in the attack.

Though their original core was Euhemerist-historical (in 1724 he still insisted upon the personality of the hero), Fréret's *mémoires* are a troublesome agglomeration of seemingly irreconcilable viewpoints, both in his religious philosophy and in his scholarship. He manifestly changed his opinions during the four decades that he pontificated in the Academy. There are dissertations such as the one on Bellerophon published in 1729, as farfetched a historicization of myth as any of the seventeenth-century scholars had perpetrated, despite the introduction of cultural history and the dazzling show of learning to account for the transmutation of each element in the tale.[18] Bellerophon crossed the sea from Greece to Lycia on his Pegasus, defeating the Chimera with the aid of the ever-faithful winged horse — this was the common tradition. In Homer Pegasus is absent altogether; in Hesiod he joins in the killing of the Chimera and then flies up to heaven to be employed by Jupiter in carrying thunder and lightning. Pindar introduces Pegasus as Bellerophon's mount and locates the scene of his harnessing with Minerva's aid not far from Corinth. At the hands of Fréret Pegasus became a boat, not a horse; the fountain of Pyrene where he was harnessed, a place to which the sailors repaired to take on fresh water before departure; and the harness a rudder, which the crew were accustomed to carry with them when debarking lest their ship be stolen. Fréret had borrowed the idea for his translation from Plutarch, who had identified Pegasus as a war vessel lighter and longer than the ships of the pirate-subjects of Amisodar who were ravaging the coasts of Lycia and whom the hero Bellerophon forced to seek refuge near Mt. Chimera. Fréret lent verisimilitude to his interpretation by recalling that ancient ships had animals carved on their prows — Herodotus, for example, described the goat figures on Samian vessels. Chimera, in a variant Fréret etymology, meant mountain goat, and probably the whole prow of the pirate ship was called a chimera by metonymy. As for the role of Minerva, it was quite appropriate for her to supply a rudder since she had already supervised the construction of the Argo, was occupied with the arts and sciences, had provided the Argonauts with a "speaking wood" from Dodona which directed them through perilous waters. Poetic traditions which gave Pegasus and Chimera marine ancestries further bolstered his interpretation. Chimera in Hesiod was born of the nymph Echidna by Typhon and there was reason to believe that Echidna was the offspring of the love of Medusa and Neptune; similarly Pegasus was born either of Medusa's blood or of the same coupling with Neptune, all of which, despite its meanderings, definitely associated the struggle of Pegasus and the Chimera with the sea.

Fréret then welded these poetic, dramatic, historical, and etymological materials into a grand hypothesis which envisaged the Chimera as piracy disturbing trade, Bellerophon as reasonable, peaceful shipping interests, and the myth celebrating his triumph as the poetic description of a typical eastern Mediterranean battle of Greeks against Phoenician pirates, an actual conflict for which there were many counterparts such as the events beshrouded in the Perseus fable.

While some of Fréret's *mémoires* specifically rejected the introduction of physical science into the study of ancient history, others went as wild as Whiston or Shuckford in identifying ancient comets or dating floods like the Ogyges and Deucalion by extrapolating astronomy backward. There are moments when Fréret piously holds to a theory of primitive monotheism, and then again at times he seems touched by philosophico-religious scepticism, so that the imprint of his name on the scandalous works which Holbach published has plausibility. Newton's opponent was surely not a normative eighteenth-century Euhemerist, though his attempt to distinguish himself from his colleagues was not always as successful as he imagined. Fréret was of the *avant-garde* but still in the Euhemerist tradition.

Viewed in broad general terms, the nature of the historical evidence which the Euhemerist mythographer was seeking and finding in the myths underwent a change in the course of the eighteenth century. Political Euhemerism was still the basic attitude of an Abbé Banier, a Shuckford, a Jean Le Clerc; but more and more at the hands of a Fréret, Banier's younger colleague, myth was divorced from personality and became a vehicle of human achievement, the annals of the history of civilization and culture, of the progress of the arts and the sciences. Myths were socio-philosophical prehistory, embroidered recollections of the moments when a nation learned to sow wheat, to cultivate the vine, to forge implements, or when it abandoned plunder for commerce. The movement of heroes was the colonial history of the Mediterranean and to follow the tracks of the adventurers was to trace the migration of peoples. "Ceres becomes the inventor and the goddess of agriculture because the same ship which brought her cult into Attica also transported wheat and farmers there," [19] was a characteristic Fréret interpretation. Myths of the battles of the gods were covers for religious wars among the priests of old autochthonous religions and new conquering cults introduced by invaders; the fighting gods had been used to symbolize wrangling priests. Myth interpretation still had a Euhemerist tinge (a seafarer named Bellerophon who led an expedition had probably existed), but the myth also bordered on historical allegory, for Bellerophon became a symbol for the wiping out of piracy and the triumph of commercial civilization.

In some of these eighteenth-century interpretations the allegorical element and the historical seem to fuse. They often do in Fréret despite his mockery of ancient symbolism as outmoded. There does arrive a point, however, where the myth as history is so far removed from any individual identifiable action attached to a real person and a specific place that the break with Euhemerism seems quite complete. Surely when the myth emerges as a spontaneous social expression of a stage in the religious or psychic development of nations or civilization as a whole it can no longer be tied down to Euhemerist history. Theories of this character, the grand structures of Vico, de Brosses, Boulanger, Court de Gébelin, were novel perceptions which sharply departed from conservative Euhemerism; they were insights beyond the ken of Isaac Newton, though Fréret would have understood them.

Among run-of-the-mill mythographers throughout the continent a far more crude and orthodox Euhemerism than Fréret's held sway. Passages from the ancient Phoenician Sanchuniathon's historical writings, which Philo of Byblus is supposed to have discovered and which Eusebius included in one of his tracts

against the heathen, were translated into European languages —
Newton owned Bishop Cumberland's version — and were widely
commented upon in direct support of the thesis that apotheosized
dead heroes were the origins of the gods. The classical studies
published in the *Mémoires* of the Académie des Inscriptions et
Belles-Lettres habitually treated the gods and the heroic figures
of Greek fable as ordinary sovereigns: Jupiter, Saturn, Cadmus,
Jason, Medea, Hercules were scrutinized like members of a royal
family, their reigns dated and their exploits recounted. The
word "hypothesis" occasionally crept into the title of a *mémoire*,
but ordinarily the mythical adventures, stripped of their marvelous aspect, were "straight history," corrupted to be sure, but
capable of being restored to a version of events which would not
tax the credulity of an average eighteenth-century literate man.
These academic mythographers became prehistory or protohis-
tory specialists, using the only texts available to re-establish a
connected story that would harmonize with chronological records
as preserved in traditional authorities.

About 1700, while French Catholic scholarship shied away from
too searching an investigation of Scripture — Simon and Astruc
were exceptions — Protestant England, following the seventeenth-
century Dutch tradition, was simultaneously absorbed both in the
problem of Biblical exegesis and in the explication of pagan
myth. And understandably enough a plain Euhemerist interpretation of pagan religion meshed with a literal reading of the historical books of the Bible to arrive at a universal concordance,
establishing "connections" among all the great civilizations, har-
monizing sacred and profane history, tracing influences during the
shadowy period not explicitly described by the Greek historians,
making the appropriate identifications with Biblical names, and
above all dating the parallel histories of empires. There was a
driving passion to frame one history for all of mankind. The
eighteenth century was still unaccustomed to a segmented historical world with inevitable lacunae; it demanded a continuum
in which the generations of men succeeded one another with the
orderly certainty of a chapter in Chronicles.

The orthodox view of the world history of religion, always the
main thread of universal history and culture, posited a primitive

monotheism revealed to Adam which was kept alive among the antediluvians through Noah and had a number of outstanding exponents like Lamech. Among the postdiluvians the monotheist tradition survived intact only in the heritage of Shem, when the patriarchs received a new affirmation of God's existence. From them the monotheist Judaic transmission, with deviations and lapses into sinfulness, ran directly until the Christian revelation. The Bible, if it stood alone, could account for the multiplicity of heathen nations and the confusion of languages, but for the diversity of idolatries there was no clear-cut rationale. Hence the opportunity for fancy-free theorizing and exegesis to piece together a consecutive history of the different pagan religions in the Mediterranean basin. No more than their predecessors could eighteenth-century scholars resign themselves to the existence of Varro's thirty thousand individual gods. The number had to be reduced to a handful, whose worship was diffused from a common center, however circuitous the routes. While the Euhemerist-historians were by no means agreed about the paths of migration of the major gods among Egyptians, Phoenicians, Chaldeans, and Greeks, their massive tomes rested upon the same preconception, which was itself a recasting of the ancient demonological theory. The Church Fathers had argued that the idolaters were inspired by demons and fallen angels, who could not invent a completely new religion — they were not creative beings — and therefore had to ape the true revelation to the Hebrews. The seventeenth- and early eighteenth-century historian, though dispensing with the demons, still availed himself of the doctrine. Pagans could only corrupt what they had learned from Noah and his Israelite descendants, and the establishment of the channels of diffusion from Judaea became the primary object of antiquarian scholarship. Guillaume de Lavaur's *Histoire de la fable conférée avec l'histoire sainte où l'on voit que les grandes Fables, le Culte et les Mystères du Paganisme ne sont que des copies altérées des Histoires, des Usages et des Traditions des Hébreux* (1731) was the definitive French academic systematization of this thesis.

Later in the century historians of ancient paganism ventured to dispense with Judaic origins, and other major centers of civiliza-

tion found modern protagonists who extolled the prior antiquity
of their gods and their culture. There were Egyptian, Chinese,
Babylonian, Phoenician diffusion theories. In 1799 Sir William
Jones appeared with the mighty challenge of the Hindus as teachers of the Egyptians in his famous essay "On the Gods of Greece,
Italy, and India." The work of this pioneer Orientalist heralded
the Aryan thesis to which the nineteenth-century German scholars devoted themselves; at the time, however, it was another spe-
cialist's passionate espousal of an original center for idolatry,
not unlike the earlier work of the erudite French abbés of the
Académie des Inscriptions. Jones went to the same great lengths
to assure the orthodox that whatever the merit of his hypothesis
might be it would "in no degree affect the truth and sanctity of
the Mosaic History." [20] But the thesis had its obvious hazards.
A less cautious French Orientalist writing at the same time, Louis
Mathieu Langlès, became so captivated by the Hindu diffusion
theory that he bluntly maintained the Five Books of Moses and
the five Chinese Books of Kings were mere derivations from the
five Vedas.

The traditional interpretation of Greek mythology as a corruption of Hebrew history also came under attack from another
source, the new schools of Biblical criticism, one of the most daring innovations of seventeenth- and eighteenth-century thought.
If Bacchus was Moses disfigured, then primitive monotheism,
Judaic diffusionism, and the authenticity of the Bible were corroborated. But what if Moses was posterior to Bacchus? The
unique significance of the first dispensation was then open to
doubt and the Hebrew tradition became nothing more than another mythic compilation. Voltaire, in chapter 28 of the *Philosophie de l'histoire,* had insisted that Moses was a recent figure because no Greek before Longinus had ever mentioned him. Other
philosophes tended to exalt the prior antiquity of Zoroaster or
Sanchuniathon. The historicity of the Bible and the traditional
Judeo-Christian belief that Moses was the actual author of every
line in the Pentateuch were questioned by a long line of scholars
from Isaac de la Peyrera through Spinoza, Hobbes, Jean Le Clerc,
Richard Simon, and Astruc. The arguments and anathemas of
orthodox apologists like Gabriel Fabricy and Jacopo Belli did not
carry the day.

Throughout the eighteenth century etymology remained the most reliable scientific tool for tracing the migrations of the gods from one part of the Mediterranean to another. Seventeenth-century philologists had exercised their ingenuity to derive the names and adventures of the gods of Egypt, Phoenicia, Chaldea, and Greece from the early history of specific individuals whose lives had been narrated in the Pentateuch. Adam, Noah, Abraham, Isaac, Jacob, Moses, and their consorts, not to mention minor figures in the genealogies of Genesis, became the prototypes for hosts of pagan gods. The remotest auditory approximation of a Biblical name and that of a Greek deity was the point of departure for an identification. In the *Réflexions critiques sur les histoires des anciens peuples* (1735) Etienne Fourmont was particularly adept in transforming Hebrews into Greeks by stages: the original Biblical Lot became Lota in Phoenician, Otla by corruption, and finally the Atlas of Greek mythology. The exegetical technique was based upon a fusion of two ideas, one ancient and one modern. The rabbis of the Talmud had built up a vast structure of law by interpreting every single letter of the Torah and by weaving etymologies from the flimsiest of word similarities. (Etymological explanation of name-origins was of course standard procedure in the Bible itself.) In addition a modern empiricist could observe that in the transmission of words from one person to another or one people to another mistakes were likely to creep in through the fallible senses of man. Since the phenomenology of error is virtually infinite, there was hardly a pagan god who could not be unmasked as a patriarch of Judaea. *In extremis* the deity could be derived from a misunderstanding of a Hebrew substantive descriptive of some natural event.

In Holland and in Germany there flourished whole schools of etymologists who developed technical *expertise* in relating the mythology of Greece to Hebrew history. The most famous performance of the century in this field was Gerhard Croese's "Ομηρος Εβραῖος (1704), which interpreted the whole of the *Iliad* as a pagan reworking of Joshua's assault against Jericho and the adventures of Odysseus as a transformed account of the wanderings of the patriarchs from the destruction of Sodom to Moses. This parochial scholarship had come to have rather set rules, like the Talmudic laws of exegesis. Noah could be recognized as a dual personality split up between Cronus and Zeus, or the attributes of two Biblical figures could be combined to make one Greek. But the art had somehow exhausted itself by the eighteenth century, after the original titanic efforts of Vossius and Bochart, and the dissertations of the German theological faculties, for all their profusion, were the works of feeble epigoni. Newton's *Chronology* was by no means emancipated from the fundamental preconceptions of the more traditionalist etymologists, particularly their obsession with the Israelite origins of pagan civilization.

For Newton as for other Euhemerists the genealogies of the Greek gods were really national political histories; his explanation for their posthumous deification is characteristically eighteenth-century, though the same idea had been proposed in antiquity: men apotheosized heroes in gratitude for great deeds of public utility such as the introduction of arts and sciences or the defeat of powerful enemies. Euhemerism was so profoundly ingrained in Newton's thinking that in some passages he described the tendency to transfigure heroes as a natural proclivity of mankind, operative even among the Israelites. In the *Commonplace Book,* assiduously poring over the nuances of meaning of each word in Scripture, he posed the Midrashic question why Moses was buried in a place which "no man knoweth," and responded in the Euhemerist spirit, "That is for fear of Idolizing him." [21]

Throughout his histories, all the accounts of the Old Testament, of the ancient historians beginning with Herodotus, though not before, and of the classical mythographers were accepted as literal truth. If they seemed to be at variance Newton usually adhered to the Biblical version. Explanations of Greek myth were in the restricted rather than the loose Euhemerist tradition. There was nothing unique in his attempt to coordinate such Euhemerist interpretations with his scientific explication of what purported to be ancient Greek astronomy. English contemporaries like Whiston and Shuckford and Frenchmen like Fréret were engaged in similar scholarly exercises. Halley's comet had made it fashionable to try to identify other comets in ancient myths and to account for the cataclysms recorded in the Bible and in the classics scientifically. The great tumult aroused by Newton's *Chronology* was over the manner in which he employed Euhemerist and scientific tools and his consequent conclusions, and the cross-Channel debates should be looked upon as internecine school controversy among men who accepted the same fundamental premises. This sparked the violence of the argument, the fiery charges and countercharges. Among allegorists, Euhemerists, and psychologists, with rival theoretical approaches to myth, there was not enough common ground for fencing within the rules of a set game. Newton, the English divines who wrote "Connections," and the French academicians had a "system" of mythology which is to be sharply distinguished from the pure allegorism of the Renaissance and the psychological interpretations of primitive religion, which grew in importance everywhere in Europe toward the second half of the eighteenth century, in Vico, Hume, de Brosses, Boulanger. The arguments in the *Chronology* dispute centered upon factual particulars, not grand conceptualizations. Fréret was willing to concede that Japheth was Neptune but bridled at merging him with Python or Typhon.

Newton usually saw organized pagan religions as political institutions founded by princes. In the accepted manner of seventeenth-century scholars he attributed the conformities among religious practices and the names and attributes of the gods in the Mediterranean world to diffusion through conquest, colonization, and commerce. Differences were the result of natural error incident to communication from one nation to another. Newton accepted the identification of Greek and Egyptian gods and heroes with the traditional kings of Greece and Egypt commonly made by mythographers and chronologists. Sesostris was at once Osiris, Bacchus, Hercules, and Belus; Thoas, King of Lemnos, had forged arms for the monarchs of Egypt and was deified as Vulcan.

The brute-worship of the Egyptians was more perplexing for a Euhemerist than the anthropomorphism of Greco-Roman religion; so abhorrent was it to an eighteenth-century man of reason, so degrading of human dignity, that in explaining it the Abbé Banier lapsed back into pure Renaissance allegorism (and so did Edward Gibbon) rather than face the ugly reality of the adoration of animals. In the *Chronology* Newton, equally repelled by brute-worship, developed the ingenious theory that in the beginning the animal hieroglyphs of Egypt were ordinary writing and that the animal forms of the king-gods were merely pictorial, symbolic representations of actions for which the kings had become famous.

Newton's predominantly Euhemerist interpretation of the origins of pagan religion was interwoven with orthodox Christian conceptions of primitive monotheism. Even when the Israelites or other peoples fell into idol worship there was at least a glimmer of true divinity in their most abominable cult practices. This was Calvin's position in the *Institutes* and it emerges from Newton's notes on "Idololatria" and "Religio Ethnica" in the *Commonplace Book*. Of the idolatrous Danites he wrote, "And yet it is most reasonable to think that they worshipped the Images with respect to the true God because they acknowledged the true God in them." [22] Newton explained away Solomon's idolatry as an erroneous though comprehensible belief in "intermediate beings," a persuasion into which he had been induced by his foreign wives and concubines. Newton was of course in this field annoyingly eclectic on occasion, like most of his contemporaries, and along with his predominant orthodox Euhemerism and apparent belief in innate primitive monotheism he had at times a tendency to trace the "purer" forms of heathen religious worship like Zoroastrism to the sacred tradition of Abraham via the Brahmans, the common seventeenth-century orthodox theory which made paganism a corruption of Judaism. The constituent elements of Newton's history were generally orthodox and Protestant; the same conceptions were represented contemporaneously by erudite Huguenots living in Holland, men like Le Clerc or Pierre Bayle's enemy, the pastor Pierre Jurieu. Primitive monotheism, occasional astral worship, and Euhemerist deification of kings were combined in one system.

Samuel Shuckford's *The Sacred and Profane History of the World Connected* (1728), the writing most immediately competitive with the *Chronology*, is another illustration of the contemporary English tendency to present antiquity as one concordance of plain political history. This is the work of a pious man, no Deist, and he does not reject out of hand all miracles, but the greatest number of the wonders of God described in the Pentateuch are explained away as ordinary natural events. The theory

of Bishop Ussher and the rabbis that the rock at Mount Horeb
followed the Israelites through the wilderness is refuted — there
were other water supplies. When Shuckford did credit a miracle,
such as the speaking of Balaam's ass, he went to great lengths to
demonstrate that it was a necessary miracle, that its ends could
have been achieved in no other way, that even the Lord conformed to the scientific law of parsimony. Shuckford dated all
Biblical events with exactitude, fixing the forty years' wandering
in the wilderness between 1491 and 1451 b.c., and he located
geographically all places mentioned in the Bible, setting the Garden of Eden somewhere between Korna and Bassora, a decision
which he could not have reached lightly in view of the scores of
contemporary volumes proposing alternative sites. The miracle of
the storm of hailstones and the Joshua incident of the sun and
the moon arrested in their course were reconciled with authenti-
cated astronomical evidence. Shuckford brought further confirmation of the miracles from the Chinese annals, and he set men's
minds at rest about any fatal consequences to the solar system
arising from these prodigies.

If Shuckford was still somewhat cautious in dealing with Scripture, he allowed himself free play in establishing the concordance
of mythology with Biblical history. Wherever it was even remotely
possible he established a connection between the Hebrews and
the Greeks. Among other things, he made Lelex of Lacedaemo-
nia an Israelite. The whole theogony of Hesiod became unadorned political history. The devouring of his children by Cronus merely meant that he sent them off to school in foreign parts,
and the vomiting up signified their return. Zeus, a contemporary
of Moses — this was the axis of world history — was a wise ruler
of Crete surrounded by worthies whom later politicians divinized.
He was an enlightened despot of antique times, who worshiped
the heaven and the earth, administered justice through subordi-
nates, taught his subjects arts and sciences. He was by definition
an orderly, centralizing monarch, and when one Prometheus tried
to instruct the people in science without a license he exiled him to
the Caucasus.

In the traditional manner Shuckford explained why later generations divinized Jupiter and the Cretan elders who had helped

govern his kingdom (not forgetting Neptune who was head of the king's navy and Pluto who established funeral customs and was a kind of chief undertaker). Princes traced their origins to a deified ancestor out of craft, to frighten or persuade their subjects into more ready acceptance of their rule. And royal advisers humored their lords and encouraged them in a real belief in their divinity to render them bold and fearless in carrying out an expansive foreign policy. On occasion, Shuckford recognized, the practice of deification had a more homely origin: the daughter of a noble who had the habit of walking alone in isolated valleys was reported impregnated by a god to save the family from infamy. By appropriate harmonization of Apollodorus, Diodorus Siculus, Pausanias, the Phoenician Sanchuniathon, fragments of the Egyptian Manetho, and Euhemerus, Shuckford achieved a perfect conciliation with Scripture, in general along the lines of Sir John Marsham's *Chronicus Canon* (1672). This nonsensical history of the universe is of interest not only because it was translated into foreign tongues and was widely quoted in the polemics of the age, but as a perfect example of the Euhemerist historicizing temper in the first half of the eighteenth century.

Other variations on Euhemerus were elaborated both in France and in England by scholars and theologians who despite their patent common orientation tended to be opinionated and aggressive in defense of the particular historical reality which they discovered in a myth. Abbé Foucher of the Académie des Inscriptions et Belles-Lettres developed a doctrine of theophanies akin to Euhemerism and proceeded to find them among all religions everywhere in the world, Assyria, Chaldea, Egypt, Phoenicia, India, Peru, even the Celts. His colleague Abbé Fourmont, one of the most learned linguists of the age, spun out a really intricate web. The Chaldeans had begun the abominable practice of deifying heroes; the Israelites heard of it from them; the Phoenicians adopted the vice and apotheosized the Hebrew patriarchs. The names of these worthy Israelite ancestors were altered in the course of transmission among the heathen and they suffered even more frightful distortions when as pagan gods they were diffused into Egypt. Whence the Greeks, adding their portion of error, derived the Olympians. This combination of Euhemerism and pan-Babylonianism worthy of a German scholar of Bagdad Railway days had managed to conciliate the idea of Hebrew name origins for the gods with Sanchuniathon's theory of Phoenician influence in Egypt and Herodotus' historical account of the migration of the gods from Egypt to Greece — the evidence a veritable jungle of etymologies from all the ancient languages.

Bishop Warburton knew Fourmont's work, but preferred a theory of Egyptian to Chaldean origins for divinization since, unlike the French *érudit,* he did not know Chaldean. The Warburtonian version of Euhemerism is a compendium of characteristic eighteenth-century English reflections on political behavior imposed upon the ancient inhabitants of the Nile Valley. The Egyptian masses were never taught the simple fact that gods were deified heroes because of their rulers' fear that with this degradation of the gods to human stature the whole political and religious structure of society would collapse. The growing eighteenth-century awareness of a stratified society combined with Euhemerism produced a common enough explanation for the perplexing coexistence of Egyptian monotheist wisdom among the priests and brute-worship among the masses, though Warburton's history of the Egyptian rite of animal worship as a form of dead-hero apotheosis, the heart of his doctrine, was dismally tortuous. In the beginning, ran the argument, Egyptian religion was "natural" and consisted of astral worship, a pure form of primitive religion. Man had turned toward the heavens in gratitude for the powers of life. This wisdom of the primitive astral religion, along with the history of the early kings of Egypt represented as animals, had been recorded in hieroglyphs on monuments by the benign priests of the earliest times. When at a later period the politicians came upon the idea that religion was a convenient weapon of authority they introduced "local tutelary Deities" throughout Egypt. Their manner of deifying heroes was based upon an astute understanding of the psychology of the common people. The gods were confined to one area, because the rulers knew that the people would reverence more a god "whose Peculiar they were supposed to be: for, when undistracted with other cares, he would be supposed at full liberty to attend to the minutest concerns of his own People." Another cunning reflection of the impostors was their sense of the "selfishness and pride of the worshippers who would be for ingrossing a God to themselves; and raising honour to their Country from this imaginary property."[23] This localization of the deities also served the purpose of the central power of Egypt by keeping the nomes and their separate deities from uniting against the Pharaoh — part of a divide-and-rule stratagem which accounted for the preservation of a multiplicity of gods. Many of these interpretations had already been brought together and summarized in Plutarch's *Isis and Osiris,* but Warburton paraded them as newborn from his episcopal brain.

It was latter-day wicked Egyptian priests, not the original sages of the Nile, who inspired in the people religious reverence for the ancient hieroglyphs which were ordinary symbols of dead kings in animal form, a pictorial language once understood by everybody. And from this adoration of the symbol of the animal the purblind masses turned to the worship of the animals themselves, encouraged in their abominations by the ruler priests and politicians. Warburton had a "reason" for virtually every aspect of primitive pagan religion. His doctrine that all gods were "local heroes deified" after this invention of Egyptian priestcraft had been diffused throughout the world entailed a number of difficulties. How account for the fact that the deities of essentially local origin had such similar characteristics? The universal features of astral worship were readily comprehensible, but why should "local" deities have identical attributes? Never at a loss, Warburton asserted that heroes in all times and places were very much alike, hence the gods who derived from them markedly resembled one another; their common symbolic attributes had originally been intended to divert attention from their personal blemishes.

The Warburton interpretation of hieroglyphics was the section of his turgid, lumbering *Divine Legation of Moses* which was most attractive to eighteenth-century continental thinkers, and it was quickly translated into French and Italian.[24] Strangely enough it earned its author a European reputation as a *philosophe,* and his theory of hieroglyphs, quoted with approval by Condillac, de Brosses, and Caylus, ultimately found its way into the *Encyclopédie,* where it was cited by name and accepted as philosophical writ. The similarity of the Warburtonian to the Newtonian hypothesis on brute-worship, which the vain bishop would never have conceded, was recognized at the time by at least one English cleric — Bishop Clogher.

In the *Histoire du ciel,* the Abbé Noël Antoine Pluche had historicized myth as a weapon of Christian apologetics. While he did not venture to preach the burning of the classical authors like an obscurantist early Church Father, the purpose of his work was to disparage the gods in public esteem by demonstrating their rather low utilitarian "mechanical" origins — they were not even human — a sort of *reductio ad absurdum* of Euhemerism. He drew upon a host of mythographers to reconstruct an authentic history of the origins of Greek and Roman religion in Egypt, proving in passing the uniqueness and purity of the physics of Moses and the errors of all the ancient philosophers, as well as those of Descartes and Newton.

In the beginning the Egyptians were a simple people worshiping a spiritual god. The Abbé subscribed to the current theory of primitive monotheism, the best orthodox account in accord with the Old Testament. Exactly when abominable idolatrous practices possessed the Egyptians he could not surmise, but it had happened naturally, through error, misconception, and stupidity. As the earliest peoples in the temperate zone were agricultural, their leaders instituted pictorial symbols informing them when to plant, sow, and reap, when to expect the winds and the rains. A utilitarian code for primitive farmers was the original purpose of the signs of the zodiac: the cancer is a crab which crawls backward, the capricorn a goat which climbs upward, the virgin is related to reaping, and the kids to spring birth. But how could these symbols apply to Egypt, where, though they were identifiable among the hieroglyphs, the planting season was not in harmony with the agricultural year described in the zodiac? The Abbé Pluche saw victory for his thesis in this very anomaly, for here was proof positive that the signs of the zodiac were foreign importations, brought from an alien land by descendants of Adam and thereafter preserved by Egyptian tradition and custom. Since the signs could not account for all of the hieroglyphs, Abbé Pluche devised reasons for later additions which were related to the flooding of the Nile and public announcements required by the irrigation system: staffs indicated the depth of the water, other symbols its increase or recession. In this manner Egyptian hieroglyphs were reduced to ordinary acts of public administration, based on astronomical observation, fulfilling mean agricultural needs.

Then came human depravity. The common people divinized the pictorial symbols, forgetting their lowly origins, and trans-figured them into gods. The Egyptian priests stood by and ob-served the process which corrupted their pure primitive mono-theism, but they were helpless in the face of popular ignorance and fanaticism. What can our own bishops avail, cried Pluche, against contemporary superstitions in Christian France despite their regular denunciations of the evil? The priests of Egypt withdrew into their temples, storing away the true significance of the signs of the zodiac and the hydraulic measuring rods which the people were worshiping as gods. Their belief in monotheism, in future reward and punishment, was cautiously reserved for a select few. Thus the mysteries were passed on to Eleusis and Samo-thrace, and when the good Cicero was initiated into them under dire oaths all he really learned, as he hints in his treatise *On the Nature of the Gods,* was the simple fact of monotheism and a good deal of rather commonplace information about the time for sowing and the time for reaping.

The fantasies aside, what Abbé Pluche did was to depreciate the Egyptian gods and their Greek derivatives as Euhemerus had once done, support the orthodox thesis (including Hebraic ety-mologies for Greek goddesses), vindicate the Bible, and make his aristocratic contemporaries blush to ornament their chambers with objects as vulgar, mean, and lowly as a peasant's agricultural implements in disguise.

However much they differed in details of interpretation, Shuck-ford and Abbé Pluche, Warburton and Abbé Banier, Fréret and Newton were all of the same stripe, latter-day Euhemerists who banished every enchantment from man's dream of the ancient world. Essentially the same procedure was being applied with respect to the miracles of the Bible and the myths of the Greeks. Both were reduced to events which could be narrated in the

commonsense language of the café. To popularize, to render
plausible, to make credible the incredible persisted as the great
historic act of the age. The same temper which impelled Richard
Simon and Astruc to historicize the composition of the Pentateuch
and William Whiston to naturalize the miracles of the Bible expressed itself in Banier's de-allegorizing of mythology. Thus divines and secular historians both participated in the attempt to
expunge the marvelous, the divine to preserve his religion from
jibes that it was "enthusiastic," fanatic, and superstitious, the
secularist to shrink the orbit of the irrational and the extravagant.
"Greek religion not mysterious" was the manifesto of Euhemerist
abbés and bishops. "Christianity not mysterious" was the Deist
echo. In fact, "Nothing is mysterious" soon became the credo of
the age and all truths were declared to be self-evident.

CHAPTER IV

The Birth of the Gods

"There is an universal tendency among mankind to conceive all beings like themselves, and to transfer to every object, those qualities, with which they are familiarly acquainted, and of which they are intimately conscious. We find human faces in the moon, armies in the clouds; and by a natural propensity, if not corrected by experience and reflection, ascribe malice or good-will to everything, that hurts or pleases us. . . .

"Nay, philosophers cannot entirely exempt themselves from this natural frailty; but have often ascribed to inanimate matter the horror of a *vacuum*, sympathies, antipathies, and other affections of human nature. . . .

"No wonder, then, that mankind, being placed in such an absolute ignorance of causes, and being at the same time so anxious concerning their future fortune, should immediately acknowledge a dependence on invisible powers, possessed of sentiment and intelligence. The *unknown causes*, which continually employ their thought, appearing always in the same aspect, are all apprehended to be of the same kind or species. Nor is it long before we ascribe to them thought and reason and passion, and sometimes even the limbs and figures of men, in order to bring them nearer to a resemblance with ourselves."

— David Hume, *The Natural History of Religion* (1757).

1

The Rationalist Myth of Origins

ORTHODOX BELIEVERS in the Christian tradition and the Deist heirs of Lord Herbert of Cherbury had solved the problem of the beginnings of religious emotion with dogma. If the idea of God was innate, or a direct revelation to Adam, there was nothing more to be said on the subject of origins. The theological difficulties surrounding the birth of primitive idolatrous, as differentiated from true, religion were not insuperable. It was a commonly accepted idea that idolatry had its inception sometime after the deluge during the dispersion of the Noahides. In the popular *Histoire générale des cérémonies religieuses de tous les peuples du monde* the Abbé Banier had suggested that idol-worship was an extreme reaction of people to the flood, which they believed had been visited upon mankind because of the rampant atheism of the antediluvians. In their terror and bewilderment men took to adoring virtually anything. Since the Bible had not established a firm historical moment for the first degeneration from primitive monotheism to idolatry, there was latitude even among the orthodox for divergent opinion both about the causes of this perversion and its precise date. Saint Epiphanius had fixed upon Abraham's grandfather, Saint Augustine upon the age of Jacob and Leah, Hugo of St. Victor upon Nimrod, Eusebius, and Gerardus Vossius in his wake, upon the sons of Mizraim (the Egyptians), Lactantius upon the Phoenicians. The inveterate compromiser Abbé Banier was satisfied that idolatry had started simultaneously in Egypt and Phoenicia. Maimonides had identified primitive paganism and astrolatry under the name Sabaism; primitive star-gazing had led to the worship of the constellations, which in turn had brought about their concrete representation. His views of the origins of idolatry at the time of Enoch formulated in the *Guide to the Perplexed* and in the *Commentary on the Mishna* were known to Christian Hebraists and were widely adopted by English eighteenth-century divines, especially after Dionysius Vossius had translated the *Avoda Zara* into a Latin treatise, *De Idololatria* (1641).

Human corruption after the fall or demonic mischief was usually sufficient explanation for idolatry in most Christian literature. "Man having been created in the image of God," wrote Marc Lescarbot after his experience with the heathen American Indians, "it is fitting that he should recognize, serve, adore, praise, and bless his Creator, and that he should exercise all his passion, thought, strength, and courage in worship. But, human nature having become corrupted by sin, this beautiful light which God had first given him became so obscured that man has sometimes lost the knowledge of its origin." [1] When necessary, specific naturalistic psychological motives could be introduced to bolster the general religious premises. Chapter XIV, verse 15, of the Book of Wisdom gave rise to a hypothetical chain of events, commonsensical and plausible; it was conjectured by Christian apologists that a dead man whose portrait was preserved by his household at first as an object of loving regard in the course of time became an ancestor worshiped as divine. Idolatry was thus a bad habit which had slowly crept up on mankind. Pagan Euhemerism, assimilated by the Church Fathers and passed on to Christian Europe, was another "cause" for idolatry, usually presented with the grotesque historical furbelows of a Bishop Warburton or an Abbé Pluche.

Bossuet's *Discours sur l'histoire universelle* (1681), which incorporated the traditional account of the birth of idolatry about the time of Abraham, was typical of the orthodox Catholic position throughout the eighteenth century. The original worship of the true God had at first been maintained both by direct, living tradition from Adam and by the fact that it was in conformity with the light of reason, a truth so clear it seemed ineradicable. "But reason was weak and corrupt, and as men

became distant in time from the origin of things they confused
the ideas which they had received from their ancestors. Unruly
children or badly brought-up ones no longer were willing to
believe their decrepit grandfathers whom they hardly knew after
the passing of so many generations. Stultified human understanding could no longer raise itself to the perception of intellectual
things. Men no longer wanted to adore what they saw. Idolatry
spread throughout the world." [2] Bossuet combined a thin residue of the demonological theory ("the spirit which had corrupted
the first man") with natural Sabaism and a utilitarian variant
of Euhemerism (worship of "the authors of inventions useful
to human life") as circumstantial elements in the corruption
of primitive monotheism. On the whole the ingredients of the
Bossuet theory were not too different from the later Deist exposition: there is forgetfulness, the weakness of reason, absorption
in the sense impressions of nature, and respect for the useful.

The Deist inquiry into why men had not persevered in the
rational religious convictions of their first parents and had lapsed
into the abominable cults witnessed everywhere throughout the
world usually became a study of psychological degeneration in
a historical no man's land. Deists tended to favor the political-
imposture doctrine of the ancients, or they resorted to a variation
on the habit theory. John Toland conjectured a concatenation
of events which brought on the evil accidentally. Wise men in
Egypt had innocently named a planet after one of their gracious
monarchs. With the passage of years the ignorant people came to
believe that their deceased ruler was not buried beneath the
earth, but was somehow present in another form in the heavenly
body which bore his name. From the idea of immortality to idol-
worship of the fancied immortal was an easy transition. For
Toland paganism thus had its initial source in rational error and
misunderstanding; the wicked priests only later capitalized on
a human weakness.

To the extent that it was feasible, both the orthodox and the
Deists had explained away the more ridiculous and cruel aspects
of pagan ritual. They modeled a respectable religious primitive
who would not be too alien to contemporaries. They idealized
and purified, made more consonant with human dignity and

man's innate religious nature the monstrous, weird creations of paganism, the bloody human sacrifices, the extravagant myths, the animal worship. They softened the coarseness and brutality, demonstrated that men were not naturally as blindly superstitious or as vile as the myths made them out to be. Despite idolatry the spark of the true God had been kept alive on the darkest continents of heathen barbarism.

In sharp contrast with these traditional theorists, earnest and erudite defenders of human reason and good will, or melancholy chroniclers of sin and demonic wiles, appear the historico-psychological mythographers of the eighteenth century who are now the main subject of our inquiry. Their psychologizing of religious experience in the historical context of the primitive world was one of the great intellectual revolutions of the age.

An open-eyed, childlike curiosity about the beginnings of things is one of the most endearing traits of the eighteenth-century *philosophes*. These paradoxical men of the world, so debonair and sceptical with a Horatian *nil admirari* on their lips, were in a state of profound wonder about origins. There was a general assumption that the real nature of man, of language, of writing, of political society, of inequality lay hidden in their first expressions. Since these sons of Locke believed that no idea was innate and everything human had to be learned through the experience of pain and pleasure and by association with previous stimuli, they opened the whole ancient world to historico-psychological inquiry. To the *philosophe* the study of antiquity was not a mere academic exercise but an investigation of remarkable utility, for if modern man was befuddled by false notions, the philosopher, in the course of examining the genesis of beliefs, the development of acquired capacities, and the growth of customs and institutions, would establish the moment in time when error had first crept into human reasoning. The diagnosis in and of itself would exert a therapeutic effect.

The *philosophes'* quest for origins derived from the totality of their intellectual enterprise. Sensationalists and utilitarians, they had to replace with science the Biblical cosmographic tradition propped up by more than two thousand years of commentary. Apart from the most orthodox churchmen, few intellectuals

still accepted the historical explanations of the Pentateuch with
the simple direct faith of previous generations. It is extraordinarily difficult for a high civilization to live without a set of
genesis myths, and when the Judaic ones had become shaky the
men of the new age put their mythopoeic minds to work. In a
creative outburst they devised theories about the geological revolutions of the planet, the emergence of man, the formation of
speech and a written alphabet. Their myths were rationalistic,
rather wooden configurations, for that was the style of the epoch.
They were also syncretistic. That other humanist world, the
Greco-Roman, had asked and answered the same questions
guided by reason alone and had left its accumulated solutions as
a heritage to the moderns, who read and debated them as if they
were the writings of respected contemporaries; nor were the
eighteenth-century myths as emancipated from Christian themes
as the *philosophes* prided themselves in their first flush of discovery. Over the past two centuries these imaginative inventions
have not been completely outmoded, though, like the ancient
ones, they too have undergone metamorphoses. Many an eighteenth-century myth is still recognizable beneath its present-day
scientific mask and barbarous terminological incrustations.

The most perplexing subject to an eighteenth-century man in
quest of reason was the origin of religious practice and belief.
This mystery troubled the avowed atheist even more than the
vacillating theist, and was magnified to the point where it became the great enigma of human nature. If only the philosopher
could discover what had happened in history to drive men into
absurd credulity and superstition, to transform them into fan-
tasts, mystics, cruel zealots, to cause them to lacerate their own
flesh and to immolate the bodies of others, if only this madness
could be fathomed, man would hold within his grasp the secret
of his irrationality and the key to his liberation.

The modern perception that the origins of religion must be
studied as part of a general theory of human nature is no older
than the seventeenth century, and Freud ended his life still grap-
pling with the beginnings and future of this "illusion." A group
of eighteenth-century thinkers, midway in the history of the
problem and writing for what was still a predominantly religious

society, ventured to ask Sophist and Socratic questions and to propose heterodox psychological answers. But since the Bastille was hungry for heretical authors and the Inquisition functioned actively in Italy and the Iberian peninsula, the psychology of religion was still frequently transposed as a blind into a historical investigation of primitive paganism, as it had been in Bayle and Fontenelle, indubitably safer terrain for the discussion of religious emotion. Occasional lip service to primitive monotheism should not therefore obscure the essential radicalism of their innovation.

Religious sentiment was not inborn, but was acquired by men at a given moment in time — this is the basic postulate. These eighteenth-century attempts to illuminate the origins of religion did not "hypothesize" after the manner of Rousseau, who in recreating the state of nature had refused to commit himself on the historicity of his savage. The major thinkers firmly believed that theirs were authentic reconstructions, founded on scientific evidence, of the dawn of religious consciousness.

The conjectures about the origins of religion in Vico, Hume, de Brosses, Boulanger, and Holbach, the writers under study as characteristic of the historico-psychological method of interpretation, can be resolved into a number of elements. First there was a backdrop for the drama of the birth of the gods, which involved an emotionalized description of the physical circumstances prevailing on the planet in remote antiquity. Then followed the key to the whole process, a psychograph of a primitive man, his capacities, the state of his reason, the dominant temper and mood of his life, the limitations of his perception. At a critical moment this man confronts the environment and a new emotion, "religion," is engendered. The newborn sentiment leads him to perform a series of acts. Finally, the metamorphoses of the original religious feeling throughout the historical process and its contemporary moral significance are presented. Not all purveyors of rationalist myths of origins incorporated each of the elements, and their constructions are as varied both in color and detail as the myths of the ancients, but there is a high degree of similarity among them, both in their formal, static elements and in their description of process and movement.

In the eighteenth century there was a consensus that the face

of the physical world as it was then known was not the same
as the primeval one. Any reasonable man brought up in the
tradition of Descartes and Newton, his sensibility trained by
mathematical and neoclassic forms, had to be discomfited by the
wild unevenness of the earth's surface. It seemed strange that
so battered an object would be fashioned by the skilled hands of
God when any geometer could have conceived of a nobler form.
For reasons theological or scientific, or more often an admixture
of both, inquirers arrived at the conclusion that the world of
nature must have undergone a whole succession of violent revolutions. That seventeenth-century clergyman of fantasy, Thomas
Burnet, had reasoned in *Telluris theoria sacra* (1681) that the
paradisiacal world as it emerged fresh from the hands of the
Creator, who was well informed about the spherical nature of
perfection, was "smooth, regular, and uniform," without the
blemish of mountains and seas on its surface. The deluge and
the consequent irregularities of the earth were divine retribu-
tions consequent upon human sin. By the middle of the eighteenth century less theological hypotheses were being propounded
on the precise manner in which the earth had been slowly formed
out of chaos. Writers in this field were not necessarily contradict-
ing Genesis and the Mosaic cosmography, for most of them had
thoroughly pious motives, like Burnet himself, who in his preface
declared: "This theory is being writ with a sincere intention to
justify the Doctrines of the Universal Deluge, and of Paradise,
and protect them from the Cavils of those that are no well-wishers
to Sacred History." [3] These commentators upon Genesis interpreted the text and harmonized it with the findings of the new
astronomy and the new physics. Imaginative geologists described the slow cooling-off process of the planet from an initial
flaming mass or its gradual drying out after having been totally
enveloped by waters. The Kant-Laplace hypothesis was the climax of more than a hundred years of science fiction about Creation. A legion of English divines, French abbés, Italian marquises
and monks had conjured up volcanic eruptions, floods, desicca-
tions, and igneous outbursts to account for the scars on the
rugged, wrinkled surface of the globe. The great mountain
ranges, the precipitous drops of cliffs, the tortuous meanderings

of river valleys, attested disturbances of colossal proportions whose historical record could be established. Two events in mid-century, the popularization of the discoveries at Herculaneum, with their reminder of the Vesuvius disaster, and the great Lisbon earthquake, though not the prime causes of this heightened interest in the revolutions of the earth, drew sharp attention to problems which had already been agitating the geologist and the theologian for decades. Most of the causes assigned for the protrusions and cavities in the crust of the earth pretended to be rigidly scientific, to rest on a new knowledge about gases, about the attractions of bodies, about the erosive power of water. As a corpus of information the fanciful systems — one part Bible, one part classical tradition, one part astro-physics, and one part nature observation — left a profound impression on the mentality of the age.

In the wake of Thomas Burnet theories multiplied — the works of William Whiston and John Woodward were the most noteworthy and controversial — showing that the Biblical flood was really a historical event which had occurred at a datable period in the geological annals of the world, a natural disaster caused by an oversized comet which, approaching too close to the earth, had in obedience to Newton's law wrought havoc with the waters. "A comet," William Whiston proved in the *New Theory of the Earth* (1696), "descending in the plain of the Eliptick, towards its Perihelion; on the first Day of the Deluge past just before the Body of our Earth." [4] Johann Gottfried Herder, who heaped scorn upon these apologetic fabricators of an arid *physica sacra* from the sublime passages of Genesis, numbered similar "systems" in the hundreds; Scheuchzer actually analyzed fifty separate hypotheses. Literary testimony from Greek mythology — the floods of Ogyges and Deucalion — and from Lucretius, newly transmitted annals from the Chinese in the translations of the Jesuit missionaries, and legends of American savages corroborated the historicity of the deluge. Throughout the eighteenth century ecclesiastical and secular writers disputed learnedly from the evidence, as they had since Benedictus Pererius, *Commentariorum et disputationum in Genesim* (1594–1600), over whether there had been one universal flood or a

series of local ones, whether the deluge had been a unique occurrence or had been repeated many times, whether the waters had
been sweet or saline, whether it had been a miracle or a natural
geological revolution, whether America too had been submerged;
but everyone was in agreement that an aqueous cataclysm had
occurred.

In a work on the fossil crustaceans published in Venice in 1740
Antonio Moro [5] conjectured that God created the world a perfectly smooth marble sphere on the outside and that it rolled
gently in an atmosphere of water. Its interior was stuffed with
earth, multicolored minerals, crystals, salts, and precious gems;
at its very center burned a fire. On the third day God commanded
an explosion of this internal fire, which burst the outer marble
casement of the globe and brought forth the primary mountain
chains. Then the fish were created and they swam about near
the summits of the mountains. When at a later date new volcanic eruptions occurred the primary ranges crashed into the
waters and were covered by the secondary mountains — all of
which served to explain the existence of marine fossils in the
bowels of the earth. For proof Moro adduced the classical traditions on the relationships between earthquakes and volcanoes
and the contemporary behavior of Etna and Vesuvius. Seashells
discovered in mountainous areas far inland fired the imagination
of amateur scientists, collecting them became a mania — Rousseau indulged himself in this passion too — and scores of historical reasons for the presence of marine specimens in the heart of
Europe were spawned overnight, including the delightful Voltairean quip that they were the luncheon debris of untidy pil-
grims. For those unconvinced that a flood alone had deposited
sea creatures on the mountaintops, a more fashionable late-
eighteenth-century explanation was the accelerated rotation of
the earth either through divine intervention or as a consequence
of natural causes. Experiments were conducted with spinning
globes to simulate the extraordinary propellent motion of the
planet which had dispersed the crustaceans.

While English theoreticians had used the marine specimens
discovered on the mountaintops to vindicate the Biblical account
of the flood as an actual historic event, the Italian Catholic schol-

ars tended to consider this a most hazardous form of apologetics, since for them the deluge was a miraculous and not a natural event. But however contradictory the rival systems may have been in their scientific and theological implications, they exuded a common spirit and recalled the same convulsive early history of the globe. For the more literal Bible commentator the universal deluge had lasted a mere forty days, for the "scientific" geologist the catastrophes had extended over hundreds, perhaps thousands of years; yet the emotional content of their works was identical. Worlds had been destroyed. Antonio Moro treated John Woodward with contempt as villainous, limping, and slippery; Costantini refuted both Moro and Woodward; Buffon made fun of Burnet and Whiston; and Jacopo Belli in *Il Santo libro della Genesi difeso da' nuovi assaliti de' moderni pensatori* (1788–1796) considered them all tainted with heresy. But in defining the spirit of the prehistoric world they struck the same terrifying chord.

As a consequence of the wide propagation of these scientific fantasies, in all the historical reconstructions of primitive religion aboriginal man does not stand on solid ground, but the good earth quakes beneath his feet. Prior to the exploration of the southern seas in the seventies, the image of nature was not tranquil, balmy, eternally placid. Paradisiacal motifs can be found, but serious men, intent upon knowing what the world was really like in the beginning, after their study of contemporary geology and paleontology could no longer believe in the poet's dream of a lasting primeval Arcadia. Count Buffon, *Intendant du Jardin et du Cabinet du Roi,* a member both of the Academy of Sciences and the French Academy, author of the *Théorie de la terre* and *Les époques de la nature,* was the official mid-eighteenth-century French historian of the revolutions of the globe, quoted with approval throughout Europe by *philosophes* and pious expositors of Genesis alike. Whether or not he plagiarized Boulanger's manuscript *Anecdotes de la nature,* a contemporary charge, is of less import than the striking conformity of his descriptions of the "convulsive movements of the earth" with the reconstructions of Vico, de Brosses, Hume, and Boulanger. Since Buffon no longer conceived of creation as a unique sublime act which in a flash, by fiat, had yielded a perfectly spherical globe, to cover imputations of irreligion or apparent contradiction with the Bible he prefixed his catastrophic history of nature with a bit of exegesis worthy of the rabbis. When Moses reported that God had created heaven and earth, the inference was unwarranted that He had made them as they were thousands of years later, and a day in Genesis was not the equivalent of an ordinary day, for prior to the fixing of the sun and the moon day and night could not have had meaning. This pious commentary accompanied by a certification to the Sorbonne that nothing in his work contradicted the Mosaic cosmography allowed Count Buffon to distinguish seven epochs, not days, of creation in his *Tableaux successifs des grandes révolutions de la nature,* all cataclysmic, extending over millennia. The skeletons of crustaceans and wild beasts and the impressions of plant life on rocks deep in the bowels of the earth could not be explained by passing inundations since most of the specimens discovered did not belong to the continent of Europe; the fossils were incontrovertible evidence of global catastrophes. While Count Buffon was circumspect and vague about the precise date of the appearance of the species man after the other terrestrial animals, he implied that human beings had already existed during the final cracking of the land masses and had witnessed the awesome submersion of Atlantis.

If a writer were unfolding the drama of the birth of the gods in Catholic France or Italy, whose censorship was to be reckoned with, and he wanted to remain within the pale of the Church, he had to set mankind in a locale that was not too flagrantly contradictory to the Genesis myth of origins and he had to provide for Adam's direct recognition of the God with whom he spoke. For this purpose the flood turned out to be a literal godsend, a most convenient breaking point in universal history. Vico, de Brosses, and even the heretical Boulanger erected a historic wall with the deluge. Whatever the antediluvian religion — it might have been monotheist — there was agreement that gentile man's religious history had begun anew with the dispersion of the Noahides. Vico, the most cautious of the mythographers, explicitly excluded the Jews from the profane history of the postdiluvian world, so that he could present his spectacle without apologizing for the irreligious character of the first brutish primitives. De Brosses followed suit, though with less remarkable consistency. Only Hume in latitudinarian Protestant England did not have to deal with Adam in any specific sense, and his pagan world was built without reference to the creation myth in Genesis.

Among the historians of primitive religion the dominant feeling of the environment was uniformly harsh, bleak, and cruel. In *Les époques de la nature* Count Buffon himself painted in lurid colors the shivering savages who had endured the early revolutions of the globe, a romantic portrait which was normative for the whole group of rationalist mythographers of the birth of the gods. "These men, profoundly affected by the calamities of their first state, and still having beneath their eyes the ravages of the inundations, the fires of the volcanoes, the chasms opened by the earthquakes, preserved an enduring and almost eternal memory of these misfortunes of the world. The idea that it must be destroyed by a universal deluge or by a general cataclysm; the reverence for certain mountains on which they had saved themselves from the inundations; the dread of those other mountains which burst with fires more terrible than thunder; the sight of the combats of Earth and Sky, the source for the myth of the Titans and their assaults against the gods; the belief in the real existence of a malevolent Being, the fear and the superstition which are its first product; all these sentiments based upon terror from then on possessed the heart and the mind of man forever. Even today he is hardly yet reassured by the experience of time, by the calm which has succeeded these centuries of storms, even by the knowledge of the effects and of the operations of Nature; a knowledge which could only be acquired after the establishment of some great society in peaceful lands." [6] Hume came nearest to being emotionally noncommittal about the primitive world, for he drew in benign natural details as well as forces of destruction, but even in his essay painful images were always the more poignant and perseverating. De Brosses, nourished on the testimony of the early travel literature, found savage nature consistently hard. Vico and Boulanger unveiled a postdiluvian world that was a veritable apocalypse of violence.

Eruptive, convulsive, threatening nature, overwhelming in its power, was the primary source of the impressions written upon the *tabula rasa* of the primitive mind. If thoughts about the world can only derive from sensations as they are awakened by nature, the character of the environment becomes the crucial determinant of the *esprit* of early man. Montesquieu's climatological theory of the laws was applied to the religious temper of the primitives. A paradisiacal setting after the manner of Diderot's *Supplément au voyage de Bougainville* would have encouraged a gentle religion of adoration and thanksgiving; a dismal physical landscape over which thunder rolled and lightning flashed could only bring forth a religion of terror. The effect of geological catastrophes upon primitive man had been traumatic.

The idea that the primitive ancestors of contemporary Europeans had a psychological make-up, a human nature, that was essentially different from Hume, de Brosses, and Vico, and that it was similar in general character to contemporary aborigines, to children, to benighted common people — in a word, that there was a distinctive primitive mentality — had been gaining ever greater force in European thought since the seventeenth century. There are even hints, though only hints, that madness too could be assimilated to this state of being. The momentous analogy was fed by volumes of empirical observation. Europeans had been watching and writing about savages for over two hundred years; a growing interest in child behavior is attested in works on education; and madmen, particularly demoniacs, had been the subject of medical analysis during the seventeenth-century outbursts of witchcraft. At the turn of the century Fontenelle had still regarded the difference between the primitive mind and the contemporary principally as one of degree; in later eighteenth-century writers the mentality of the primitive became more distinct, individualized to the point where a different human nature was recognized. Turgot even suggested that this early stage involved a different mode of perception from later metaphysical and scientific thinking — his famous anticipation of the Comtian law of three states.

A rational *philosophe* comprehended the theories of Harvey and Newton, knew of the existence of that "other" world of scientific-mathematical law which explained the movement of the planets, the geological strata, the meteorological violence, and even the physiological source for the passions of the individual. The savage had only simple emotional reactions to the external world. If the savage ceased to be necessitous and if the child were taught, their natural faculties might come to understand the law of this other world of true causal relationships, but the primitive had not yet had an opportunity for such development and his knowledge was limited solely to hasty reflections upon his sensations.

From Locke stemmed the notion that the most common characteristic of the mentality of primitives, children, savages, idiots, and illiterate people was its essential simplicity, its pictorial vividness, and above all its concreteness. In one of his manuscripts Locke had explained idolatry as the consequence of a natural human tendency to fall back and rest upon ordinary sensible objects and images. Generalized thinking, the complex combination of ideas, was so difficult that few people could remain in the realm of rational, unemotive abstraction for a prolonged period of time. That primitive man was a concretizer in his thought, his speech, and his first efforts at writing was a widespread conception in the eighteenth century, held by thinkers as diverse in their views as Vico, Warburton, Monboddo, Condillac, Astruc, Hume, and Turgot. Bishop Warburton's formulation of this idea in *The Divine Legation of Moses* (1738–1741) turned out to be one of the frequently quoted texts on the continent. "For men so conversant in *matter* still wanted sensible images to convey abstract ideas. . . . Thus we see the common foundation of all these various modes of writing and speaking, was a picture or image, presented to the imagination through the eyes and ears, which being the simplest and most universal of all kinds of information (the first reaching those who could not decipher the arbitrary characters of an alphabet; and the latter instructing those who were yet strangers to abstract terms), we must needs conclude to be the natural inventions of rude necessity." [7] In his *Observations on Man* (1749) David

Hartley explained the anthropomorphic conception of God among the children of the most pious Christians and Jews as deriving from their incapacity to conceive of the abstract and the invisible.

The problem whether savages were or were not capable of abstraction had caught eighteenth-century missionaries on the horns of a dilemma. On the one hand many of them confessed that from their observation the barbaric languages were sorely lacking in words expressive of abstractions, and they reported to their superiors on the extraordinary difficulties which communication about matters spiritual entailed under these circumstances. On the other hand they could not relinquish the idea that at least a spark of the conception of divinity had been preserved among the wildest and most ignorant tribesmen. Often the same Jesuit relation afforded contradictory evidence on this score. The European theorists, however, who read these accounts tended to bestow far greater weight upon the data which revealed the savage incapacity to abstract — even at the risk of unorthodoxy; and this applied to men like Vico, Warburton, and Herder who remained within the confines of their respective Christian churches as much as it did to David Hume who strayed.

The one emotion pervading primitive life as portrayed by the psychological historians of religion was terror. Upon first thought nothing seems more alien to eighteenth-century consciousness than ideas of fear and trembling. The optimist *philosophes,* exulting in their science and progress and self-evident reasonableness, seem to flee the darker recesses of the human soul, whose secrets await the romantics of re-Christianized Europe in the nineteenth century, to be probed by a Kierkegaard or by a Dostoevski. Actually the currents of opinion and the tones of feeling in the Age of Enlightenment were far more varied than was allowed by later simplistic accounts. The psychology of fear and its relation to religion was an area of knowledge upon which eighteenth-century thought shed great light, though it was, of course, by no means a complete intellectual novelty, since in this sphere too the *philosophes* drew heavily from the writings of Greek and Roman antiquity reintroduced into Christian society with the Renaissance.

When Petronius and Statius wrote "Primus in orbe deos fecit timor" the fear-theory had long since been a part of the Western rationalist tradition. The pre-Socratics, who first ventured naturalistic interpretations of the worship of the gods, had already fixed upon man's fear of death and his terrible anxiety in the face of natural prodigies as the most plausible explanation for the origin of religious awe among mankind. Sextus Empiricus in his treatise *Against the Physicists* cited Democritus of Abdera as the original source for the doctrine that the gods were born of fear. "For when the men of old time beheld the disasters in the heavens, such as thunderings and lightnings, and thunderbolts and collisions between stars, and eclipses of sun and moon, they were affrighted imagining the gods to be the causes of these things." [8] In Cicero's dialogue *On the Nature of the Gods*, Lucilius Balbus quoted Cleanthes the Stoic as authority for four reasons accounting for the formation in men's minds of ideas of the gods, the third of which is the Democritus fear-theory embellished. "The awe inspired by lightning, storms, rain, snow, hail, floods, pestilences, earthquakes and occasionally subterranean rumblings, showers of stones and raindrops the color of blood, also landslips and chasms suddenly opening in the ground, also unnatural monstrosities human and animal, and also the appearance of meteoric lights and what are called by the Greeks 'comets' and in our language 'long-haired stars,' such as recently during the Octavian War appeared as harbingers of dire disasters, and the doubling of the sun, which my father told me had happened in the consulship of Truditanus and Aquilius, the year in which the light was quenched of Publius Africanus, that second sun of Rome: all of which alarming portents have suggested to mankind the idea of the existence of some celestial and divine power." [9]

In the classical texts fear of the gods is a spontaneous reaction of men when confronted by calamity, without institutional mediation or intervention, a terror aroused directly by the untoward events of life. This doctrine, which in Democritus was sufficient explanation for religion, among more eclectic thinkers was joined to a late version of Euhemerism in which tyrants, bent on strengthening their own dominion, wickedly used the prodigies of nature and their knowledge of human fraility and natural terror to create gods out of dead heroes and to deceive the common people into the belief that the gods were the authors of the marvelous and the dreadful. The original conception of this psychology of imposture can be found in the fragment of Critias' drama on the Sisyphus myth.

The God of the Old Testament as He survived from Judaism, both Pharisaic and Essene, in primitive Christianity had inspired terror on solemn occasions — during the granting of the Decalogue on Mount Sinai and in eschatological prophecy. Though the Church Fathers, in their polemics against the pagans, adopted both the fear-theory and Euhemerism in order to denigrate the false gods, the idea of the fear of the true God as a natural human feeling and even a manifestation of piety was not despised. The great preachers of the Reformation and the Counter-Reformation were not loath to identify religion with hellfire and to terrify their listeners into conformity with one or another orthodoxy by a graphic depiction of the exquisite torments of the future state. All these fearful Judaic and Christian images were inevitably reflected in eighteenth-century rationalist interpretations of the origins of primitive religion.

The most magnificent ancient expression of the fear-theory was the philosophical poem of Lucretius. In this form it had the profoundest effect upon the minds of Europeans, after the Renaissance discovery of the text. World literature has few more gripping passages than the description in the third book of the torments of religious fear, the anticipatory terror of the punishments inflicted by the gods in Tartarus which poison man's whole existence and embitter his every pleasure. There is even a glimpse of the floating uneasiness, the undefinable disquietude rooted in fear of the gods which so envelops a man that he can find no place for himself; he rides off to seek surcease from anxiety and then turns back again to the haven of his villa, disturbed, distraught, he knows not why. Lucretius paid his debt to Epicurus, "discoverer of truth"; but it was his poem which most closely approached in tone the aristocratic philosophical morality of the Age of Reason. In every psychological discussion of the origins of religion the verses of Lucretius were either quoted directly or were echoed, for his golden passages, like the "images" he described, found their way into the souls of his eighteenth-century readers. Vico's autobiography bears testimony to the powerful influence of Lucretian thought upon Neapolitan youth at the turn of the century, and though he pretends to have outgrown him the telltale marks are everywhere in his writing. Thomas Jefferson had eight copies of the poem in various editions and translations in his library; the Baron d'Holbach had twelve. The influence of Lucretius was recognized to be so dangerous to revealed religion that Cardinal Polignac's feeble counterattack, a versified *Anti-Lucretius* (1747), won him a measure of fame among the pious.

Finally, the two philosophical giants of the previous generation, men whose names were not often spoken but who were among the unacknowledged masters of the *philosophes* — Hobbes and Spinoza — had included in their monumental works subtle versions of the theory that found the natural source of religion in fear and anxiety. Of eighteenth-century writers who psychologized the origins of religious emotion and cult practices, the most skillful invariably paraphrased these great heretics.

By mid-century the fear-theory in some form was commonly held by orthodox and *philosophes* alike. For the more devout like the Italian Marquese de Gorini Corio in his *Antropologie* (1761) it was fear and pride; among the radical *philosophes* it was fear and ignorance; but it was always fear. The Jesuit Lafitau confirmed the fear-theory from his observation of Indians. "One sees these poor people when they perceive the approach of a tempest overwhelmed by violent apprehension, rush to their cabins, crouch around their fires, their elbows on their knees, their faces hidden by their hands. In this posture they weep and express their terror until the storm has completely passed, because they say he who is shouting at them is gravely irritated with them and is threatening to destroy them." [10] The Diderot-Grimm *Correspondance littéraire,* while reluctant to accept the more extravagant apocalyptic versions, joined the eighteenth-century fear-theorists. "How magnificent is the philosophical opinion which attributes the origins of the first religious ideas of ancient peoples to the physical revolutions of our globe. . . . Man, the victim of great physical calamities, must have sought their cause in some unknown power. He must have created the gods and made himself the object of their loves and hates. Animals who have escaped danger soon forget it and the memory returns only when a new danger approaches and bears down upon them. But the imagination of man, aroused by perils which threaten his existence, terrified by the vast phenomena of nature, must soon have created the system of rewards and punishments and the myth of a god of vengeance. . . . You will find, Sophie, that in his conduct the God of hosts is a being capricious, cruel, fantastic, vindictive, and ferocious. He tries to lead people into crime in order to have the barbarous pleasure of punishing and exercizing his vengeance upon them." [11]

Most eighteenth-century rationalist myth-makers of the birth of the gods were polemical and argumentative because they were writing with the competitive religious history of Genesis looming in the background. Depending upon their individual persuasion they either conciliated the Mosaic tradition with their own theories, passed it by in dramatic silence, secularized it, or heaped ridicule upon it. Even when these historico-psychological theorists seemed least discursive they were by implication always battling rival and more respected traditional doctrines — Euhemerism, allegorism, diffusionism, primitive monotheism. Vico, Hume, de Brosses, Boulanger, and Holbach were above all moralists utilizing the history of the origins of religion and mythology for the education of the human species. But here they diverged most fundamentally. Vico, after the flirtation with the Neapolitan Lucretians in his youth, had written a new civil theology; the others were militant members, more or less covert, of the anticlerical crusade, who diagnosed religion to eradicate it and analyzed myth to banish it from human consciousness. The alternative to the primitive mythopoeic world which they unveiled was reason. Here again there was a divide: with Hume and perhaps Vico the confidence that reason as an enduring human state of consciousness could be attained was rather feeble; in Boulanger, Holbach, and even de Brosses the revelation of the true primitive was the major premise of a theory of rectilinear progress. The Turgot-Concorcet idea of perfectibility — the culmination of eighteenth-century philosophy — always took for granted the benighted primitive unearthed by the radicals of mid-century.

2

Vico:

The *Giganti* and Their Joves

*T*HE MAN is out of place — that is the rather stereotyped traditional verdict on Vico. He was born, lived, and died in obscurity in Naples and was not heard of until almost a century after the publication of his major work, when the young French historian Jules Michelet romanticized him in a free translation and popularized him throughout the continent. The real history of Vichian thought is more complex. He was profoundly appreciated in eighteenth-century Italy, though generally not until after his death, and he was revered as a great seer by jurists of stature, such as Gaetano Filangieri. Outside of Italy his influence was not significant until the nineteenth century, though it is known that Montesquieu bought a copy of the *Scienza Nuova* while on his travels, and Goethe rhapsodized about him in the *Italienische Reise* under an entry dated Naples, March 5, 1787: "In [his] fathomless depths the newer Italian legists greatly refresh themselves. . . . Upon a cursory perusal of the book which they communicated to me as a holy work, it seemed to contain sibylline presages of the good and the true . . . grounded in serious reflections on the past and experience. It is wonderful when a people has so venerable an ancestor; Hamann will someday become a similar codex for the Germans." [12] But even if Vico was noticed sympathetically, as he was by Court de Gébelin and the Abbé du Bignon, or reviewed in the international learned journals, the *Acta Eruditorum*, the *Journal des Sçavans*, the *Mémoires de Trévoux*, he was rarely understood. When Fausto Nicolini expanded Benedetto Croce's modest bibliography and discovered the Vichian impress virtually everywhere in world philosophy and history after 1750, he grossly inflated the Neapolitan's European role.

In modern Italy Vico has been resurrected as part of the cultural *risorgimento* and has been raised on a pedestal, a native philosopher of equal rank with the French Descartes, the English Hume, and the German Kant; but since the Italian state was from its inception torn by a spiritual civil war over the role of Catholicism, two Vicos were recovered, one religious and devout, the other secular and merely conformist, each mirroring the beliefs of rival commentators. The Vico whom no one wanted in his lifetime has been fought over for decades by Croce and his Catholic antagonists. This partisan debate does not, however, concern us, no more than do recent attempts to enshrine Vico among the fathers of existentialism.

Since Vico was nourished on a smattering of the Church Fathers, on the late scholastics, on the new philosophies of Bacon and Descartes, on the political theory of Grotius and Pufendorf, on the Renaissance humanists and the Roman jurisconsults, on the seventeenth-century mythographers and chronologists, on Plato and Aristotle, the Stoics and Lucretius, and since this born glossator strewed learned references with abandon throughout his works, he can be read in the spirit of any one of them, even those whom he explicitly attacked. He pretended to the geometric spirit of Descartes, the idealism of Plato, the respect for everyday reality of the lawyers, and the precision of the scholastics. In form and style his turgid and obscure work belongs to the seventeenth-century erudite system-makers and decadent humanists; in content, however, it breathes with a spark of new life. One must abandon critical judgment of his etymologies and Roman legal history in a temporary suspension of historical disbelief to soak in those profound reflections and majestic affirmations which reverberate long after the mean errors of detail have been forgotten.

Vico discovered that history was a form of cognition, and like all revealers of new areas of consciousness he was so exultant that he declared it to be the only, or at least the primary, form of truth, superior to mathematics. That presumption in itself would have jolted an eighteenth-century gentleman dabbling in the sciences and may in part account for Vico's rejection by the Enlightenment of the North. Before Vico, history had been a chronicle of battles and the struggle for power among the chiefs of polities. The tone of life remained ever the same in these descriptions, only the protagonists, the dates, and the locale changed. Vico's new history had no individual figures; the dramatis personae were nations and classes within nations, and the polities had one distinguishing quality — their time. The two eyes of history were geography and chronology. Arrest one of the four or five peoples that he considered appropriate physical units of study, particularly the exemplar nations Greece and Rome, at a given moment in its development — the beginning, the middle, or the end of the life cycle — and Vico could define its spiritual essence. As a formal historical schema he adopted Varro's three traditional ages, of gods, of heroes, and of men, a cycle experienced independently by each of the great nations of antiquity without significant influence upon one another. Vico was the original auto-inventionist. Nations passed through stages by an inner power of growth upon which foreign intrusions, even relations of commerce and war, exerted at most a feeble effect. The cycle had been reinitiated among the barbarian peoples of Europe after the fall of Rome, and under similar conditions the same pattern would be repeated again and again though there were an infinity of worlds. His own age of enlightened monarchy and law was the epoch of rational men in the second round of *ricorsi*.

What is moving in Vico is not this rather hackneyed triad, already old in his day, worn even thinner since by a long line of philosophers of the rise, maturity, breakdown, and disintegration of nations, states, societies, civilizations — depending upon the selection of the universe of discourse — but the substance, the feeling, the spirit of his characterizations. A segment of time in the life of a nation had a unique nature, a reality as true as a philosophical idea, and this nature was all-pervasive. Each age lives, speaks, acts, thinks, governs, legislates, dreams in its own language and idea system; it has a distinct metaphysic, a cosmography, a logic, an economy, and a politics; above all it has a psyche, to whose historic metamorphoses Vico imparted brilliant attributes. A heroic emotion could not be expressed in a rational age, nor a

divine law of barbarian times have relevance to a modern legis-
lator, for an age was exclusively divine or heroic or human, and
no expression in religion, custom, war, language, writing, symbol,
law but bore the mark of the dominant temper. In the age of the
gods, the childhood of the world, "whatever men saw or imagined
or even did themselves they took to be divinity." [13] The twelve
greater gods were really symbols for twelve epochs during each of
which men had invented some novelty in response to human need
and utility. Since in the divine age men feigned that every one of
their achievements was an operation of a god who had acted
through them as mere instruments, the god's name was a historical hieroglyph. Thus the age of Saturn, the golden age, was
the age of grain, Saturn being derived from "sati," sown fields.

For many eighteenth-century *philosophes* history was either en-
tertainment, a moral homily of a secular order, or an ugly spectacle of human vice and idiocy, the unlovely prolegomenon to the
Enlightenment. It was difficult to discern philosophical sense in
a combination of acts whose human motivation was overwhelmingly bestial and self-seeking. If men were driven by their uncontrollable lusts, how could their history be rational or subject to
exposition in scientific terms? There was a fundamental cleavage
between philosophy and history, between abstract scientific truth
and the behavior of tyrants, barbarian leaders, conspirators, as-
sassins, robber barons, soft and decadent luxuriating sybarites.
History was not the world of philosophers or a realm of philosophic contemplation; the sages had been victims of history more
often than its creators. In nature law reigned, Descartes's or
Newton's law, but in human affairs there was only chaos.

Vico appeared with arguments, dialectical and scholastic, to
prove the contrary. Faced with the spectacle of human barbarity
through the centuries, he bestowed meaning upon it. What blasphemy to imagine that God would reveal to man the secrets of
the mechanics (the history) of the physical world and keep hidden the truths of the world of minds, the metaphysical world.
For decades the Neapolitan professor of jurisprudence wrestled
with the myriad projections of human experience, for no fact was
alien to the historical process, and twice he was defeated in his
struggle with the mass of materials. He himself expressed dis-

satisfaction with the first *Scienza Nuova* of 1725; he corrected the
text and issued another edition in 1730, but no sooner had a
copy emerged from the press than he covered it with marginalia
and emendations. The third time, in 1744, he was content.

The web of history was passion, cruel necessity, wild desire,
but though individual acts were not rationally premeditated and
predictable, the whole formed a civil theology, clear, unified, and
purposeful. Each isolated human act was motivated by self-inter-
est, base desire, irrational fear and terror, fantasy, imagination,
superstition — and yet the totality of human behavior in political
societies obeyed law. Man the actor freely willed the individual
deeds of passion, but by a strange dialectic, through his passions
he also was the creator of the idea. Hegel's "cunning of reason"
was not a novel doctrine in European thought. Man was an instrument of divine providence, but he was also man living in myth,
religion, law, language, battle, the ceremonials of marriage and
death. He was a being at once thinking, willing, and feeling —
always in the spirit of his age. In everyday existence he expressed
himself through volition and sentiment far more often than in
abstract thought, but his ultimate destiny was rational perfection.
Metaphysics had hitherto concentrated on the illumination of the
spiritual nature of man as an individual; the *Scienza Nuova* condemned this mean restriction of the domain of "metaphysic." It
was far nobler to study God's way in the history of civil customs
"by which the nations have come into being and maintain themselves in the world." [14] The Cartesian philosophical analysis of the
processes of abstract reasoning was insufficient; before Vico lay
the vast historic plain of God's works in the sensate world of trembling with terror, punishing, fighting, loving, hating, talking.
These real expressions of man's nature were not to be denigrated
as transient error, corrupt matter distant from the true revelation
of pure spirit — the Aristotelian, the medieval, and the Cartesian
verdicts upon the uses of history. There was no longer a hierarchy
of being, for God had manifested himself in every aspect of human
existence. Vico rehabilitated the everyday commonsense world as
a new glorification of the Deity. Thus even the vulgar details of
mythology, scorned by the theologian as a refuse-heap of idolatrous abominations, assumed great significance, became sources of

knowledge, a record of the gentile nations' faltering quest for God. Primitive religion was not nonsense, idiotic babbling, but man's first striving toward the divine truth. Pagan laws and customs were no empty accidents or shadows of truth; they were necessary stages in the attainment of rational justice. God's order, the principles of the laws of nations, were embodied in the most remote corners of human experience.

The three stages, divine, heroic, and human, were not ranged in a progression of ascending values in the late eighteenth- and nineteenth-century sense, a unilinear advancement from what is recognized to be the less good to the better. There are three separate human natures — *tre spezie di nature* — each of which has its virtues and its potential weaknesses, though the rational human age, when sustained by Christianity, is the most perfect. By far the largest portion of Vico's work was devoted not to the man of reason but to the interpretation of the primitive, uncovering the poetic wisdom of the first ages of mankind. Vico's revelation of the "true Homer" transformed the poet of the Christian gentleman into a minstrel of barbarism; after his reinterpretation of feudal law early Germanic kings lost their pious religious attitudes and became counterparts to the rough leaders of the expedition against Troy. This absorption in the first two ages rather than the third betrays a secret admiration for the "crude minds of the first founders of the gentile nations, all robust sense and vast imagination." [15] He appreciated the qualities of these barbarians as had no other philosopher since the late classical world. In the study of primitives, who in response to fears and desires established religions, created languages and poetry, built civilizations, Vico captured the spirit of a world that was alien, even repulsive to the rational man of the Enlightenment.

A bold new theory of the origins of gentile religion and a novel explication of myth were two pillars of the *Scienza Nuova*. In the 1744 edition Vico introduced his drama of the birth of the Joves with a magnificent poetic and historico-psychological evocation of primitive man.[16] In outward form his narrative invites comparison with the learned commentaries on the early chapters of Genesis that were still being compiled in the eighteenth century by Italian monastic scholars; but this external habit covered the most heterodox ideas about original man.

After the waters of the deluge had receded, Vico narrates, the races of men descended from Ham and Japheth reverted to a wild state of nature and scattered over the great forests of the earth in savage migrations. The divine plan required a lapse of time so that the earth might dry off from the wetness of the flood and begin to emit certain exhalations of matter igniting in the air. The natural drying process required varying time periods in different places, only a hundred years in Mesopotamia, two hundred years elsewhere. As soon as the dehumidification was completed, the "sky fearfully rolled with thunder and flashed with lightning," and the primitive man-giants, dispersed on the forested mountain heights among the dens of the beasts, took fright. Thunder and lightning were not ordinary occurrences which might have escaped primitive man's notice, but wholly unprecedented, terrifying natural explosions. In Vico's epic the savage giants were forced by the sudden rumbling to raise their eyes heavenward and thus to become aware of the existence of the sky for the very first time. At that moment, when the *giganti* lifted their heads, in an instant of awesome fright the gods were created by man. The wild savages had heard their own shouting and growling often enough before when preparing for the kill; when they perceived the sky bursting with violence they envisaged the heavens as one great animated body and named it Jove, a god "who by the whistling of his bolts and the noise of his thunder was attempting to tell them something." [17]

Vico's postdiluvian was monstrous in size because he was abandoned by his mother after a brief period of suckling and he had inhaled the invigorating vapors of the soil fertilized by his own filth, but he was already a man endowed with the primary instinctual responses of humanity — above all the fear of death. And it was precisely this terror which drove him to imagine the first human invention, the idea of a god. In the same frightful process curiosity was aroused, the mind was opened to reason, religion and civilization were born together.

Throughout the second book of the *Scienza Nuova* Vico left vivid traces of those personal experiences and perceptions which had inspired his vision of the birth of the gods. The key intuition was the association of primitive consciousness with what he had learned from direct daily observation about the psychology of children and the common people among whom he lived in the heart of teeming Naples in the Vicolo dei Giganti. Even minor details of his mythic fantasies can be related to Neapolitan folklore — the belief, for example, that children who play in dirt will grow strong and healthy. The variants and manuscript notes with which he bordered every text he published have numerous comparisons between *il mondo fanciullo* and the primitives. Vico had also seen the "vulgar" who, when aroused by strange phenomena, "make of all nature a vast animate body which feels passions and effects"; [18] he had heard them say that a "magnet loves iron"; he had watched children "take inanimate things in their hands and play with them and talk with them as if they were living persons." [19] Primitives were endowed with the same "corporeal imagination," a capacity to "feign" the living existence of natural bodies, and then to believe what they had just feigned. From the travel literature, particularly the recent work of the Jesuit Lafitau, Vico learned that the American Indians animated and called gods whatever power in nature surpassed their feeble understanding. Finally the empirical evidence had been synthesized into an axiom of human behavior, true in all ages: "That the human mind, because of its indefinite nature, whenever it is lost in ignorance, makes itself the rule of the universe in respect of everything it does not know." [20] When novelty breaks in upon man's consciousness he looks for an analogy in "what is familiar and at hand," and if no analogy is discoverable, as a last resort he projects himself with his passions and desires into the new phenomenon. The Sophist moral dictum that man is the measure of all things was changed by Vico into a rule of psychology: "man makes himself the measure" by projection.[21] That general eighteenth-century insight which identified the mentality of ancient primitives, contemporary savages, children, and peasants found one of its most fertile applications in the Vichian theory of the origins of religion.

Vico rejected Van Dale and Fontenelle and aligned himself in the Democritean tradition. "Fear first created gods in the world . . . : false religions were born not of imposture but of credulity." The Christian orthodoxy of this pagan perception was moreover vouched for by Eusebius, who had also taught that the first people invented the gods "from terror of present power";

to which Vico was quick to add in what seems to be a stricture against Hobbes, "not fear awakened in men by other men, but fear awakened in men by themselves." [22]

The creation of a Jove in man's own image was proof of a fundamental axiom of the *Scienza Nuova*, "that the world of civil society has certainly been made by men, and that its principles are therefore to be found within the modifications of our own mind." To placate wrathful Jove the first act of men was the suppression of a bestial lust, the end of promiscuous copulation with women and the installation of life in the cave with one alone, followed by the setting up of a family society. The initial propitiation of Jove was a self-denial, a curbing of the wild sexual instinct. Fear made the gods, and the gods made men curtail their appetites as an act of appeasement. Thus had Providence operated in the world, that out of terror of natural phenomena and the false image of a Jove man instituted civil society. An act of will leading toward a rationalization of human behavior was born of passion. Though he failed to establish the psychological relationship between terror and sacrifice, Vico recognized the universality of the inhuman rituals to which primitive men had abandoned themselves in order to calm the anger of the gods, and he humbled the *superbia* of the Europeans who, proud of their descent from the rational Greeks and the noble Romans, were revolted by the bloody rites of the Aztecs and the Incas. In the early ages all Mediterranean peoples had behaved in accordance with the same rule of barbarism.

Vico broke with the tradition of the Renaissance humanists who had imputed rare wisdom to the most ancient gentiles. If scholars wanted to learn about primitives they should have begun with "these first men, stupid, insensate, and horrible beasts," [23] not with creatures of fully developed rationality. He ridiculed the writers of the natural-law school who made aborigines enter into civil contracts and establish religious ceremonies on the basis of a perception of orderliness in the world.

Vico's portrait painted by Francesco Solimèna, preserved only in a mediocre nineteenth-century copy, reveals a brooding, anxiety-ridden philosopher. In the *Scienza Nuova*, perhaps the grand projection of his psychic nature, fear continued to loom as the dominant human emotion long after the passing of the epoch when gentile religion and family society were first founded. At every critical moment in the development of barbaric mankind fear of death, of brutal punishment by superiors, was the major "necessity" which brought forth historic innovation. Key Vichian transitions from one age to another were invariably the consequence of violent "irrational" outbursts among men which inspired terror in their fellows. The more dark and mysterious the source of a historic institution, the more wonderful appeared God's works. When Vico had to explain the peopling of the western Mediterranean he refused the commonplace idea that it was the result either of an extension of commerce or of imperialist expansion. Men could be driven to migrate and colonize only by a cause of extreme *necessity* which welled up from the very bowels of the commonwealth. There had been a civil war within heroic society. The *famuli,* grown weary of serving their noble lords, had revolted; among the defeated rebels many had been slaughtered outright by the heroes; others in terror of death "committed themselves to the hazards of the sea and went in search of unoccupied lands along the shores of the Mediterranean, towards the West where the coasts were not then inhabited." [24] The barbarian aristocratic heroes had acted from blind passion and their victims from fear, not for such nice and proper rationalist motives as the spread of empire and the furtherance of trade, fitting expressions only for the last age of men.

"The fact is that all the nations sprung from Ham and Japheth," wrote Vico, "first developed their native languages inland." [25] The burden of his argument was the autochthonous development of nations in every sphere of their existence and above all in those two sublime realms which were most distinctively human, religion and language. His absolute and uncompromising autoinventionism ran afoul of major Christian traditions. The Church Fathers had seized upon the confusion of tongues incident to the building of the tower of Babel to account for the multiplicity of languages throughout the world and the abandonment of the sacred antediluvian speech in which Adam and Noah had conversed with God. Vico, in defense of his conception, modified patristic opinion with a cautious gloss: the Scriptural confusion had occurred only

among the descendants of Shem, in the language of the "easterners"; the other two branches of the human species, the sons of
Ham and Japheth, the dispersed gentile nations whose history he
was writing in the *Scienza Nuova,* each had a separate and completely independent linguistic evolution. While this commentary
on Genesis may have squared him with the Church Fathers, it
was a direct affront to his especial bêtes noires, the diffusionist
etymologists, who "traced all languages of the world back to
the origins of the eastern tongues," usually Hebrew through Phoenician intermediaries. A polemic with latter-day Christian scholars, however exalted their reputations, was a call to glory which
he could not resist. In the first *Scienza Nuova* Vico had already
illustrated the unique development of the language of the Latins;
the same rule, he demonstrated in the third edition, prevailed
throughout the gentile world. The solid core of a national tongue
had always been fashioned *inland,* in isolation, in mountainous
hideouts after the flood; the paltry number of "foreign" words
were insignificant late addenda to an already fully matured means
of verbal expression, introduced toward the end of the heroic
period, when commerce and war finally brought the peoples down
from the high places to coastal areas and intermingled them. The
etymological history of native words reflected a natural order of
ideas: "First the woods, then cultivated fields and huts, next little
houses and villages, thence cities, finally academies and philosophers: this is the order of all progress from the first origins." Foreign etymologies were not grounded in history, for they were
"mere stories of words taken by one language from another."

These Vichian excursions on language were directly pertinent
to his theory of the origins of religion and pagan myth. Since all
the creations of man forging his own nature were parallel developments through time, the same evolution held true for religion as
for speech. The gods and myths of the gods were not diffused from
a common center any more than were languages, and conformities were not a consequence of importation but rather spontaneous
expressions of human nature that was fundamentally the same in
the diverse areas of postdiluvian dispersion when men were confronted with elementary necessities of an identical order. "Uniform ideas originating among entire peoples unknown to each

other must have a common ground of truth." [26] The invention
of a god, a language, a myth, a law, a custom was always — and
this is reiterated throughout the *Scienza Nuova* — an indigenous
emanation of the human spirit, never a borrowed tool. Vico's
thesis swept into the same discard the voluminous seventeenth-
century etymological scholarship of Vossius and Bochart and the
contemporary Euhemerist diffusionists of the Académie des Inscriptions et Belles Lettres, Fourmont and Banier.

Superficially Vico's explication of myth retained a certain affinity with historical Euhemerism. While he was an aggressive opponent of the narrow theory which made all gods deified heroes,
an imposture to serve political ends, he was in the common eighteenth-century tradition in utilizing myth as a serious factual source.
He was closer to Fréret than to the Abbé Banier, to those who
read myths as revelations of broad cultural trends than to the
literal-minded abbés and English deans who looked for the covert
family scandals of ancient royalty in Hesiod. But the Vichian theory broke the limits of Euhemerism and bordered on historical
allegory, a new symbolism. Myth was at once the language of
primitive man and a hieroglyphic record of major developments
in the history of humanity.

In searching for categories in eighteenth-century mythography,
one is sometimes tempted to establish a division between those
Euhemerists who maintained that, however fantastical the later
accretions of a myth, originally flesh and blood personages with
specific names had lived, acted, died, and been deified, and those
myth interpreters who considered even the names themselves
fortuitous; but this bifurcation is not always fruitful. Though
Vico, far more thoroughly and consistently than even Fréret, trans-
figured every divinity and hero in the myth into a cultural symbol,
the *Scienza Nuova* still betrays a slight trace of the "straight" historical idea that real human beings with these names and characteristics at one time existed. One of Vico's acute insights, drawn
from child psychology, was bound up with this conception. The
first Hercules may possibly have been historical; what is important
is the existence of many other Hercules figures who did not originally bear the name, whom popular speech of the infantile age of

mankind fused into one hero and identified by the same appella-
tion. Any man who has played with children — and Vico had
eight of them — knows that they continue to call all remotely
similar persons by the name which they have first associated with
their parents. But so thin a tie to the traditional historical school
is a feeble subsidiary element in Vichian myth analysis. The profound meaning of mythology for Vico lies not in its vestiges of
personality but in the historic fact that it was the universal language of gentile nations in the early period of their existence,
narrating their own cultural progression.

Every item in the great heroic legends of the Mediterranean
world was subjected by Vico to cultural-historical interpretation.
The Dido myth, which he located toward the end of the heroic
age of the Phoenicians, is a good illustration of his method. From
Dido's migration to Carthage he learned of a rather complex
socio-political development, a series of events for which there
were counterparts among all gentile nations. There had been a
heroic contest in Tyre between rival groups, and the vanquished,
symbolized as a woman in heroic diction because they were the
weaker, fled to Carthage and founded a colony of refugees. Memory of the conflict was preserved in the legend that Dido professed
to have left Tyre to escape the hatred of her brother-in-law. Another example of Vico's succinct translation, element by element,
of a myth of one stage of the historic humanization process is
Degnità 79: "On Mount Parnassus, in front of the temple raised
to divine justice (which was later the dwelling of the Muses and
Apollo, the god and the arts of humanity), Deucalion with Pyrrha
his wife, both with veiled heads (that is, with the modesty of
human cohabitation, meaning marriage), seize the stones that lie
before their feet (that is, the stupid brutes of the former savage
times) and make them into men by throwing them over their
shoulders (that is, by the discipline of household economy in the
state of the family)." [27] For Vico myth never dealt with the minor
personal political events of Mediterranean kingdoms, but with
momentous occurrences in the gradual socialization of mankind:
the origin and genesis of pagan religion, the establishment of
families, the invention of speech and writing, the institution of

marriage and burial rites, the rebellion of the clients for the right
of equal participation in human ceremonials, the defeat of rebels
and their migration to foreign countries to escape death.

Neither the Orpheus nor the Hercules around whom the mythic
cycles revolved, no more than the Jove whom the *giganti* created,
was a real historic person. The Hercules of myth was a "heroic
character of the founder of peoples." [28] The tendency of nations
to create archetypes symbolic of social-historical moments in their
existence persisted from the first "feigning" of a Jove through the
creation of Aesop the moralist slave, who was not an individual
man in nature, but an imaginative type or "poetic character of the
socii or *famuli* of the heroes." [29] Boulanger later wrote a long
essay in the same spirit on Aesop as a symbolic social type of the
oriental peoples, though in his intricate manner he assimilated
him with Solomon, a mingling of images from different nations
which Vico would never have allowed.

Vico fought every one of the diffusionist hypotheses of the
spread of gods and demigods, Pythagorean, Egyptian, Phoenician,
and even Judaic, despite the fact that the latter was as common
an orthodox favorite among learned eighteenth-century Italian
monks as it was in German theological faculties. The diffusionist
systems had invariably involved a translation of pagan deities, an
imitation of customs, and a borrowing of language forms from
some central source — all concepts that were to Vico gross perversions of true history; and his refutation was both rationalist and
historical. Ancient peoples were secretive about their religion,
rather than facilely communicative, he insisted with a wealth of
evidence, hence the very foundation of the diffusionist theory was
sapped. Egyptian hostility to the admission of foreigners, especially Greeks, was notorious; religions were hidden from their own
plebes by the priestly castes, a fortiori they were veiled before
strangers. There had been no encounter between the Greeks and
the Romans before the Tarentine war, proof of the autochthonous
development of nations. "So well acquainted were the first peoples," Vico exclaimed ironically, "even when they were not sepa-
rated by water and not far apart by land." [30] The whole traditional history of the eastern Mediterranean which had been
founded upon the transmission of ideas and religions by philoso-

phers, great legislators, and poets — Anacharsis the Scythian, Hermes Trismegistus, Orpheus — was undermined. Judean diffusionism was attacked on the ground "that the Hebrews in the times of Homer and Pythagoras lived unknown to their nearest island neighbors, to say nothing of remote nations overseas." [31] Moreover, there was Jewish antagonism to the propagation of the Mosaic law lest it be profaned by traffic with the gentiles — witness the rabbis' curse on the Septuagint. His quarrel with those who considered the myths of the gods to be sacred history corrupted was not a mere school controversy among rival mythologists, for it involved the heart of the Vichian system, the demonstration that in each pagan nation the civil theology of the *ricorsi* had been operative independently, without revelation or alien intervention, through human necessity and utility alone.

Vico's reliance upon a law of internal development made him postpone incidents of cultural fusion as long as possible in world chronology. Even when there was actual human contact Vico denied influence; conquest did not necessarily alter the dynamics of the soul of a people. Though the Egyptians held the Hebrews in slavery, neither paid heed to the other's spiritual development. Only on the rarest occasions was the life-cycle of a nation interrupted by total defeat in war, and when this occurred the people ceased to exist as a historic entity.

That myths, the crude, primitive language of early nations, had been used by philosophers and legislators to inculcate moral humane virtues upon the ignorant masses, an axiom of the allegorist tradition, was for Vico false and anachronistic. Even as allegories the licentious myths could not have been enlisted for the moralization of mankind by wise ancients, for there was always a risk that they might be taken literally and, instead of spiritualizing men, would reduce them to beasts. Obscenities in myth were not primitive, authentic survivals of the divine epoch, but later accretions of the decadent stages of the last "human" age. "The treacherous reefs of mythology will be avoided by the principles of this Science, which will show that such fables in their beginnings were all true and severe and worthy of the founders of nations, and only later (when the long passage of years had obscured their meanings, and customs had changed from austere to dissolute, and because men to console their consciences wanted to sin with the authority of the gods) came to have the obscene meanings with which they have come down to us." [32]

Vico is none too precise about who devised the original myths; sometimes he described the *fabula* as if it were generated spontaneously by the popular imagination of mankind, a presage of the romantic theory of the great epics; in other passages the "founders of nations" seem to have done the actual composition, though their inventions were spiritual expressions of the barbarous age and not the rationalistic and didactic personal creations of law-givers. The Vichian theory ran counter to the learned tradition which had imputed occult wisdom to the fathers of Greece and Rome and to the early Egyptians. These nations revered by European society were in their beginnings mute and without language, like all other savage peoples in their infancy, and they too experienced the travail of slow growth. Only in the last epoch of their cycle were the Greeks and the Romans rationalists. The twelve tables, as he had already shown in his *Princìpi del Dritto universale,* were no legislative prototypes for enlightened humanity but "crude, inhuman, cruel, uncivilized and monstrous." The very conception which imputed sagacity to the heroic and barbarous progenitors of nations was the fruit of the late classical world whose historians, inquiring into human origins, judged of the remote ancients as if they were intellectual contemporaries — another example of projection — instead of realizing that they had been uncouth aborigines.

After his death Vico's postdiluvian feral man and the graphic depiction of the origins of pagan religion in the terror of the wild giants led to a disputation, in the course of which the inconsistency of Vichian history with Scripture was laid bare in a long series of formal scholastic propositions; for though Vico had remained discreetly silent on the history of the chosen people and had deferentially excluded them from his *Scienza Nuova,* the Bible had not been reticent about the gentile nations whose genesis Vico portrayed with circumstantial detail. Rousseau's *Discourse on Inequality* had been quickly recognized as heretical and its similarity, however far-fetched, with Vico's first stages of mankind in the *Scienza Nuova,* had cast grave suspicion upon the orthodoxy of the late Neapolitan professor. The equation of the writings of Boulanger, a rank atheist, with Vico's theory was even more condemnatory. The Dominican theologian Giovanni Finetti, author of the *Apologia del genere umano, accusato di essere stato una volta bestia* (1768), was the leader of the denunciators, the *antiferini;* the defenders, marshaled under Emmanuele Duni, whose *Saggio sulla giurisprudenza universale* (1760) eulogized Vico as the "gloria eterna della nostra napolitana nazione," were called the *ferini.* If this was not a controversy of the magnitude of the Guelphs and the Ghibellines it nonetheless touched men's souls.

To pinpoint the verses of Scripture from which Vico had deviated was easy. He had presumed that at the time of Babel the descendants of Ham and Japheth had no language, flagrantly contrary to the text. But the brunt of the attack was concentrated on Vico's portrait of feral man himself, an affront to Divine Providence, pernicious for religion, aid and succor to the *libertini.* This was a grave accusation to level against the memory of the dead Vico, who had envisaged his lifework as "una Teologìa civile ragionata della Provvedenza divina." Fine words, retorted Brother Finetti, but what kind of creatures had Vico made the first postdiluvians? "They are neither men nor beasts. What monstrous anomalies! They are men because they are provided with the potential faculty of thinking and living humanly; they are not men because for whole centuries they are universally deprived of active thought and a human way of life." [33]

The Catholic Vico had outraged his contemporaries with a primitive whose nature had no connection with the sophisticated eighteenth-century Neapolitans who paid court to the great cardinals and to the Spanish rulers. They seemed to belong to a different species. The lonely giants without family were mere concupiscence. They hunted the beasts of the forest and they cohabited with women like animals. Even mother-love was not enduring among them. Vico had made the man-giants subject only to passion and utility to demonstrate by the law of development the wondrous way of God with gentile mankind. For Vico the feral state was a necessary interlude because he could conceive of no civility without a prior ray of religious consciousness, but for the orthodox he was skirting the brink of heresy when he introduced this mute creature who knew neither love nor speech. Could the good God who had made man in his own image have allowed the race to degenerate into such bestiality?

Despite the charges of the *antiferini* Vico himself had meant the resurrection of the primitive world to serve profound moral and religious purposes. In the loftiest sense his work was an apologetic, a demonstration that God in His wisdom had transmuted private vices into public virtues (the influence of the Mandeville fable has been noted before). "For out of the passions of men each bent on his private advantage, for the sake of which they would live like wild beasts in the wilderness, it had made the civil orders by which they may live in human society." [34] It was an act of piety to establish the true history of man's ascent from the feral state and to demolish the false one, thereby founding God's law upon sound demonstrations, not erroneous ones which had a tendency, when disproved in a rationalist age, to lead men into atheism. Finally there was for Vico a dire warning in this revelation of the blood and flesh primitive, an admonition to mankind that if they departed from the rational way of life which they had achieved under divine guidance and abandoned themselves to vices, to hypersophistication, like the decadent Romans of the late Empire, humanity would again "fall back into the dregs of Romulus." The warning has a contemporary resonance that is terrifying; the prophet of Naples foretelling the doom across the centuries had an uncanny insight into the psychic ills to which the rationalist society was heir. "Thus in the midst of their greatest festivities, though physically thronging together, they live like wild beasts in a deep solitude of spirit and will, scarcely any two being able to agree since each follows his own pleasure or caprice. By reason of all this, providence decrees that, through obstinate factions and desperate civil wars, they shall turn their cities into forests and the forests into dens and lairs of men. In this way, through long centuries of barbarism, rust will consume the misbegotten subtleties of malicious wits, that have turned them into beasts made more inhuman by the barbarism of reflection than the first men had been made by the barbarism of sense." When the final stages of depravity had been reached, the extreme remedy of Providence was a necessary purification through a reinitiation of the historic cycle, a return to the primitive simplicity of the "first world of peoples," to the "piety, faith and truth which are the natural foundations of justice as well as the graces and beauties of the eternal order of God." [35]

Were the *ricorsi* inevitable, was the recurrent cycle the inexorable fate of mankind in a rational Christian world? What did Vico the Catholic make of the drama of redemption? Instead of aligning him either with the Catholic or the secularist school, why not recognize the persistent tension in the Vichian moral world of the Lucretian of his youth and the Christian of his later life? Despite his exaltation of Providence, the appearance of Jesus does not seem to have played a crucial role in the history of the gentile world unfolded in the *Scienza Nuova*. Nor does the slow rise of mankind from the barbarism of the dark ages after the disintegration of Rome seem to have been affected one way or another by the ministrations of Christianity. Hercules struggling with the dark forest of the earth, a battle which will be repeated throughout time, appears to be the more eternal Vichian symbol of mankind.

3

Mr. Hume's *Natural History*

BETWEEN the rationalist apologiae for the truths of revealed religion current in eighteenth-century England and a naturalistic interpretation of religious experience there was no great divide. The act of apology itself involved a momentous leap — objectifying the problem — and once this gap had been bridged the reduction of religious mystery to mere anthropology could not be long delayed. Viewed in retrospect the barbed arguments and snide illustrations of religious superstition which punctuate Hume's work appear less heretical than the effrontery of the subject itself. The defiance was emblazoned in the words "The Natural History of Religion." In 1757 Mr. Hume blandly informed his public in a polite essay that he was prepared to analyze religion as an aspect of human nature. There was to be a natural history of religion as there was a natural history of flora and fauna. A few years previously, in 1748, the Baron de Montesquieu had published an evaluation of the relative effects which the three rival monotheist creeds had exercised upon moral behavior, but he had cautiously prefaced that comparative study in Book X of the *Esprit des Lois* with a prophylactic admonition that he was investigating only the worldly, institutional embodiments of religion and was not presuming to encroach upon theology. Hume's "natural history," after a perfunctory obeisance to the one and only true faith, audaciously proceeded to study the psychological roots, the origins in time, and the etiology of religion. The general tenor of Hume's theory, forthright and pointed, sharp and critical, indifferent to traditional adaptations of sacred history, is an index of the speed with which European

consciousness was evolving during these years. A naturalistic interpretation of religion was a far bolder act of disrespect to
official opinion than any important English work that had appeared since the tracts of the early eighteenth-century Deists,
Toland and Collins and Woolston. The posthumously published
works of Lord Bolingbroke (1754) were its only contemporary
rival in impiety. Bishop Warburton — who tried to get Hume's
essay suppressed — was alert to its heretical implications despite
the mild-mannered phraseology and had his man Hurd issue a
warning blast immediately it was published. The very title of
the essay is provocatively reminiscent of John Trenchard's *Natural History of Superstition* of 1709. Its substance is in the same
psychological tradition that flows from the Epicureans through
Hobbes and Spinoza, through Bayle and Fontenelle, a current
swollen by tributaries from Shaftesbury and, more recently, from
Hartley. There were French and German translations within a
few years; and during the next decades when the problem of the
origins of religion was heatedly debated on the continent,
Hume's essay was a pivotal point of attack or a stronghold of
defense. It became the classic naturalistic interpretation of religion. The French translator of 1759, an antagonist, grasped the
fullness of its bitter morality, the abolition of psychological distinctions between the sources of polytheism and monotheism:
"How did the human mind come to devise a religion? This is
the problem which Mr. Hume proposes to resolve. Polytheism
is the most ancient religion. Idolatry the most ancient cult. Both
the religion and the cult were born of the passions, the ordinary
passions which the daily events and scenes of life excite in the
human heart. And theism has emerged from the very bosom of
idolatry. This is the basic solution of the problem." [36] For Johann
Georg Hamann, the Magus of the North, who rendered the text
into German though he never published his version, Hume's
work was that of a seductive anti-Christ. Orthodox Italian theologians like Jacopo Belli, reviewing the heresies of the moderns
on the eve of the Revolution, fixed upon the essay as a major
fount of impiety. Among French atheists of the second half of the
eighteenth century the *Natural History* was a new canon.

Nothing in the age of lucid reason could equal the beauty and conciseness with which David Hume formulated a problem. The opening of *The Natural History of Religion* stated the case for the century: "As every enquiry which regards religion is of the utmost importance, there are two questions in particular which challenge our attention, to wit, that concerning its foundation in reason, and that concerning its origin in human nature. Happily, the first question, which is the most important, admits of the most obvious, at least the clearest solution. The whole frame of nature bespeaks an Intelligent Author; and no rational enquirer can, after serious reflection, suspend his belief a moment with regard to the primary principles of genuine Theism and Religion. But the other question, concerning the origin of religion in human nature, is exposed to some more difficulty." [37]

In this essay *le bon David* was not scrutinizing the nature of philosophical religion, whose dilemmas he had skillfully debated in the *Dialogues Concerning Natural Religion,* a work written almost simultaneously but cautiously hidden away in a drawer and unpublished during his lifetime. The *Natural History* turned instead to the "other question," the religious beliefs and behavior of the masses of mankind, viewing them clinically as a widespread reality of conduct and not as an approach to truth. The subject of the *Natural History* is thus not Hume's idea of God but the popular religion of the overwhelming number of human beings in the world, from whom he felt sufficiently detached to analyze their motives without apparent involvement. Even the monotheism described in the essay should not for a moment be related to his own intimate philosophical perception of the world. Except for an occasional compliant genuflection to the powers of Church and State which any "knower" can recognize, the *Natural History* has few ambiguities. At times its overwhelming pessimism about human nature seems so pervasive and the hostility to Christianity so flagrant that one wonders whether the circumspect Hume did not secrete the wrong dissertation.

Before Hume plunged into his inquiry on the "origin of religion in human nature," his central topic, he had to commit himself on the general character of religious emotion. What was its place among the passions as he had defined them in his previous

works? Early in the essay he excluded religious sentiment from
among the primary instincts and specifically labeled it secondary
and derivative, thereby deliberately setting himself in opposition
both to Deist and to orthodox thinkers for whom the idea of a
God was an original emotion inherent in mankind. Religion for
Hume was not even a natural endowment of the same order
as the instinct for sex, a desire for food, a love of children, or the
emotions of anger and gratitude, for it was neither as universal
nor as necessary as any of these basic human feelings.

What then was primitive religion? It could conceivably be
treated as a purely rational process — and many Deists held this
opinion — a realization of the unity and harmony of the universe.
Hume summarily rejected the idea that religion in its origins in
remote antiquity could ever have been a consequence of rational
cognition. He was no more sympathetic to the view that natural
religion was deduced by primitives from the contemplation of
the scientific order of nature than he was to the dogma of innate
primitive monotheism. Such traditional theories of the genesis
of religion were dismissed because they were fundamentally incompatible with his hypotheses on the nature of primitive mentality, the character of early man's perceptions, and the tone of
his feelings. As for the controversy, simmering since Bayle, over
whether the empirical evidence of voyage literature proved that
all nations without a single exception harbored religious sentiments, Hume adopted a sceptical attitude. Nations of atheists
could possibly exist, though they were certainly not numerous.
He thus cast further doubt on the innateness of the idea of God,
since the orthodox theory allowed for no anthropological sports,
without in any way diminishing the importance of his inquiry
into an emotion widely manifest in human nature throughout
history.

Primitive man was devoid of general thoughts about the character and functioning of the universe not because he lacked the
faculty of reason, but as a consequence of his miserable condition;
he had no opportunity to reason. Hume did not accept Rousseau's depiction of primitive mankind as humanity asleep or in
a state of unreflective being, for he could not envisage man without consciousness. The image of primitives in the acorn-eating

stage, virtually without awareness of their own existence, set Jean-Jacques apart from the French and English thinkers of the age and drove his theories across the Rhine to the eastern frontiers of civilized Europe, where his savages were first really appreciated in Königsberg and Berlin. Hume's primitive was more akin to Fontenelle's, a born cause-seeker, an inquisitive rational creature, a man with the capacity to ponder on his own sensations; but he had neither the leisure nor the prior knowledge necessary to conceptualize one God, the prime mover of a natural order. Primitive man like ordinary persons in all ages was simply incapable of apprehending the rational mechanism of the world. Even a philosophical gentleman of England with his capabilities intact, thrust back into the environment of primeval mankind, could not have conceived of the plan of a harmonious universe under a single direction. If he reasoned about nature at all, his first conscious impression of the forces raging in the world was likely to be not one of unity but of diversity, of conflict, of contradictory, clashing powers. Such a pluralist conception of the sources of power would have been born directly, with quick sensibility, from man's own experience with the chaotic energies of nature, now bringing him a bountiful crop, now destroying his substance in bursts of violence, now filling his rivers with fish, now burning his wretched cabin. No commonsense primitive could impute a single divine cause to such opposing actions. The regularity of the frame of nature and the perfection of its laws escaped his notice, for the primitive took the uniform experiences of his existence for granted. It required a trained and highly developed intellect such as only a small minority were endowed with in any epoch to encompass that broad view of the wonderful meshing of the parts in the natural order which ravished the philosopher.

The primitive, all passion and desire, was not a rationalist, despite his capacity to reason. He reacted with wonder only to the great cataclysms, to extraordinary manifestations like thunder, lightning, earthquakes, volcanic eruptions. He had to be aroused emotionally in order to perceive, and far from discerning a constant principle in the world, whenever he was terrified he infused natural phenomena with his own immediate feelings.

"There is a universal tendency in mankind to conceive all beings like themselves, and to transfer to every object, those qualities with which they are familiarly acquainted, and of which they are intimately conscious." [38] This was the Humean version of the common eighteenth-century projection theory. The primitive made a distinct god of each separate expression of power, a god who willed as he did, an affronted god who must be angry, a hostile god who might desist and protect if appropriately propitiated. The primitive mind, when driven to establish causes, could only fix upon immediate, proximate answers; the notion of a remote cause, the beginning of a chain, was alien to him, for this capacity too was associated with the power of abstraction. Milton's Adam in the full perfection of his faculties, wrote Hume, might have sprung into being asking questions about a first cause, but that was not the real primitive, "a barbarous, necessitous animal . . . pressed by numerous wants and passions." [39] One had to look elsewhere for the font of religion than in a savage appreciation of the perfection of nature. Religion was born not of reason but of a passion, and a sordid one at that, was the burden of Hume's blasphemy.

Gods were originally invoked in connection with specific concrete events of life because uninstructed aboriginal man was incapable of an abstract conception of the universe. The very idea of a power behind an event would never have occurred to him if he had not been provoked by direct passion, "the anxious concern for happiness, the dread of future misery, the terror of death, the thirst for revenge, the appetite for food and other necessaries." [40] The stimulating emotions Hume listed were invariably painful ones. "Agitated by hopes and fears of this nature, especially the latter, men scrutinize, with a trembling curiosity, the course of future causes, and examine the various and contrary events of human life. And in this disordered scene, with eyes still more disordered and astonished, they see the first obscure traces of divinity." [41] Hume's primitive was no La Hontan savage with an innate sense of the Great Spirit, nor was he a Warburton Sabaist who, overcome with awe as he gazed at the heavens, initiated astral worship. Original man was too oppressed by sheer necessity to contemplate.

Hume made an absolute commitment to the chronological primacy of polytheism rather than monotheism in the history of religion — a pointed inversion of the traditional sequence. This was another flagrant heterodoxy, a topsy-turvy order which neither Vico before him nor de Brosses after ventured to affirm without disguises and subterfuges. It is necessary to revert half a century to Bayle and his contemporaries to discover the same brazenness. "The further we mount up into antiquity, the more do we find mankind plunged into polytheism. No marks, no symptoms of any more perfect religion. The most ancient records of the human race still present us with that system as the popular and established creed." [42] The teachings of a few philosophers and the theism, albeit impure, of a few nations did not merit serious attention as exceptions to his basic generalization. Hume rejected those pious travel writers who found traces of monotheism among the savage idolaters of the new world; he was no "state of nature" primitivist, and neither contemporary barbarism nor ancient texts afforded him adequate evidence of a widely diffused rational theism. Without a romantic cult of the religion of the heart among the ignorant multitude or faith in the naked savage's natural insight into the true God, this theorist of middle-class civility, this scrupulous social scientist, could not give credence to a hypothesis of monotheism before men had records and were civilized.

The entrenchment of theism had required civilization, experience, the passage of centuries. The collective mind of mankind had moved slowly from a lower state of consciousness, polytheism, to a higher one, monotheism, through time. Hume's primitive man rose from the inferior, the concrete, to the superior, the abstract, in an Aristotelian progression. In the "natural progress of human thought" the perfect was realized by abstracting from the imperfect over a long period of time, a rare evolutionary concession on Hume's part, a theme significantly paralleled by d'Alembert's description of the birth of the idea of God in the *Discours préliminaire,* first published in 1751. Hume's idea that the primitive stage of consciousness was sensate and pictorial had by the mid-eighteenth century become widespread enough to penetrate even the most improbable minds, for example that of Bishop Warburton, Hume's irate censor, whose ingenious history of hieroglyphs had been composed with this fundamental preconception. The identification of the early mind with the concrete, the visual, as contrasted with the abstract capacity of the civilized man can of course already be found in Fontenelle and Vico, and even earlier in the father of them all — John Locke. A more recent work, David Hartley's *Observations on Man, his Frame, his Duty and his Expectations* (1749), had illustrated this principle with profuse examples from the behavior of children, ordinary people, even brutes, whose lack of an abstract capacity turned out to be the prime characteristic which distinguished them from the human. While Hartley, who hobnobbed with Anglican bishops, would never presume to doubt primitive monotheism, his psychology of pagan religion bolstered Hume's theory: "Idolatry, heathenish and popish, has made a much quicker and more extensive progress in the world on account of the stability and vividness of visible impressions and ideas, and the difficulty, obscurity and changeable nature of abstract notions. And image worship seems to have been derived in great measure from this source." [43]

What is novel in Hume is his notion of the manner in which man's capacity to abstract — and the idea of divinity as a cause is the first abstraction of moment — came into being among primitives. In the genetic process the mind first distinguished "the nobler parts of its own frame from the grosser," and once having discerned this distinction in itself projected the more abstract part of human nature, its intelligence, into a divinity. Contemporary psychologists might be interested in the fact that Hume envisaged the first step away from primitivism as an act of "differentiation." Emotionally Hume still retained the pejorative attitude toward the body and matter and sensation which his culture had inherited from Plato and Aristotle. Emergence from the primitive was thus a movement from the conception of the whole world as matter undifferentiated, from simple ideas based on mere sensation, of man himself as well as the gods and nature, to a realization that there was pure spirit in himself and in God.

Hume's arguments against primitive rationalism and primitive monotheism were interlocked. If the savage could ever have reasoned about the "frame of nature" he would never have lapsed into idolatry; reasoning power would have sustained him in his theist belief forever had its original source been the intellect. Had reason been so diffused among the generality of early mankind that it permitted a deduction about "the order of the universe," that very reason would have preserved the concept. If ever a widespread popular idea was founded upon simple, easily communicable, straightforward reason it would not be destroyed. Historic fact was of another character; it could be perverted in time — and in Euhemerist fashion Hume used the demigods as illustrations of distorted historical heroes to prove his point — because (here too he followed Fontenelle) men loved exaggeration, were careless about testimony, had frail memories. But if the mass of people had by reasoning, as distinct from empirical evidence and from passion, arrived at a truth it would have remained unchallenged and unimpaired, for a rational, self-evident truth is immortal. The possession of an abstract capacity preserved abstractions. Hume's scepticism about the ultimate endurance of philosophical religious conceptions among the masses of people arose from the fact that for the multitude all religion, even monotheism, was *not* the product of reasoning about the natural order but had its roots only in passion and, what was perhaps most dangerous, a passion not very different from the fear-ridden emotional reaction which had given birth to the first glimmerings of primitive polytheism. The monotheism of the popular religions was not a rational insight into the unified works of nature, but a mere haphazard, the outgrowth of the maximization and generalization of particular deities and their attributes until one omnipotent God was imagined; or it was a religious reflection of a state of society in which a single monarch had engrossed absolute power. But this religion, resting on the idea of inflated power, was far from the philosopher's religion, which depended on his perception of the true scientific order of nature. Only a few rare minds had ever entertained a pure conception of rational theism and their belief had been, as he showed in the *Dialogues*, more akin to philosophy than to religion. There was nothing to make the

historian of Puritan and Quaker enthusiasts, the victim of three-
hour Calvinist sermons in his boyhood, the traveler in Catholic,
saint-adoring Italy, the pained reader of the testimonies of educated witnesses to the miracles of Abbé de Pâris, conclude that
superstitious concretizing religion had in any way diminished
with time and that reason was extending its sway. The wise were
to understand that Hume demonstrated the lowly inception not
only of polytheism but of theism itself in superstitious primitive
terror, and neither religious form had ever cast off the fetters of
its miserable beginnings. In the end the fundamental distinction
between popular polytheism and popular theism was merely
sociological, not epistemological. Polytheism and theism imparted
different political tempers to the societies they dominated, but
both were false world-views, for no conception based upon an
immanent god who intervened in human affairs could be palatable to the philosopher.

A well-nourished and complex psychology of fear informed
Hume's whole vision of primitive religion, indeed his view of
virtually all actual non-rationalist religious experience. Though
he was still in the tradition of the ancient fear-theory of the
origins of religion, he sophisticated the concept of fear and related it to hope, so that "fear-hope" became the composite source
of general religious feeling. For many years before he undertook
to compose a natural history of religion he had been analyzing
what he called the direct passions, among which fear and hope
had occupied a central position. In his *Dissertation of the Passions,* which was published along with the *Natural History* and
illuminates it, he had arrived at a set of subtle hypotheses about
the coupling of one passion with its opposite, fear with hope,
and the frequent movement back and forth between one sentiment and another. These polar emotions, rarely pure, were often
so fused that it was only a matter of slightly upsetting a delicate
balance when one or another predominated. He generally tended
toward an appreciation of the superior potency of fear; the state
of uncertainty between expectancies of grief and joy, pain and
pleasure — the original forms of fear and hope — was in itself
characterized by a vague feeling of fear. Hume had dissected
the emotion of fear aroused by the sudden appearance of the

unfamiliar, for any novelty bore with it the possibility of pain and evil, and he left beautifully chiseled passages on the perseveration of such primary emotions, likening them to the resonance of orchestral chords long after the original mechanical stimulus to the instruments, the laying on of the bow, had stopped. Since Hume was analyzing a historical-psychological problem, the content of primitive man's perception of the external world, in the first instance the key to the dynamic process had to be sought not in rational understanding either of unity or diversity but in something more basic, in primary emotions. In hitting the rock bottom of fear and hope Hume had reduced religion to a natural consequence of primitive experience.

Though Hume distinguished formally between the polytheism which had its origin in primitive man's frantic attempt to allay fears aroused by his savage state and the more civilized man's theism, his conception of one God, he could not hold fast to any theory of progressive evolution. Despite Turgot's earnest attempts to convert him, he always remained outside the ranks of the newly convinced believers in the idea of progress. While at times he used such phrases as "the natural progress of human thought" to describe the change from polytheism to monotheism, "progress" should not be infused with anything like the optimism it later acquired in Condorcet; elements of the older meaning of mere movement still clung to the term. Section VIII on the flux and reflux between polytheism and theism is a blunt denial of the idea of progress. Here Hume appears a sceptical, cyclical theorist in the classical tradition. "Men have a natural tendency to rise from idolatry to theism, and to sink again from theism into idolatry." [44] The dynamics of this process of oscillation between polytheism and theism is one of the weakest parts of the essay. Having attained monotheism by elevating their deities to the point where they conceived of attributes of unity and infinity, simplicity and spirituality, the common people were then unable to persevere in the contemplation of abstract power and lapsed back into lesser but more concrete symbols of gods. This descent into idolatry was ultimately followed by a new resurgence of the generalizing force. "The feeble apprehensions of men cannot be satisfied with conceiving their deity as a pure spirit and per-

fect intelligence; and yet their natural terrors keep them from
imputing to him the least shadow of limitation and imperfection.
They fluctuate between these opposite sentiments. The same infirmity still drags them downwards, from an omnipotent and
spiritual Deity to a limited and corporeal one, and from a corporeal and limited deity to a statue or visible representation.
The same endeavor at elevation still pushes them upwards, from
the statue or material image to the invisible power, and from
the invisible power to an infinitely perfect Deity, the Creator and
Sovereign of the universe." [45] Although in Locke's unpublished
notebooks, to which Hume of course had no access, this psychological necessity of ordinary people to cling to corporeal images
had already been offered as the explanation of idolatry, Hume's
law of religious alternativity was acceptable to virtually no substantial body of religious opinion in mid-eighteenth-century Europe, since it conformed neither with theories of the degeneration of primitive monotheism into polytheism, nor of primitive
deism subject to merely superficial variants, nor even of primitive
fetishism purified and sublimated with time into loftier conceptions.

Hume's essay ended with a none too hopeful assimilation of
popular religious practices in all times and places and their identification with primitive religion; the rites of positive religion
had fulfilled the same function throughout the ages, to allay
superstitious terrors. Even Alexander, the great hero of antiquity
who mocked the gods in his moments of triumph, had recourse
to auguries when frightened. Ordinary people everywhere still
conceived of their gods, whether one or many, in concrete, practical terms, as agents they invoked for particular utilitarian purposes. His conclusion that the vulgar and the primitive mind
were the same was thoroughly Baylian — his moral posture
appears to be a more elegant, subtle version of the French writer
— and he even used the same illustrations. Hume's primitive,
frightened, irrational, often cruel and disgusting in the magical
rites he devised to quiet his terrors, was recognizable in all times
among children, among religious fanatics, among victims of
priestly charlatanry, among madmen. The realities of popular
religion, particularly image-worshiping, miracle-making, super-

stitious Catholicism (which he could revile without reprisal from ecclesiastical authority), and enthusiastic Calvinism, which had reified the torments of the future state, made Hume despair of the possibility ever of converting the mass of mankind to a semblance of rational religion.

The spiritual history of mankind becomes a conflict eternal between the pressing need to find immediate, concrete causes of dreadful phenomena, however frivolous, in order to quiet terror, and an equally natural tendency to rise slowly to a perception of a first cause which might be graced with elements of spirituality. In neither state could mankind settle back comfortably. The Humean doctrine betrayed even more profound elements of despair than the mutual negation of spiritualizing and concretizing principles in religious conduct, especially in those passages where he sketched an embryonic sociology of religion, a paradoxical counterpoint between the respective moral personalities molded by polytheism and monotheism. The roots of his idea in Pierre Bayle's *Pensées* and in John Trenchard are unmistakable. Of all the attacks upon the dominant religions of Europe this was the most telling. Montesquieu before him and Turgot his contemporary, in an effort to evade metaphysical and theological controversies on the truth of Christianity, had devoted themselves to extolling its social utility. Along came Hume and undermined the foundations of the new-styled apology by casting doubt upon the salutary moral consequences of the triumph of monotheism over polytheism. In the light of the humane values of the eighteenth-century *philosophes,* the spirit of tolerance inherent in the very loose nature of popular polytheism rendered it the less painful and more endurable error, superior to the vulgar "theism" which had replaced it. The institutionalized religions of Europe, contemporary havens of monotheism, had amply demonstrated their proclivities toward absolutism, bigotry, and the cruel persecution of dissenters. While polytheism ultimately allowed for the flowering of a courageous spirit, monotheism fostered an abject, subservient nature. In a footnote Hume bordered on a Nietzsche-like identification of Christianity with a slave religion. On Hume's new ledger of the virtues and the vices — a perverse adaptation of the Calvinist one of his

youth — monotheism was far more often generative of vicious
character types than was polytheism.

The eighteenth-century myth-makers were not simply giving
rein to their free-roving fancies when they wrote tales of the
dawn of religious consciousness. All of them had a moral pur-
posiveness which inspirited their myths. Hume was not merely
exercising his scholarly, philosophical curiosity, pursuing his life
work, the treatise on human nature, studying man in one of his
most baffling manifestations; he was also communicating to the
age his own sad convictions about the limitations of reason as
the guide to life among the overwhelming majority of mankind.
The contemporary religionist, he taught, was not acting from
desires, needs, and perceptions essentially different from those
of the first primitives who experienced this sentiment, since the
fear of future events still possessed every one of us and remained
the fundamental source of religious feeling.

It was not only the historic fact that fear had made the gods
which absorbed and depressed the eighteenth-century psycholo-
gist of religion. Hume was an "associationist" — whether he followed Hartley or not — and in his experience the emotions of
fear and anxiety were normally linked with rage, anger, vin-
dictiveness, a bitter persecuting spirit, a melancholy temper. Fear
of God was not an isolated and distinct feeling for it was always
flowing over into other sentiments, and any religion which had
its primary source in fear became entangled with these other
emotions. If the fear of God was moderate and became related
to love, Hartley had reasoned in what he called his Theopathy,
the religious emotion would remain sound; but should the fear
become exaggerated, then religion would inevitably degenerate
into superstition, into the false belief that God was extraordinarily severe in his punishments, vengeful, and cruel. A man who was
superstitious, obsessed with fear, tended to develop a narrow,
absolutist, splenetic character. By association all of the unsalutary
emotions would merge with one another, so that what was initially anger or rage at a hurt or at a "denial of gratification" —
the phrase is Hartley's — would ultimately be transformed into
fear and then into cruelty. Throughout his essay Hume drew
upon the psychological analysis of the dour enthusiast, the reli-

gious fanatic, a figure delineated by Shaftesbury in the *Characteristics*, John Trenchard in the *Natural History of Superstition* and the *Independent Whig*, Bayle everywhere in his works, Hartley in the *Observations on Man*. Hume the historian of seventeenth-century Puritanism had worked in a great clinic of religious absolutists and he had observed their behavior with a moralist's eye.

For both Hartley and Hume the ultimate source of religious feeling, the combination of hope and fear, was in turn reducible to the sensations of pleasure and pain. Man naturally hoped for pleasure and feared pain and his religion embodied these fundamental psychological attitudes. Hartley saw the ideas of a malevolent and of a benevolent god simultaneously at play in the psyche; in their hyperbolic manifestations these feelings became harmful, and when a man was shaken by unfounded terror of evil forces which he imputed to Providence, he was a victim of superstition. A normal awe, perhaps even a reasonable fear of God seemed natural and sound to Hartley, but the enthusiast who imagined that God had a special care of his person and destiny suffered from a hypertrophy of images which in themselves were benign. Hume carried over basic elements of Hartley's Theopathy into the natural history of religion. Primitive man was exaggeratedly hopeful and exaggeratedly terrified, when a normal, rational, Humean view of the world would have taught him to expect both his share of pains and his share of pleasures.

Religious feelings born of fear molded an ugly character — by eighteenth-century standards of utility as laid down in the *Enquiry* — and led to vicious actions both against the person of the enthusiast himself and against his fellows. Hume made an attempt, as did his predecessors who diagnosed extravagant religious fanatics, to comprehend behavior so irrational and contrary to utility as self-lacerations in the name of religion. He did not summarily dismiss them as madness, and yet he failed to hit upon a plausible explanation of this strange violation of reasonable principles. He approached but did not quite arrive at modern analytic theory. Since it was an axiom of behavior that most men lived in terror of the future, the religionist sought to appease the impending wrath of unknown limitless power.

But the performance of mere rational acts, leading a good life for example, could not be considered adequate, for such ordinary moral behavior was deducible on simple grounds of reason. The religionist had to give his God more, to sacrifice something, to cause himself pain in order to placate the wrathful, all-powerful one. Hence the self-inflicted tortures which characterized the behavior of all religious enthusiasts throughout the world.

What was the remedy against superstitious, fanatical religion? It lay in overcoming the obsessive terror of future events. And how could this be achieved? The majority would never be liberated and would remain steeped in prejudice, but a few chosen philosophers could arrive at the realization that the future held the prospect not of pain alone but an admixture of the pleasurable and the painful that was the fabric of existence. If this would rid them of terror, it would free them from dependence on positive religious performances. Any religious ideas that remained would be born of the purely rational contemplation of the causal unity of all things. The Humean moral solution was profoundly Epicurean and Lucretian. Most of mankind would continue to behave like primitives in matters of religion — that was their fate. Those who could had an obligation to emancipate themselves from its toils and perhaps help others to move in the same direction, though Hume was sceptical of any mass success even under civility. "The whole is a riddle, an enigma, an inexplicable mystery. Doubt, uncertainty, suspense of judgment, appear the only result of our most accurate scrutiny concerning this subject. But such is the frailty of human reason and such the irresistible contagion of opinion, that even this deliberate opinion could scarcely be upheld; did we not enlarge our view, and opposing one species of superstition to another, set them a quarreling; while we ourselves, during their fury and contention, happily make our escape into the calm, though obscure, regions of philosophy." [46]

4

Président de Brosses:
In Memory of the Little Fetish

*T*HE PRÉSIDENT Charles de Brosses was far from an original genius, and nothing he ever published was a polished literary masterpiece. This typical eighteenth-century polygraph tried his nonprofessional hand at a wide selection of vexatious contemporary intellectual problems without achieving mastery or great distinction in any one of them. He was a man of insatiable curiosity about the origins of things, particularly language and religion, but he never outgrew the dilettante. While attending to his judicial duties as head of the Parlement of Dijon and writing memoranda on public affairs, he managed to compile a two-volume work on the beginnings, mechanics, and development of language which was adapted by Turgot for the *Encyclopédie* — *Traité de la formation méchanique des langues et des principes physiques de l'étymologie* (1765) was its final title — and to publish a collection of all existing exploration accounts of the southern seas, the *Histoire des navigations aux terres australes* (1756), a record which served as an impetus to Bougainville's voyages of discovery. Throughout his life he was preoccupied with the early history of Rome and he collated the fragments of Sallust in an original manner, albeit his textual reconstruction, the *Histoire de la République romaine, dans le cours du vii⁰ siècle, par Salluste* (1777), has not been appreciated by classical scholars. The vast history of mythic times which he planned in the 1740's, an *Histoire des origines ou des temps incertains et nébuleux,* never came to fruition. As a writer he is

most widely known for his *Lettres d'Italie,* which grew out of a
whirlwind tour undertaken in 1739–1740, the great event of his
life. De Brosses's descriptions of paintings, books, music, excavations, the society of the cardinals in Rome and Naples, the world
of the Venetian courtesans, are among the most vivid portrayals
of eighteenth-century Italy, and a recent Italian edition of his
work is today enjoying some vogue. Though in Naples de Brosses
was a frequent guest of the Cardinal Troiano Acquaviva, to whom
the first *Scienza Nuova* was dedicated, and the sherbets at his
parties are dilated upon with enthusiasm, there is no reference
to Giambattista Vico.

Modern literary scholars have been intrigued by de Brosses's
plagiarisms and by thorny problems surrounding the authenticity of his letters. As a person he is best remembered because of a
bitter quarrel with the aging Voltaire over payment for fourteen
cords of wood from the estate of Tournay which the philosopher
of neighboring Ferney had leased. Voltaire, who never forgave
an affront, avenged himself by preventing his landlord from being received among the forty immortals of the French Academy.
His altercation with Voltaire apart, de Brosses was a loyal friend
and defender of the *philosophes* in high places — he had dined
with the nonagenarian Fontenelle, a link with the first generation of the Enlightenment — and he cultivated relations with
distinguished foreign intellectuals like David Hume, the famous
naturalist Charles Bonnet, and Jean Jallabert, professor of
philosophy at Geneva.

When the Président de Brosses was elected an honorary asso-
ciate member of the Académie des Inscriptions et Belles-Lettres
in 1746, the major preoccupation of the *compagnie* was still
the explication of mythology; Fréret was Permanent Secretary
and the members were animatedly engaged in the exchange of
historical fantasies which they had uncritically projected into the
Greco-Roman corpus of myth. Their horizons had begun to extend beyond the confines of Europe to religions throughout the
world, but the Euhemerist spirit of Abbé Banier, deceased in
1741, still hovered over them. During three sessions in May 1757
and again two years later, this staid learned society which had
seen better days was disturbed by the erudite Burgundian noble,

a strange little gnomelike figure, who came propounding a dissertation so contrary to the prevailing doctrines on mythology that the academicians refused to publish it in their *Mémoires,* though his earlier effort, the learned *Description d'un ancien vase ciselé, trouvé dans le duché de Permie, et de quatre mss. en langue et en caractères de Tangut et des Kalmouks, nouvellement trouvés dans les ruines de la ville d'Ablakit en Sibérie,* had been respectfully received. Since it could never pass the censor, de Brosses had his rejected work printed secretly in Geneva in 1760 under the title *Du culte des dieux fétiches.*[47] In mid-eighteenth-century France it was respectable to be an allegorist or a Euhemerist-historicist in treating of myth and primitive religion. Charles de Brosses was neither — he was a fetishist.

Somehow de Brosses has never surmounted the contempt of Voltaire and as a thinker he has rarely been taken seriously. During the days of their brief friendship Voltaire used to sign his letters to de Brosses *anti-Fétiche,* playfully recalling the anonymous publication to flatter him; in his anger after the dispute he mocked him publicly as a miserable little *fétiche.* At the time of its appearance the book was briefly noted by the *Mercure de France,* which in May and September 1760 printed an exchange of inconsequential polemical letters on the de Brosses thesis, and Court de Gébelin, a rival revealer of antiquity equally unacceptable to the Academy, reviewed it with critical detail in his *Monde primitif.* It was remarked upon in the literary correspondence of the day but created no great stir. De Brosses's name was first publicly attached to the work when Naigeon reprinted it during the Revolution in the second volume of the *Encyclopédie méthodique.* The term *fétichisme,* which de Brosses invented, was ultimately accepted by the French Academy in 1835. By one of those quirks in the history of thought, during the crucial formative period of his life in 1842–43 Karl Marx was reading and digesting in his notebooks a German translation of de Brosses. The term "fetishism of commodities," though much transformed, is still a recognizable intellectual derivative which would have made the French aristocrat shudder. It was probably Auguste Comte who, by adopting the de Brosses concept as the definition of a stage of human consciousness in the *Système de politique positive,* resur-

rected the book and saved it from complete oblivion. Lytton
Strachey's charming little essay on the Président de Brosses omits
all reference to it. Two hundred years have passed since de Brosses
alarmed his fellow academicians with a *mémoire* which described
the astonishing conformity of ancient Egyptian brute-worship with
contemporary Nigritic adoration of fetishes and on this foundation
erected a universally applicable theory of the progress of religion.
And while the work is still mentioned perfunctorily in summary
histories of anthropology, it has never been examined in the intellectual context of the eighteenth-century attempt to define
primitive mentality and the nature of early religious experience.

Du culte des dieux fétiches must be coupled with David
Hume's *Natural History of Religion,* for the crucial third section
of the de Brosses book covering the psychological genesis of
fetishism among primitive mankind [48] is a literal translation from
Hume's essay, except for the excision of a few daring impieties,
the insertion of a sanctimonious caveat here and there by the
Catholic jurist, and the substitution of his own neologism
fétichisme for Hume's polytheism in an effort to bring the alien
part into harmony with the rest of the dissertation. Though the
translation from Hume is unmarked by quotations, the text at
one point does refer to an anonymous eminent foreign writer
from whom a number of the ideas were derived. This was clearly
not an act of plagiarism in any ordinary sense of the word, for in
later years de Brosses, in a letter full of extravagant admiration
for the Scottish philosopher, wrote that anything worth while in
his little book on Egyptian religion owed its inspiration to Hume.
He frankly explained his omission of Hume's name as an act of
caution necessitated by the furor raised at the time among "the
people of the bigote and the makebates" [49] by the publication
of Helvétius's work. (The daring of *De l'esprit* had delighted
him and he proudly wrote Jallabert: "The Tolands have not
yet written anything as sharp even in England.") [50] The relations
between Hume and de Brosses were always amicable; they spent
many days together in intellectual converse when Hume visited
Paris, and during the period of his harassing controversy with
Jean-Jacques Rousseau Hume communicated to de Brosses
through Madame la Présidente de Meinières his own version of

the weird incidents which were titillating philosophical coteries on both sides of the Channel.[51] De Brosses knew English, and even before its official publication in 1757 he may have had access to the Hume text, a printed copy of which had found its way to the continent two years earlier. His translation was original, not the affectedly pious and shocked rendering of the essay into French given in the third volume of the *Oeuvres philosophiques de Mr. D. Hume* (1759).

That the de Brosses treatise was a work influenced by Hume the Grimm-Diderot literary correspondence perceived immediately and reported to its subscribers, though it did not remark upon the verbatim translation of some twenty pages. The remaining portions of the two texts, however, are strikingly different. Hume focused on the nature of Greco-Roman polytheism as the exemplar popular religion, while de Brosses had his eye on the explanation of a more baffling religious phenomenon, Egyptian brute-worship. Their primary sources, too, are different, Hume deriving from the Greek and Latin corpus almost exclusively, with auxiliary support from Bayle and Fontenelle, Hartley and Spinoza, while de Brosses was deeply immersed in travel literature and in the seventeenth-century polyhistors. Hume is one of the most controlled and elegant essayists of all time; de Brosses is clumsy and turgid, sometimes confused and inconsistent, an autodidact aristocrat with a fixed idea who scorned the art of fine diction. While Hume "reasoned" about primitive man *ex hypothesi* like a closeted philosopher, de Brosses had acquired from his reading and editing of voyage accounts real insight into savage mentality, a sense that was alien to Hume.

Rancor against revealed religion is far less flagrant in de Brosses. Hume was writing in mid-century England where, despite the bombastic threats of pompous Anglican bishops like Warburton, who could not tolerate contradiction of their own learned theories on pagan religion, actual prosecutions by the attorney-general were rare; the only concession Hume made in his text (Millar was initially afraid to publish it) was to introduce a conciliatory avowal of theism which sticks out like a sore thumb. At the time de Brosses delivered his original dissertation before the Académie des Inscriptions et Belles-Lettres, *philo-*

sophes were still being imprisoned in France and books burnt by the public hangman upon condemnation by the Sorbonne. Despite the fact that the manuscript had circulated in Paris and had aroused mild controversy, de Brosses took precautions to envelop its publication in great secrecy; he wished to create the impression that it had been printed without his permission, and he made complicated arrangements for the clandestine shipping of his own copies into France to avoid detection. The pouch of Dufour de Villeneuve, the Intendant of Burgundy, obviously with his consent, was the vehicle of transmission. The temper of Rome was quite different and de Brosses had no hesitation about having the book sent to his Italian acquaintances, among them the Cardinal Domenico Passionei, librarian of the Vatican. Charles Bonnet, quick to sense the heretical implications of the work, was worried lest his friend should be molested by the authorities. "There are in Europe great countries where I still recognize all sorts of Fetishes," he wrote from Geneva on April 9, 1760, "I am afraid lest the priests of these Fetishes, irritated by the allusions of the author, might want to make of his person, or at least of his book, a sacrifice to their idol. I know that he is not too afraid of them. I should prefer, however, because of the concern which I entertain for his tranquillity, that he might remain forever unknown to them." [52]

De Brosses was convinced that he had finally solved the problem of *Egyptianisme* in a novel manner. Neither the classical writers on Egyptian religion — Herodotus, Diodorus Siculus, Cicero, Plutarch, Ovid, Iamblichus — nor modern commentators like the great Athanasius Kircher, the Abbé Pluche, and Bishop Warburton, nor iconographers like Dom Montfaucon had been able to face up to a literal interpretation of the images on obelisks, mummies, and papyri which depicted human beings in postures of adoration before beasts and creatures half man, half animal. There was too profound an insult to human personality in the spectacle of wise Egyptians prostrating themselves before loathsome beings of a lower order. Such ceremonials seemed to reverse the design of nature itself, a hierarchy in which man was the supreme creation. If the irrational behavior of Greek and Roman pagans worshiping their gods in statues of human form

was difficult for men of reason to cope with, the conception of
naked brute-worship was too abhorrent even to contemplate.
There had to be some arcane meaning to these animal gods.

A long array of feeble explanations had been concocted in
antiquity in an attempt to evade the reality of zoolatry, and the
moderns had generally paraphrased them and introduced only
minor variations. Abbé Nicolas Caussin's *Symbolica Aegyptiorum
Sapientia* (1631) was characteristic of seventeenth-century allegoric interpretations. The most pretentious explication was still
the century-old, elephantine set of four Latin folio volumes entitled *Oedipus Aegyptiacus* by Athanasius Kircher of the Society
of Jesus, one of the most learned monstrosities of all time. Hieroglyphs were there demonstrated to be the secret repositories of
a great fund of ancient Egyptian wisdom. Using analogies and
indulging freely in flights of scholarly fancy, etymologies based
on the remotest phonetic resemblances of words in different languages — his text was bedecked with quotations from twenty
tongues — Kircher showed that every branch of knowledge,
medicine, architecture, music, theology, geometry, had already
been fully developed among the Egyptian priests. He knew the
classical corpus, rabbinic literature, the cabala, Hebrew and
Arabic philosophy, and through his devious interpretations every
Egyptian pictorial image on a mummy, an obelisk, on the wall
of a tomb, on papyrus, assumed concrete scientific or theological
significance. The Isis, Osiris, Horus trinity was a prefiguration
of Christianity. *Oedipus Aegyptiacus* became a monumental cultural history of mankind, since all other religions and metaphysical and scientific systems, except of course the direct revealed
traditions of Judaism and Christianity, were derivations, corruptions, modifications of priestly Egyptian wisdom written down in
hieroglyphic language. This was symbolism gone wild; but since
Kircher had access to the missionary reports of his order from
Asia, Africa, the Americas, his body of factual information even
on contemporary cults overwhelmed any potential critics for
decades, and it was not until the eighteenth century that dissident
alternative theories were advanced. Dom Bernard de Montfaucon's treatment of *La Religion des Egyptiens* in *L'Antiquité expliquée et représentée en figures,* after reviewing the interpreters

since Plutarch, adopted a militantly sceptical position toward all of them and reserved a heaping measure of Benedictine contempt for the Jesuit *érudit*. In *The Divine Legation of Moses* Bishop Warburton was equally mocking. "Inflamed by the glory of a Discoverer, he [Kircher] launches out in search of this unknown World; guided by some of the latest Greek writings, in conjunction with the earliest Egyptian hieroglyphics. . . . By this direction he steered at large: and it is pleasant to see him labouring through half a dozen folios with the writings of late Greek Platonists, and the forged books of Hermes, which contain a philosophy, not Egyptian, to explain and illustrate old monuments not philosophical." [53] If the new interpreters were not essentially more respectworthy than Kircher — and they pilfered his facts while they rained blows upon him — they had at least the merit of relative brevity.

By the eighteenth century there was less tendency to regard the animals as symbols of Christian virtues and vices in a theological system like Kircher's mammoth construct, and a growing penchant for the projection into the brutes of contemporary secular moral ideals. They were more often symbols of labor, of the fecundity of nature, of the beast's utility to man, of productivity, of historical, political, or cultural fact. The humans incised on the obelisks who appeared to be worshiping animals were interpreted as counterparts of reasonable eighteenth-century citizens of the world manifesting their reverence for progress and gentleness in a symbolic manner, sort of ancient Freemasons. Through metamorphoses of the animal gods orthodox ideas of primitive monotheism could be preserved, and the interpretation of brute-worship became an explanation of how men, for praiseworthy didactic reasons, fell into what seemed to be an adoration of animals. Ancient Egyptian religion was vindicated and a modicum of human dignity was preserved. If pressed, those who reluctantly conceded that the images depicted ordinary worship resorted to the idea that this was a very late Ptolemaic corruption of Egyptian religion. The good God could not have launched men as brute-worshipers, even though through their own iniquity they might have degenerated into this piteous state.

For some eighteenth-century mythographers the animals were

originally battle-standards of warring Egyptian nomes which in time had come to be adored, or they were once head-pieces on the cuirasses of warriors, worn to inspire terror among the enemy. Contemporary travel reports with illustrations of savages wearing horned headdress, in Père Lafitau for example, lent plausibility to these originally Roman interpretations. The Abbé Pluche's ingenious conceit in the *Histoire du ciel* which made the animals useful signposts in the Egyptian irrigation system was entirely in the spirit of the age. In the maze of eighteenth-century conjectures, pure allegory and historical allegory became intermingled. For Euhemerists Egyptian animal worship represented a commemorative cult of great events in the early history of Egyptian civilization. The introduction of agriculture under a heroic Pharaoh was symbolized by the adoration of a bull who was the Pharaoh. Among the purveyors of such conjectures had figured none other than Isaac Newton himself in the *Chronology of Ancient Kingdoms Amended*. The animals in the Osiris myth became symbols of Egyptian military history, and the tearing apart of the body of the god a mythic record of the invasion of Egypt by the Hyksos. Bishop Cumberland surmised that this cover story had been devised by the priests to hide the shame of the Egyptians, who were extraordinarily sensitive about national defeats.

For those unconvinced by pure allegorism there was a more complex solution to the meaning of the images in the revival of the ancient doctrine of the double-truth which was so fundamental to most eighteenth-century thinking on the nature of the gods. The portraits of Egyptians worshiping brutes was a literal depiction of a religious reality as far as the Ptolemaic masses were concerned, but the exclusive Egyptian priesthood always had known better and in their mysteries had secretly preserved monotheism. The people had been precipitated into the darkness of brute-worship by trickery. This was the common Deist doctrine applied to Egyptian religion in John Toland's *Letters to Serena* and in Henri de Boulainvillier's unpublished "Abrégé d'histoire universelle," a work which may well have been available to de Brosses in a clandestine manuscript. Bishop Warburton's chapters on Egyptian religion were far the most intricate variation on the Deist system of the "true Original of Animal Worship." Only when the beginnings of the cult in the adoration of hieroglyphs had been entirely forgotten were the animals worshiped directly for their own sakes by the ignorant common people. Warburton had severely restricted the duration of real brute-worship; the dominant ancient cult of Egypt had been monotheist or reasonably astral, as befitted wise Egyptians.

While such antecedents may have influenced de Brosses, he ventured far beyond them. In the face of almost two thousand years of accumulated *figurisme* he took a new look at the images — he had reported on a few Egyptian figurines in his *Lettres sur l'état actuel de la ville souterraine d'Herculée & sur les causes de son ensevelissement sous les ruines du Vésuve* (1750) — reread the classical accounts, and announced that Egyptian religion was always, from its inception, animal-worship pure and simple. This fresh perception had no doubt been suggested by the examples of conformities between ancient and modern paganism which had been accumulating for a number of centuries in the travel literature, more specifically by the comparison of the Greek priest and the *fetissero* of Guinea in the writings of Pierre Bayle and Balthasar Bekker around 1700. The analogy which had touched Bayle off in the reports of the First Merchant Willem Bosman's *Voyage de Guinée* is found again in de Brosses and it is supplemented by the testimony of Père Loyer [54] and other accounts from Nigeria, though the travel record most closely akin to de Brosses in the interpretation of fetishism, Le Sieur Vaillant, *Relations des costes d'Afrique appellées Guinée* (1609), is somehow never mentioned. De Brosses inflated the Baylian analogy into a general theory and identified all primitive Egyptian religion as fetishism of precisely the same nature as the contemporary savage cults described by the missionaries and the factors of the great trading companies. The Sphinx ceased to be an enigma and became merely a largish fetish.

More than half a century after Bayle, de Brosses was still fighting allegorism, only he had transferred the argument from Greco-Roman to Egyptian religion and the brute-worship engraved on the obelisks, a pictorial world which Bayle had ignored. Though de Brosses's book has usually been classified as anthropology, the expressed primary purpose of its author, as in most studies of conformities between the ancient pagan world and the savages, was still to illuminate antiquity, to penetrate the mystery of Egyptian religion, whose hieroglyphic texts and cult objects were becoming increasingly provocative to the collectors and antiquarians of Europe; the understanding of contemporary primitives was peripheral.

A goodly portion of the essay, polemical in the manner of eighteenth-century antiquarians, was a refutation of the allegorical interpretations of Egyptian religion which had been repeatedly advanced since antiquity. The method of argument was rationalistic rebuttal. If brute-worship had its origins in symbolic adoration of the useful, why then did Egyptians reverence noxious creatures like lizards? Why were the same animals adored in one area and despised in others? If these figures were representations of divinity, what possible attribute could an onion symbolize? If the animals were originally symbols of ferocity or bravery emblazoned on military standards or on the helmets of warriors, how was it that a substantial number of the creatures depicted were vile, loathsome, pusillanimous things like moles and rats? Even if there was an element of truth in the conjecture that the animals ornamented the battle flags of rival nomes it was more plausible to imagine that they were first worshiped for themselves and then adopted as martial symbols, even as the images of Christian saints came to illustrate standards long after they had been glorified for other reasons.

De Brosses not only dismissed the allegorical interpretations on rational grounds, but he offered an explanation of their historical origins, one which Jean Le Clerc had already given half a century earlier. Allegorism was essentially the creation of pagan apologists during their battle with the Church Fathers. Similarly he traced to the same age of religious controversy the orthodox Christian doctrine that all pagan myths and worship were a degeneration of Adamic monotheism or a corruption of Biblical history. This patristic thesis had been the Christian *riposte* to the pagan charge that there were numerous conformities between heathen and Christian ritual and belief. De Brosses treated both theories as nonsensical residues of an ancient dispute which had no right of survival in the Enlightenment.

If not circumscribed, de Brosses's revolutionary hypothesis of a stage of universal fetishism among all nations was flagrantly contradictory to the assumption of primitive monotheism, at least to the idea that an element of the knowledge of the true God had been transmitted from Adam. As long as a mythographer or historian of religion recognized brute-worship as a degeneration of monotheism or as a mere symbol he remained within the bounds of religion, but de Brosses's insistence on the unqualified postulate that these animals were from the earliest times worshiped in and for themselves skirted on heresy. This great judicial officer, a man of repute and position, was unwilling to break openly with the Church, and though he was a member of the philosophical sect he tried to humor official opinion in his publications even when they appeared anonymously. Probably out of caution de Brosses found the solution which, in appearance at least, allowed for a conciliation of the traditional religious position with fetishism: the deluge served as a convenient break in the history of mankind, permitting de Brosses to give lip service to the primitive monotheism of the antediluvians and at the same time retain universal fetishism for the postdiluvians. "Everything was forgotten, everything became unknown. This new state of so great a portion of the human species, which has its necessary cause in a unique event, is a state of infancy. It is a savage state from which various nations have slowly raised themselves, but from which many others have as yet only partially emerged." [55] The fetish cult became operative only after the flood, among the dispersed descendants of Ham and Japheth, and Shem was allowed to preserve the Adamic monotheist tradition relatively intact. If the Jews were virtually excluded from profane history, the brute and fetish worship of savage peoples throughout the world might be set forth as fact without serious risk.

While the motives of Vico, who had availed himself of the same flood to posit a feral stage and a naturalistic fear-theory for the origin of the Joves, are difficult to fathom, the aspect of mere formal compliance in de Brosses is unmistakable because the diluvian thesis is flagrantly at variance with the spirit of the essay. De Brosses struck at the vital doctrine of the fall, and orthodox polemicists were quick to recognize that the reinitiation of gentile history with the postdiluvian world was a subterfuge. *Du culte des dieux fétiches* was outrageous because of its stark view of savage man, utterly devoid of a spark of true religion, worshiping animals and things.

The de Brosses definition of fetishism was so all-embracing that it covered the divinization of or the imputation of sacred power to any object, animate or inanimate — trees, birds, beasts, rocks, springs, rivers, groves, staffs, weapons. Jallabert became so infected with his friend's theory that he began to see stone fetishes in all the remaining statues in Genevan churches. Once the fetish had been raised as the central figure of primitive religion, the whole classical and patristic corpus describing pagan ritual and the travel-book portrayals of heathen worship throughout the world which had been accumulating since the voyages of discovery were suddenly bathed in the monochrome of an *idée fixe*. In the enthusiasm of his new perception de Brosses made fetishism swallow up every conceivable form of rite and belief without distinction of time or place. The world ancient and modern, backward and enlightened, became alive with fetishes and vestiges of fetishes. In effect de Brosses labeled any hierophany a fetish.

In ancient Egypt fetishes of every variety, personal, local, and national, had played a prominent role, as the classical writers testified. Sacred animals were carried on journeys; when killed, either intentionally or accidentally, they became the cause for bloody wars of vengeance. The hieroglyphs which de Brosses had inspected on the obelisks in Rome and in the illustrations of the works of Kircher and Montfaucon were pictorial depictions of fetishism, men on bended knee offering sacrifices to animals. Diodorus Siculus had reported on monkey-worship in Egypt, Plutarch on the clandestine murder of fetishes during calamities. Mycerinus, according to Herodotus, had encased his daughter in a cow in order to have her worshiped, evidence that the Egyptians then recognized animal but not human idolatry. The Israelite adoration of the golden calf was a wicked fetishist habit which they had acquired during their years of bondage. The famous Sanchuniathon fragment quoted from Philo of Byblus by Eusebius, which eighteenth-century writers prized as an authentic source on the early history of pagan religion and which some dated prior to Moses, was interpreted by de Brosses as a witness of fetishism rather than Euhemerism, the more common usage of the Phoenician "historian." Persian fire-worship was not symbolic, as Thomas Hyde had intimated in his famous work on Zoroastrian religion, but literal fetishism. The Roman auguries were fetishes. Suetonius had described Augustus avenging himself upon a statue of Neptune after a disaster as if it were a fetish. The Germanic tribes worshiped trees, and the fairies of medieval legend were nothing but remnants of the Celtic adoration of springs. De Brosses detected a trace of fetishism in the Hesiod myth of Saturn devouring stones instead of his children. Selden's classical work on the Syrian gods furnished him with numerous examples of fish- and dove-worship. The rock adored by the Arabs before Mohammed was a fetish, and the Israelite Urim and Thummim were smaller stones of the same character.

De Brosses's discovery of a profusion of fetish objects in the Scriptural record of the patriarchs was a daring, even dangerous confirmation of his thesis that the practice was universal. Abraham had a sacred grove; Rachel stole her father's teraphim; Jacob anointing a sacred stone at Bethel was performing a particularly dramatic fetishist act. To regale the abbés of the Academy with this sacrilegious interpretation of the Bible was an instance of de Brosses's occasional indifference to established opinion. To soften the blow to Father Jacob's reputation he had recourse to the doctrine of "condescension," which its able seventeenth-century proponent, John Spencer, had illustrated in his grand, orderly compilation of Judaic laws and rituals.[56] Conformities of Hebrew and pagan rites had there been explained as acts of divine complaisance: God had sometimes condescended to accept into the Jewish dispensation and to reinterpret a heathen practice if it were harmless. By proclaiming himself the God of Bethel He had rubbed the wickedness off of Jacob's fetishist performance.

Allegorists who saw the coiled serpent of Egypt biting its own tail had called it the symbol of eternity, even as very recent mythographers of the Jungian persuasion like Erich Neumann have discovered in the same image the symbol of the state of man in the uroboros. To de Brosses it was nothing but another undistinguished fetish. Utilizing the exegetical techniques of the rabbis and the scholastics de Brosses tackled critically every passage of the Sanchuniathon fragment which allegorists had interpreted to transform the serpents with tails in their mouths into something other than what they were, plain snakes. Thoth, the allegorist readers of Sanchuniathon had marveled, watched dragons and serpents with great assiduity; to what purpose, inquired de Brosses, would the exalted Thoth have devoted himself to the minute examination of these creatures if they were merely symbols?

By the side of the mountain of evidence on ancient fetishism — in a letter he excused himself for having tired his friend Hume with the boring details, but he wished the facts to speak for themselves — de Brosses juxtaposed long descriptions of identical ceremonies among contemporary savages. Wherever he turned in the voyage literature he knew so well he found corroboration of the fetishist principle: Africans worshiped beasts, rivers, the sea; American Indians the manitous; Laplanders held expiatory ceremonies when animal fetishes were unwittingly destroyed; Circassians and Hindus worshiped trees. The serpent fetishism of Egypt had been so persistent that despite the many religious revolutions which the land had experienced over the centuries, this particular superstition could still be found among the Christian Copts. Of all his sources on the identity of ancient and contemporary savage religions the work of the Jesuit Lafitau yielded the richest body of parallels. This indefatigable missionary had seen customs and practices among the Algonquins which reminded him in detail of what he had read in the classics about the Pelasgians, and the engravings of the sacrifices and initiations of the American Indians inserted in his volumes made the resemblances even more striking, for no eighteenth-century artist could draw a naked body without fixing it in a Greco-Roman posture, the only model he knew. The higher beliefs of the Indians, the superstition that every animal had a replica of itself in the land of the souls, which Lafitau had dwelt upon, seemed to de Brosses identical with Egyptian notions which led them to mummify serpents and other repulsive creatures.

But the hieroglyphs were silent images and the classical accounts only descriptions; they did not in and of themselves prove absolutely that the ancients believed these animals to be real gods. They might have been worshiping symbols. It was the thought processes behind the rites among contemporary savage fetishists, whose real purpose had been inquired into and explicitly formulated, which capped the demonstration. Equivalent actions necessarily connoted equivalent thoughts and sentiments to a reasonable eighteenth-century empiricist. From recent travelers of many nations he knew what the *fetissero* believed, and the ancient Egyptians had behaved toward these creatures precisely like the Negroes; what more positive proof was necessary for the scientific deduction that the ancients had identical religious sentiments when they prostrated themselves before the animals, that the ancient worship was actual and not symbolic. "The people understand nothing of these niceties. They only know what they see. Their religion is never allegorical." [57]

The problem whether heathens, both ancient and modern, had literally divinized the vulgar objects of their worship or regarded them as symbols of a more spiritual being may now appear to be a theological refinement. In the eighteenth century the implications of this controversy penetrated to the very heart of religious orthodoxy. The contest between the Dominicans and the Jesuits, for example, over the permissibility of certain rites among the new Chinese converts, a crucial issue in the Christianization of the mandarin class which shook the whole Catholic world about 1700, revolved around the prickly question whether the ancient Chinese dictum "Adore the Heavens" was an allowable spiritual commandment or an abominable form of idolatry, a literal worship of the sky. Volumes upon volumes of ecclesiastical subtlety, much of it still in manuscript in the former Jesuit and Dominican libraries in Rome, were expended upon the demonstration of the rival viewpoints. The older and equally fundamental conflict which divided the Protestant and Catholic worlds, the adoration of saints, also hinged in the last analysis upon the distinction between literal and symbolic acts. Against this religious background de Brosses's repeated emphasis upon the literal meaning of pagan ritual, his use of so revolting an example as brute-worship, and his discovery of vestigial elements of fetishism even in Judaism had overtones of significance far beyond his own realization.

The instinctive antagonism of his official Catholic colleagues in the Académie des Inscriptions et Belles-Lettres to this thesis was readily explicable on theological grounds alone. De Brosses proposed an even more provocative psychological explanation of the reluctance — we would now have to say resistance — to accept a fetishist theory in preference to a symbolical one. It was an unconscious expression of human egocentrism, "un effet de l'amour-propre qui agit sourdement en nous," [58] and "amour-propre" carried with it Rousseauist overtones. Only man's self-centered admiration of his own species made it seem nobler to worship anthropomorphic idols and degrading to adore animals. De Brosses the scientist was subject to no such narrow prejudices. The mercilessly objective criteria for the study of human psychology which his friend Charles Bonnet had outlined were also his. In a letter of July 24, 1761, the author of the *Essai de psychologie, ou considérations sur les opérations de l'âme, sur l'habitude et sur l'éducation* (1754) wrote: "I studied man about as I had studied insects and plants, I dissected them, juxtaposed and compared them, and I concentrated all my attention on the consequences which seem to flow most directly from my observations." [59] Charles de Brosses, the free-lance scholar who had proposed to Charles Bonnet the organization of a frank, international inquiry into the reproductive process, did not tremble before the naked truth of a little fetish. In a forthright statement of his scientific attitude he called upon contemporaries to look at the realities of human experience, not what they would like man to be or what he was perhaps potentially capable of becoming. De Brosses's daring acceptance of man in the ignominious pose of a worshiper of repulsive animals is one of the great achievements of his little book.

De Brosses used the term "fetishism" in a broad sense to blanket a whole period of religious worship intervening between a brief adoration of heavenly bodies, which along with Bishop Warburton and most eighteenth-century theorists he considered the purest pagan form, and later anthropomorphic polytheism. He did not designate three distinct stages in the evolution of

religious consciousness after the flood, and his acceptance of
Sabaism before fetishism and polytheism also bears the earmarks
of acquiescence to orthodoxy, another compromise with the idea
that a higher religious consciousness is innate in all of us. This
section of his work is woolly because the priority of astral worship was inconsistent with his bold psychology of fetishism. What
remains of interest is the idea itself, the conception that all gentile nations passed through identical stages of religious experience in progression, though not at the same tempo, that religion
was subject to a pattern of historical development which, in
greater or less degree, held true throughout the world. Vico,
theologically inspired and far less positivistic than de Brosses,
had anticipated the concept, but his full meaning, clothed in the
style of the seventeenth-century commentators, was veiled from
contemporaries. There were also passages in Turgot's famous
harangues before the Sorbonne in 1750 which hinted at the
growth of human consciousness from an animist through a metaphysical to a scientific stage, and de Brosses was a friend of
Turgot. Many attributes of the primitive mind described by
de Brosses had already been remarked by Fontenelle in the
Origine des fables, and the equation of the contemporary Aus-
tralians with the barbaric Greeks at the time when they were
first civilized by the Phoenicians, which de Brosses had introduced into the *Histoire des navigations aux terres australes,* has
a distinct Fontenellian flavor. Yet whatever multifarious influences played upon the theory of fetishism — and Hume must
never be forgotten — it stands in its own right as a major innovation in the history of thought.

While de Brosses had nothing very illuminating to say on the
transition from the astral to the fetishist stage of primitive religion — he recalled the Lucian hypothesis that each nome identified a different animal among the constellations and worshiped
it — his reflections on the imposition of the new anthropomorphic idolatry upon primitive fetishism and the manner of their
amalgamation were novel. He had a fine sensitivity for religious
syncretism (though he did not use the term he understood the
phenomenon). In Egypt, Asia Minor, China, whenever new religious forms were adopted, the old had never been completely

abandoned, because ancient religious beliefs, once they possessed men's souls, were extraordinarily tenacious. Even monotheisms like Judaism and Christianity betrayed the residues of more primitive religious cults. In the Book of Ezekiel he found traces of Sabaism, fetishism, and the idolatrous worship of dead heroes. At one point de Brosses recklessly stepped up to the abyss of heresy with a conjecture that the cross of the Christians and the Chinese might have a fetishist origin. Greek and Roman polytheism were outstanding examples of the fusion of new religious beliefs based upon the cult of dead heroes, a recent importation from Asia Minor, with the more ancient belief in fetishes. The physical attributes of the Greco-Roman deities, originally object or animal fetishes, were prior in time to the gods themselves. The stag had antedated Diana. De Brosses respected the sensible Roman rituals, which were primarily related to social and governmental functions, more than he did the religion of the Greeks, an imaginative and flighty people, but even the noble Romans had preserved fetishes. The javelin was the original fetish to which a human had later been attached.

In his account of stone fetishism the anthropomorphic Greek gods slowly took shape out of the more ancient divinized rocks, probably of meteoric origin (he had once seen a meteor in the country and he realized how easy it would be for peasants to consider these stones from the heavens sacred). Pausanias had reported that greater adoration was bestowed upon the cruder, scarcely fashioned rocks near temples than upon the finely sculptured anthropomorphic idols, proof that these older unhewn rocks were originally sacred objects with their own divine power and that only later were the names and shapes of alien gods attached to them. This grafting of the strange gods onto the fetishes worshiped by the aboriginal Greeks led de Brosses to arresting conjectures on the history of religious syncretism in the eastern Mediterranean basin. He came to consider Greek religion and mythology as a mingling of two elements, one which had pushed down from the North and another which had been introduced by invaders from Asia. Obviously borrowing an idea from his late colleague Nicolas Fréret, he identified the mythological birthplace of a Greek god as the locality where an oriental deity had first been introduced. But despite such refinements he still clung to a basic fetishist interpretation of Greek religion in his *Mémoire sur l'oracle de Dodone,* read before the Academy on May 27, 1766, though the philosophical heterodoxy was attenuated enough to allow for its insertion into the *Mémoires.* "The best way to understand what once happened in little known ages is to observe what occurs in modern times in parallel circumstances." [60]

Not everything in de Brosses is graced with the same spirit of innovation. In tracing the names of the Greek gods he was still partial to the threadbare Bochart etymologies which derived them all from Hebrew and Canaanite sources (for example, Aesculapius from Isch-Caleb). But while de Brosses was willing to resort to Euhemerism and old-fashioned diffusionist theory to account for latter-day details of mythology, fundamentally he was an independent inventionist. Fetishism was a direct expression of the soul of primitive man and was a reflection of an elementary psychological nature which was similar throughout the world.

In the third section of the de Brosses book, "Examen des causes auxquelles on attribue le Fétichisme," in many ways the most interesting, quotations from Hume are interwoven with Vichian themes (though the direct influence of Vico is extremely doubtful) and with many original perceptions. De Brosses raised again the gnawing question which Hume had posed so masterfully at the very outset of his essay on the natural history of religion: what is there in the nature of man which has caused him to invent and worship these gods? De Brosses was in a sense even harder put than Hume because he made the query in connection with the origins of fetishism, while Hume, who had never considered this cult, had restricted himself to the understanding of anthropomorphic polytheism.

De Brosses's first reaction to his own problem was an act of disturbed withdrawal. Fetishism was a form of human behavior so patently absurd that reason could not possibly come to grips with it. Fetishism was born of fear and madness; in passages informed by the spirit of Pierre Bayle he called it an illness of the mind. At moments of debility the brain had a natural disposition to invent all manner of superstitions; in the early stages of man's development, when his reasoning powers were feeble, fetishism was a normal state. Virtually no other explanation was possible. No meaning could be offered for most actions of childish play, and none for the fixations of the infancy of mankind.

"When one sees in ages and in climates that are so distant from one another that men who have nothing in common with each other but their ignorance and their barbarity have similar practices, it is still quite natural to conclude from this that man is made that way. When he is left in his natural brute and savage state, not yet shaped by any reflected idea or by any imitation, the same holds true for primitive customs and for ways of acting in Egypt as in the Antilles, in Persia as in Gaul. Everywhere there is the same mechanism of ideas, whence follows that of actions. And if one is surprised by this particular point, which does indeed seem very strange, if one is astonished to see fetishism spread among all the uncouth peoples of the world, in all times, in all places, one only requires, to explain this phenomenon, to relate it to its own cause already cited, which is the constant uniformity of savage man with himself, his heart perpetually open to fear, his soul ceaselessly avid with hope, all of which gives free play to the derangement of his ideas, drives him to commit a thousand senseless actions, when his spirit uncultivated and without reasoning power is incapable of perceiving that modicum of relationship which exists between certain causes and the effects which he expects from them. Since no one is astonished to see children fail to elevate their minds higher than their dolls, believe them alive, and then behave towards them accordingly, why should one be amazed to see peoples who constantly pass their life in an eternal infancy and who are never more than four years old reason incorrectly and act as they reason?" [61]

In the portrayal of primitive mentality, allusions to childhood and mental illness had been made with increasing frequency for about half a century by Bayle, Fontenelle, Bekker, and Trenchard. De Brosses, like Vico, had often observed and listened to children. In his "Observations sur la langue primitive telle que les enfans la parlent," a chapter of the *Traité de la formation méchanique des langues,* he reported that he owed to them the

discovery of the basic elements of primitive language. "To learn
how human speech began it is necessary to turn our eyes toward
those who start to speak it. These are children." [62] The remoter
origins of other lines of thought, quoted here in their Humean
form, may be traced back as far as Democritus and the Sophists,
particularly the fear-theory. When de Brosses deprived primitive
man of all rational power he was doubtless supplementing
Hume's essay with motifs from Rousseau's *Second Discourse,*
which had, after all, been submitted in a Dijon competition.
"We know that they live in a state of insensibility which borders
on apathy, a consequence of their limited number of ideas,
which do not extend beyond their present needs. They know
nothing and they have no desire to know anything. They pass
their lives without thinking and they grow old without emerging
from childhood, all of whose faults they retain." [63] In the *Histoire des navigations aux terres australes* de Brosses had already developed the same dismal portrait of the primitives: "Almost
everywhere they have been found in a state of ferocious stupidity,
perfidious and unapproachable. In some places they have even
appeared to lack a taste for commerce and for the novelties
which have been shown to them. They have maintained an
obstinate silence, deaf to the voice of strangers and to all signs
of friendship." [64] Hobbesian elements are not absent and the
introduction to the *Tractatus* has left its mark (among de
Brosses's many unrealized projects was a translation of Spinoza).

Once de Brosses recovered from his initial horror at the contemplation of childish, mad, sick, terror-stricken primitive man,
in good eighteenth-century manner he resigned himself to a historical analysis of the genesis of religious sentiment. The argument turned against conceptions of primitive monotheism. To
imagine that on the morrow of the flood the pitiful wretches,
without revelation and cut off from the traditions of Adam,
could with one leap reach the conception of a rational God was
preposterous. "Would those who would give to savages the head
of a Plato or a Descartes be very judicious critics?" Primitive
man followed a development that was appropriate to his nature.
"It is not in his possibilities, it is in man himself that man should
be studied. The issue is not to imagine what he might have or

should have done, but to look at what he did." [65] Hume the psy-
chologist had written that man proceeded from "objects of sense
to abstract knowledge," and de Brosses translated him verbatim.
Man could not have first conceived of an abstract spiritual God
and then fallen backwards into fetishism. He had to move from
the concrete to the abstract, from sensation to ratiocination,
from ignorance to enlightenment. During the course of civilized
history there had been many metamorphoses of religious experience: some men had grown oversubtle in their dogmas, some
abandoned them altogether, others maintained a sound core of
belief without allowing their religion to become decadent and
without leaving it — but de Brosses knew of no retrogression
to primitive forms of religion once a "purer" doctrine had become known. The possibility of primitive monotheism followed
by fetishism was precluded, and another stone was raised in the
modern structure of dogmatic evolutionism.

In an original passage, while dilating upon the crudity of the
early postdiluvians, de Brosses hinted at the significant idea,
common among twentieth-century sociologists of religion (Lévy-
Bruhl has a long didactic passage to this effect) but quite rare
in his day, that the very words employed to describe elementary
religious images had completely different connotations for savages and civilized men. "Among savages the names of God or
Spirit do not at all signify what they mean among us. In reasoning about their manner of thinking we must . . . be careful not
to attribute to them our ideas because they are at present attached to the same words which the savages used, and not to
impute to them our principles and our reasonings." [66] The word
"God" to a pagan meant any being having power over human
nature, though it was sometimes merely temporary and restricted
to a specific power. Only with maturity and the slow acquisition
of reason did most nations arrive at the moral certitude that one
omnipotent God existed.

In de Brosses's theory the development of language and religion were two facets of the general progress of the human spirit;
in this sense he was a more empirical, if less philosophical, Turgot. In his hypothesis of the historical formation of speech isolated
bands of men dispersed throughout the world began to utter the

same elementary sounds because these were determined by the structure of their physical organs which were identical. As growth continued under diverse geographic circumstances and at different rates of speed the original basic language assumed variant forms. Those ignorant peoples forced to spend themselves in labor in order to eke out their existence had many words for concrete objects but few for general conceptions, while the more highly civilized nations who enjoyed leisure invariably evolved abstract linguistic expressions. This is the same genetic evolution that de Brosses traced in the religious movement from fetishism to spiritual monotheism. Since his history of language, which appeared in book form in 1756, had been written a number of years before, his reliance solely upon Hume in the presentation of this progression seems unlikely. De Brosses's primitive mumbled and played with fetishes like a child; in his maturity man employed sophisticated abstractions both in language and in religion.

In the mood of his works on religion and language de Brosses was generally a forthright scientific progressist of the Turgot persuasion. There was a well-defined ladder of progress, and nations primitive and civilized stood on different rungs but all were inevitably moving from inferior to higher stages. The scientific, philosophical society of contemporary Europe was at the apex of the development of the human spirit and the fetishist society at the bottom; between them were ranged the various nations of the world. Bold and unflinching inquiry into every aspect of nature, both what was human and what was external to man, was a prerequisite of progress, and de Brosses felt a certain pride in venturing to contemplate ugly, fetishist man as he really was in the abject stage of superstitious terror. The primitive was unable to comprehend the relation between cause and effect — that was the source of the blind fear that culminated in fetishism. With time and the growth of reason men might learn the true relations of things in the world and the terror, if not banished, would at least be mitigated. De Brosses was an activist, committed to the acceleration of progress, which in the intellectual sphere meant the eradication of the fetishism which was still entrenched in the dominant religion of Europe. In corres-

pondence with friends, among them Voltaire before their momentous quarrel, he jestingly used the terms "fetish" and "anti-
fetish" when alluding to the obscurantist religious authorities and
their philosophical enemies. His friends knew that in revealing
the dark heart of ancient Egyptian and contemporary Nigerian
fetishism he also had in mind the survival of fetishes nearer
home.

But there is also a distinction to be made between the tenor
of de Brosses's historical anthropology, which implied the growing rationality of mankind through time, and the theses of the
Turgot-Condorcet progressists who were expecting the imminent
universal victory of the moral law through the instrumentality
of scientific discoveries. While de Brosses hailed the triumph of
reason and in a letter of February 18, 1766, to Jallabert conceived of himself as a humble worker adding a stone to the great
edifice of pure science, he was always aware of the persistence
of irrational beliefs like fetishism even in highly civilized societies. De Brosses, the friend of Bonnet, had an interest in
biological phenomena, and his sense of progression was therefore not quite as mechanistic and mathematical as Turgot's. A
new state of man was not accompanied by a completely fresh
mode of perception, for elements from previous stages of religious consciousness lingered on in even the most advanced rationalist epoch. At times, in the spirit of Hume, he seemed to
doubt whether the common people would ever be much more
than the superstitious horde that the mass of primitive Egyptians
had been at the very zenith of their civilization. While the de
Brosses thesis was later assimilated into Auguste Comte's "Social
Dynamics," in its original form it did not have the character of
a mass progressionist theory. The Baylian scepticism endured,
and de Brosses's stadial development of reason was largely restricted to an elite. "Unreasonable customs do not lose in a country in the same proportion that reason wins there, above all,
when they are consecrated by inveterate habit and by pious
credulity. Their antiquity maintains them in one part of a nation
while the other is perhaps turning them to ridicule. . . . Civility
does not exclude superstition."

An optimist progressism invaded by the aristocratic reflection

that after all the mass of people have always been ignorant
throughout history is a far more common eighteenth-century intellectual attitude than has been recognized by those who have
looked for one consistent and pervasive emotional tone. Hume
appears to be among the more pessimist, Condorcet surely among
the more buoyant optimists of the age, but a ray of progressism
can be detected in Hume's *Enquiry Concerning the Principles of
Morals* (1751), and Condorcet worried about the interruption
of rectilinear progress by the unenlightened mob. In a chromatic
scale of faith in progress de Brosses probably stands midway.
Though he copied Hume, he really either missed or turned his
eyes away from the profoundly disillusioned passages in *The
Natural History of Religion*. De Brosses could translate Hume's
words, but not the strange ambiguities of his moral position. The
President of the Dijon Parlement died with the consolations of a
religion which, at least in his circle of friends, was becoming ever
more rational, and this was evidence enough of a great human
progress over the miserable fetishists he had described. While all
men in all times were wicked — he once called himself a *hobbiste*
in a letter to Pierre Pictet [68] — rational civilization was an absolute good because it restrained and limited human perversity,
introduced palliatives.

At least de Brosses was confident enough of the superiority of
his own enlightened society to propound the merits of capturing
a new area of savagery for France and raising it from primitive
religion to civility. With the same zest with which by a none too
subtle implication *Du culte des dieux fétiches* attacked fetishist
remnants in Christianity, in his compendium of exploration narratives he called upon the French monarchy to conduct new
expeditions to the southern seas, to colonize the islands not only
for the grandeur of France but for the good of the savages, to
civilize them, to raise them from fetishism, their low stage of
development, to rational perception. This philosophical formulation of the "white man's burden" became an early fixture of
French progressist thought and recurred both in Condorcet and
in Saint-Simon within a generation.

5

Nicolas-Antoine Boulanger:
The Trauma of the Flood

A YOUNG ENGINEER who died prematurely at the age of
thirty-seven, Nicolas-Antoine Boulanger was driven by a passionate desire to compose a definitive "Spirit of the Religions," a
pendant to the great "Spirit of the Laws." With an autodidact's
zeal he had feverishly studied the customs, ceremonies, traditions,
and mysteries of ancient peoples and had sought to penetrate the
meaning of their cosmogonies, theogonies, and mythologies. He
had amassed a vast corpus of literary sources on the cultures of
peoples savage and civilized, pagan and Christian, on Jews, Mohammedans, Japanese, Chinese, Indians, Mexicans, Peruvians,
and Caribs. He knew the ancient codes of law, the historians, the
poets, and the travelers. In a warm and sympathetic introduction
to his posthumous work Diderot described him standing on the
great roads of the realm which he was constructing for the king,
with a "rabbinic author" under his arm.

The three little volumes in duodecimo which illustrated his
unique discovery were edited by the Holbach group to which he
belonged and published by Marc-Michel Rey in Amsterdam in
1766 as *L'Antiquité dévoilée par ses usages, ou examen critique
des principales opinions, cérémonies & institutions religieuses &
politiques des différens peuples de la terre, par feu M. Boulanger.*
The last chapter of his work had been detached and issued separately some five years before in 1761 as *Recherches sur l'origine
du despotisme oriental,* prefaced by a letter to Helvétius of doubtful origin, a vibrant and triumphant manifesto of the philosophic

210

crusade for progress, a presage of Condorcet, Saint-Simon, and Comte: "The adepts of Philosophy are already legion. An even greater number is prepared to follow its standards, and the religious anarchy which is continually more obvious prepares for philosophy a host of subjects whom it will be easy to conquer. . . . If this anarchy lasts long enough mankind may be thrust into a state more horrible than the first ages of its existence. People have talked about Savage Europe, Pagan Europe, Christian Europe. There may yet be worse. There must finally be a Rational Europe." [69] Boulanger manuscripts had been widely circulated in secret before their publication (Holbach had sent them to Hume, whose response was less than enthusiastic). In 1764 John Wilkes, the wild man of English politics, published a translation of the *Despotisme oriental,* a highly prized illegal work in any language, difficult to come by even in Switzerland. "I am dying to have a book which can only be found in Geneva," wrote the Président de Brosses to Jallabert, "and even there it is said to be strictly forbidden. . . . It is attributed to the late M. Boulanger, with whom I was acquainted." [70] In Paris there was published in 1767 under the name of Boulanger a counterpart to the *Antiquité dévoilée* entitled *Le Christianisme dévoilé, ou Examen des principes et des effets de la Religion Chrétienne,* but this is really a composition by Holbach and his assistants. Though the dogmatic *idée fixe* of their dead friend was adopted, the Holbachian exposure was not as rigidly monist as Boulanger's original. The Baron himself was eclectic enough to admit more than one foul source for the evils of religious superstition.

Abbé Le Gros, who devoted himself to refuting the heterodox historians of the primitive world, has reported on the testimony of the Abbé Gérard that during his final illness Boulanger summoned the Vicar of St. Severin, his parish, confessed that the "philosophical coteries" had intoxicated and seduced him, and on his deathbed sought to repair the damage caused by his scandalous irreligion. Whatever his repentance *in extremis* may have been, Boulanger's writings became irrevocably identified with the revolutionary radicals, and in 1792 they published his complete works in eight volumes as an homage to his memory.[71]

The readers of Diderot's introduction to the first edition of

L'Antiquité dévoilée learned that its late author was born in
Paris on November 11, 1722, of a respectable family, that he
served in the wars as an engineer for M. le Baron de Thiers,
joined the department of bridges and roads and was sent to
Champagne, Lorraine, and Burgundy, that he was in the en-
virons of Paris in 1751, worked on the Orleans highway in 1755,
and died on September 10, 1759. In addition to his major work
Boulanger wrote the articles "Déluge," "Corvée," and "Société"
for the *Encyclopédie,* a life of Alexander, an etymological dictionary, dissertations on Aesop, Enoch, and Elijah, Saint Peter,
Saint Roch, Saint Genevieve, and a natural history of the course
of the Marne.

Boulanger's unveiling of antiquity occurred in a moment of
sudden illumination, like Rousseau's apocalyptic vision of the
savage world. Only the stage scenery was different. While Jean-
Jacques had captured the true primitive in the forest of Saint-
Germain, Boulanger was struck with his revelation while gazing at
the enigmatic geological strata of the roadbeds he was laying.
Boulanger had by instinct, wrote Diderot, discovered the spirit
of prehistoric man and the common nature of all religions.

Unlike the natural rights theorists Grotius and Pufendorf, who
had hypothesized an original rational being *in vacuo,* Boulanger
was always devouring facts about the physical environment of
early man. Whatever one may think of the final constructs of the
eighteenth-century historians of primitive religion — Vico, Boulanger, Holbach, de Brosses, Herder — they were all militant em-
piricists in open revolt against the symbolic and rationalistic philosophy, Platonic and Cartesian. The *factum* is the *verum,* Vico
had taught. "We are going to consider and study man as he escaped from the ruins of the ancient world. . . . It will not be a
savage, a metaphysical being, or a perfect creature who has become corrupted, the chimera with which so many learned men
and scientists have occupied themselves in vain; we shall examine
a real human being in a real state," wrote Boulanger in the
Recherches sur l'origine du despotisme oriental.[72] "To return to
the true source from which all our errors have flowed we need no
metaphysical speculation, only a fact," continued *L'Antiquité
dévoilée.*[73] And Boulanger had divined that fact, the cardinal

event from which all institutions of the human polity and all religious ceremonies were derived — it was the universal deluge.

All nations preserved traditions of a flood, on this the works of antiquity were unanimous. The flood had left physical traces for the scientist in the sea shells on mountain tops and in animal fossils buried in the depths of the earth. (Jean-Jacques remembered Boulanger as a fellow conchyliomaniac in the François Mussard circle in Passy.) [74] The postdiluvian world was moreover accessible to an imaginative philosopher of primitive religion. Since the basic psychic nature of man had always been the same, primitive emotions could be resurrected by introspection ("en nous repliant sur nous-mêmes").[75] Though the records of the historical sciences did not extend back directly to the primordial world, contemporary savage societies which were still in the process of growth contained clues to the state of humanity which other nations had left behind them — the common eighteenth-century thesis from which the anthropological sciences have never been emancipated. Finally there was the world corpus of myth, the secret depository of the early history of mankind, waiting to be unraveled by a genius who could read its cryptic language.

Boulanger declared the deluge to be the *fons et origo* of all vicious legislation, all wicked political doctrines, all false and harmful religions. *Hinc prima mali labes.* "We shall there see the origin of the terrors which throughout the ages have alarmed the minds of men always possessed by ideas of the devastation of the world. There we shall see generated the destructive fanaticism, the enthusiasm which leads men to commit the greatest excesses against themselves and against their fellows, the spirit of persecution and intolerance which under the name of zeal makes man believe that he has the right to torment those who do not adore with him the same celestial monarch, or who do not have the same opinion he does about His essence or His cult." [76] If man has been cruel to man, look to the consequences of the flood, still making themselves felt through inherited institutions.

The cosmographic or scientific fable had been recognized ever since antiquity as one category in the great variety of mythographic interpretations, and contemporary Euhemerists like Abbé Banier occasionally had recourse to it for the reading of certain refractory ancient traditions. Boulanger the absolutist found that all myths without exception had a common cosmographic origin in the deluge. He violated the pluralist eclectic spirit of the *philosophes* and called forth incredulity even among those of his colleagues who loved him most. Diderot himself, though he appreciated his friend's ardor, expressed disapproval of the wild and fixated insistence upon one idea, relentlessly pursued in all his works.[77] Our own generation, which has propagated the doctrine of an equally ancient though to be sure competitive primal catastrophe in the killing of the old man, should not take umbrage at Boulanger's monist dogmatism.

Boulanger's deluge was not one unique catastrophe in the physical annals of the world. He agreed with the ancients that nature had many times before undergone a cycle of growth, maturity, and final calamity, only to be reborn, and that there were destined to be similar geological upheavals throughout all future time. The postulates of *L'Antiquité dévoilée,* however, were not founded upon the whole series of universal deluges, for these were unknowable, but rather restricted themselves continently to the last one where the evidence was securely scientific. Boulanger was sceptical of traditions which recounted the story of creation and human experience before the flood, for the deluge was a great wall beyond which no "historical being" was identifiable. The antediluvian was the abstract man of the metaphysicians and the Bible. Boulanger triumphantly revealed the first authentic post-diluvians, not noble savages, not perfect monotheists, not fallen and corrupted men, but civilized human beings caught by a terrible cataclysm which had left only tiny bands of survivors taking refuge in the hills. In Boulanger as in Vico the flood brought about a reinitiation of the human drama. Only since the flood had men had a continuum of experience which could be discovered and comprehended.

The historical deluge of Boulanger was no mere rising of the waters which gently receded after the passage of the Scriptural forty days, but the movement of tidal waves so mighty that they transfigured the face of the earth, split continents, leveled peaks, pushed forth new mountain ranges, cut valleys, spread thick layers of silt, hurled boulders. The crust of the earth had cracked and subterranean streams gushed forth to mingle with the cataracts which poured down from the heavens. A thousand volcanoes vomited water and torrents of lava at the same time. Noxious fumes and gases destroyed what the waters and the fires had spared. Compared with this deluge the Biblical event was a passing shower. When the refugees on the high places witnessed the first setting of the sun, which after a long darkness had finally reappeared, they were stricken with the fear that what had threatened to be eternal night would again return, and they cried out their lamentations to the heavens. And when at long last the regular blessing of the light was restored, who could depict the affliction of the wretched men at the sight of the wasteland which confronted their eyes? Boulanger, like Dante, averted his gaze from the dismal spectacle which he himself had conjured up. *En passant* Boulanger demonstrated that so monstrous a conception as Hell, which had tormented mankind for centuries, could never have been conceived by reasonable, natural man unless he had experienced in the flesh pangs as violent as the Hell of the religionist. In the eighteenth century John Locke stood by even the most ghastly imagist: there was nothing in the mind which had not previously been in the senses — not even Hell — and there had once been a Hell on earth.

The sparse chapters of Genesis narrating the flood were embroidered by Boulanger with the imagination of a rabbi composing a Midrash — an Holbachian devil quoting Scripture. At moments there are Talmudic turns of thought and methods of proof. Boulanger was obviously dissatisfied with the serenity of Noah and his family emerging from the ark as they were depicted in the Pentateuch. After the deluge the Lord assured Noah that as long as the earth endured there would never again be an alteration in the succession of the seasons, in the sequence of night and day, of sowing and reaping. Why this promise, asked Boulanger, if during the deluge there had not been a complete disruption of nature, if during the long and irregular nights men had not plumbed the depths of anguish?

Variations in the national myths of the deluge were explicable solely in terms of local climatic conditions (the spirit of Montesquieu endured), for some areas were consumed by fire and others were devoured by tidal waves. The Biblical "whole earth" referred only to the eastern Mediterranean. The Boulanger deluge theory departed from Scripture by hypothesizing more than one group of survivors, for the flood though catastrophic was not sudden and unheralded, and it allowed for a number of asylums on the mountaintops in various parts of the world. Commemorative cults of high places were useful empirical support, and the persistence of a belief among all nations that they were autochthonous sustained the contention that there had been more than one nucleus of postdiluvians.

Boulanger rejected as a false image, devoid of any understanding of man's nature, the idea that the handful of human beings who had escaped death in the cataclysms patiently waited for the waters to subside and the fires to be extinguished and then resumed the business of living as if nothing had happened. What would *you feel,* he challenged his contemporaries, on the morning after a universal destructive revolution of nature? Would you calmly proceed with your affairs? "What! the habitation of man, the whole earth will be destroyed, the human race will be exterminated, and the man who survives this terrible event will look upon it with indifference and with insensibility? His character will not be changed by it and his behavior will continue to be the same? He will return to his old way of life? He will cultivate the soil as tranquilly as before? He will intrepidly, even audaciously rebuild his cities? No! It should never, it could never happen so. Those who have composed history on this principle have given us only a senseless novel, empty of verisimilitude. As for myself I have seen written in nature that man was thrown into profound turmoil by his misfortunes. I saw that he trembled. I saw that he conceived a loathing for this unfortunate earth. I also read in this book that the first acts of man were determined by his emotions, that everything which happened in the course of the centuries in the moral, religious, and political world was merely a consequence of these primitive acts; finally I recognized that this first state of man renewing his social existence was the true key to our history." [78]

Living in eternal anxiety and dread at the prospect of a new visitation, postdiluvian man would never know peace. Each eclipse of the sun or the moon revived the memory of his ancient horror. A gloomy primitive, persecuted by the recollection of past destruction, lived out his days in anticipation of the renewal of calamities. When the haunted man sought for an explanation of the events which he had experienced and imagined a powerful author for them, what kind of an image could he have invented? The perpetrator of these upheavals could be none other than a cruel and vengeful god, who punished for offenses which man could not fathom.

Boulanger's postdiluvians, unlike Vico's, were not bestial savage giants. They were the survivors of a sophisticated society that had grown old along with nature, who, subjected to the trauma of the deluge, were deprived of their reason, imagined the coming of the great Judge, and invented fantasies of a pleasant future life to console themselves. The religious images of the conflict of good and evil forces, the idea of man as an exile on earth, as a mere traveler, as a stranger, the dogma of the accursedness of the world, were born in this period. Religious doctrines were the ravings of formerly intelligent creatures in a state of postdiluvian shock.

All cults, hydraulic in origin, were commemorative rehearsals of the one catastrophe which weighed heavily upon man. Since Boulanger's primitive, instituting rites and offering up sacrifices to the monstrous god, could never for a moment free himself from the memory of the flood, his festivals became dismal, lugubrious, funereal reenactments of the return of the waters of destruction and his worship a long religious dirge. Rituals preserved from remotest antiquity the grief and sadness which had once overwhelmed him. This was the "spirit" of the religions.

With a grand display of erudition Boulanger identified the telltale marks of the aqueous catastrophe in every ceremonial practiced throughout the world. Virtually any ritualistic act was in some way related to the deluge. To explain the fixation, the persistence of the one tormenting impression, Boulanger offered an empirical psychological observation: "The wretch takes a fatal pleasure in feeding on his pain; he likes to reiterate its causes." [79] The explanation of circumcision was ingenious. The first men after the flood were so shattered by the memory of the evil which they had experienced that they lost desire for life. They fled from one another. And those few who, overtaken by a contrary passion, succumbed to lust and for a brief moment indulged in an act of procreation were so filled with self-disgust and shame at the prospect of bringing children into a desolate world that they punished themselves at the source of their wanton pleasure by castration — of which the rite of circumcision was a residue.

The languages of the nations were a rich repository of irrefutable and universal psychological facts about the aftermath of the deluge. The speech of both Oriental and Occidental peoples demonstrated that the word "flood" and ideas cognate to "flood" were the same among all nations. For those eighteenth-century etymologists Vico and Boulanger (as later for Nietzsche and Freud) language more than any other human creation had encased and preserved the spiritual history of mankind. What distinguished them from their arid seventeenth-century predecessors was the novel idea that words bore with them a set of emotive tones which were clues to the true temper of antiquity. They used their etymologies not to follow, as the seventeenth-century diffusionists had, one name for a god into its corruption in another language, but to show emotional identities among all peoples by pointing out verbal similarities for both ordinary and extraordinary events. Since the flood and its accompanying psychic phenomena had left behind traces in all languages, its universality was proved, for similar verbal expressions could not have been produced by different events. Unlike the polyhistors Boulanger revealed identities arising from the common nature and experience of mankind, not linguistic approximations born of faulty historical transmission.

The ancient tradition of a flood in the reign of Ogyges had been explained naturalistically by Boulanger's contemporaries as a consequence of a change in Venus. Fréret the academician had identified the Boeotian deluge with the passing of comets. Earlier in the century typical English Newtonians like William Whiston had similarly found astronomic origins for the Biblical flood. Boulanger knew the seventeenth-century scientific theories, but unlike the rationalists — and they usually were religious and orthodox — he was not interested in demonstrating that the deluge was an ordinary event, of excessive intensity and duration perhaps, but still a natural rainstorm magnified. Boulanger did not belong to the commonsense school; he was a herald of the new romantic psychology. For him the deluge was a great divide in the history of mankind and it had to be qualitatively different from the upheavals incident to eclipses, the swirl of comets, and the falling of meteors.

Ultimately the recuperative process of nature, ever renewing creation, reasserted itself. Under the first impact of disaster men had been so overwhelmed with fear that they thought only of the next world, but after the passage of a few centuries they once more approached one another with warmth, consoled one another in their adversity, behaved toward one another with goodness, pity, simplicity — still united in fear of the Supreme Being, the persistent tone of religion. While their hearts were burdened with sadness, the postdiluvians were mild, not ferocious, brutal savages, wild and rebellious. After a further interval of convalescence, families were founded once more. The men of these primitive times banished bloodshed — the law of Noah was a residue of the universal compact — for mankind having seen the world destroyed in an instant resolved never to shed blood again. The multitude of deaths had made them abhor killing, and the religious prohibitions against the slaughter of certain animals were a recollection of the same feeling. Misfortune had softened human tempers and men were readily obedient to what they fancied to be the law of God. "The ages of the suffering of mankind were those of humanity, of cordiality, of reason." [80] Laws were unnecessary because need constrained men to afford one another mutual aid, and since there was nothing superfluous a general sense of equality was felt by all men. There was no occasion for formal dominion and wise paternal counsel naturally prevailed. This was a far nobler savage than Rousseau's.

The memory of the period following immediately upon recovery from the initial trauma had been preserved in mythology as the age of Saturn. It was, however, a golden age (details borrowed from Plato and Seneca) painted in muted colors. Boulanger accepted the depiction of Arcadian human behavior, the natural goodness, from the ancient myths, but his ardor for historic fact and reality constrained him to alter the feeling tone of the painting. We gaze not upon the smiling, fortunate man of antiquity's golden age but upon a man virtuous, kind, loving, and melancholy. Boulanger combined the emotions in an unaccustomed fashion: his sad, religious people were in their common wretchedness beneficent to one another. In contemporary eighteenth-century psychology, particularly that of the English Deists, of the Scottish school, and of Hartley, there was a very different pattern in which the pained, the hurt, the wounded, the despised, invariably became the angry and the ferocious. Rival primitives were produced from varying psychological palettes.

Why the fond recollection of the age of Saturn preserved in the annals of all nations if man was then uniformly unhappy? The memory of this world was bright only by contrast with the evil reign of the despotic legislators who followed in the East; only the enslavement of peoples under brutal monarchs made them long for the lost age of Saturn. Since there was uneven development among the various societies in the world the peoples of the East imagined that Saturn had retired to Europe, and as Europe became dominated by tyranny the dream was transferred to America, where it could now be verified. For there among the savages the reign of Saturn still endured; there men were gentle, free, and unhappy.

Since Boulanger saw the first age as golden in its moral character and miserable in its physical environment, he fell into a vexatious theory of historical evolution in which the various "progresses," moral and material, were not parallel or even harmonious. Later in the century Condorcet simplified the theory and forced all the progressions to march at a relatively uniform, orderly, even pace.

When after the passing of Saturn the Boulanger men, wretched though virtuous, continually contemplating the end of the world and the Kingdom of Heaven, finally built societies, they inevitably infused them with the spirit of the pains which they and their ancestors had suffered. Grief was institutionalized. Ultimately the recapitulation of the great catastrophe, embodied in all organized religions, became the most powerful antiprogressist force in history, because it was difficult for men living in the shadow of these lurid images to commit themselves to this world and to labor for its prosperity.

Boulanger ran counter to traditional Euhemerism and theories of the political origins of religion. He proclaimed the Vico thesis of the religious origin of politics, for both the Catholic philosopher and the member of the Holbachian "synagogue" were convinced of the primal significance of the religious temper. This was the burden of Boulanger's *Essai sur le gouvernement, où l'on prouve l'influence de la religion sur la politique* (1788). But while for Vico the creation of a religious idea became the guiding force in man's self-humanization, for Boulanger the birth of false terrors of the next world and the wasteful devotion of the whole of life to a contemplation of doom was the great pall which had descended upon mankind.

The later political vicissitudes to which Boulanger subjected the postdiluvians are feeble and unconvincing attempts at historical synthesis. Somehow the early religious family societies degenerated into theocracies, an era during which the simple, religious feelings of the golden age assumed ever more complex ritualistic and theological forms. The Supreme Being became a monarch, the immediate king of a human agglomeration, and all laws were declared to be of divine origin. God was treated as a man and civil laws were subordinated to him; the god-monarch was given a temple to inhabit, offerings animal and human to nourish him because he was conceived of as god the destroyer, an evil king who had to be appeased with bloody sacrifice. Since he was an anthropomorphic god-king, the most vital problem of existence became the foretelling or divination of his will, and out of this need grew the institutions of oracles, auguries, and auspices. A thousand conventions were adopted for this illusory purpose, ridiculous and criminal practices which multiplied with time and spread throughout the world, suffocating the natural good sense of mankind. The fantastic aggrandizement of the image of a god-monarch entailed the ultimate degradation and enslavement of man. There were no contracts or agreements possible with this Almighty One who ended up as the god of a mystical government, an invisible Sultan, surrounded by visible viziers who in his name became the rulers of society. The priestly caretakers of the god came to control vast territories among the ancient nations, and at a later date under Christianity a vicar of this god almost succeeded in subjecting all the sovereigns of Europe to his dominion.

Boulanger, like his friends in the Holbach circle, was partial to the imposture theory, but in his view of the evolution of religious institutions the deceivers were fairly recent intruders, posterior to the common experience of religious terror and the spontaneous initiation among ordinary people of memorial ceremonies which symbolically reiterated the original painful experiences of the race. Latter-day impostors who became sacerdotal rulers or tyrants merely carried over into the temporal sphere and exploited the feelings of religious subjection which were already active in man's soul, long since poisoned by fear of the Great Judge and his imminent return for further castigation.

Since the religious temper had determined the totality of all other institutions, civil government became most despotic in those parts of the world where the image of the capricious, primitive, cruel judge of mankind — the god of destruction — had been most deeply engrained. When Boulanger was confronted with the empirical problem why Asiatic religions and polities went to mad extremes in self-abasement before despots and in self-torture before the gods, he conveniently borrowed an explanation from Montesquieu: the hot climate drove men to excess. Variations in religious forms could also become projections of different social and political circumstances, the consequence of a dialectical process. While the oriental kings were initially imitations of the idea of the cruel god in judgment, and the subjects of these monarchs, affected by the heat, behaved toward them in an exaggeratedly abject manner, this political relationship was ultimately mirrored in an even more slavish worship of the gods. The attempt to explain the penitences of the religionist, so contrary to the pleasure-principle in the psychic economy, was as lame in Boulanger as it was in Hume. There is of course a presumption in Boulanger that if man ever freed himself from his ancient religious terror he would at one and the same time cast off the shackles of political tyranny as well.

The first postdiluvians had been endowed with the same hu-

man nature as contemporaries, an admixture of passion and reason. This was normative French eighteenth-century thought to
which the generations from Fontenelle through the moral progressists of the Turgot-Condorcet school would have subscribed. The
six or seven thousand years' interval since the flood had introduced no marked differences, and no changes were to be expected
throughout history. Behavioral distinctions which struck the eye
were ascribable exclusively to the impact of external conditions
upon the mechanism, an environmentalism as absolute as that of
Helvétius. Vico's man was directed by a God who, utilizing base
passions, allowed him to create conditions which ultimately hu-
manized him, the driving force always springing from his inner
creative power. External events might serve as the spark, the initial stimulus to a whole succession of human activities, they might
fire man's imagination to invent the gods, but the mysterious
genetic force in man and God's plan were the vital elements in
the confluence. Boulanger remained a more simple stimulus-and-
response environmentalist, the imaginative reporter of how conditions on the morrow of the flood told on the complex machine
of man sentient and reasonable.

There is no physiological transmission of the postdiluvian terror, nor a theological incubus of sin, merely a historical tradition
embodied in rites, myths, ceremonials. Boulanger required no
biological mechanism or race memory plasmically inherited to
account for the enduring effects of the trauma of the flood; mere
imitation and institutional inheritance was adequate, a theory
which allowed also for the relatively easy cure of the disease and
thus generated an optimism whose spirit is to be distinguished
from the traumatized humanity of Freud. "We still tremble today
as a consequence of the deluge and our institutions still pass on to
us the fears and the apocalyptic ideas of our first fathers. Terror
survives from race to race. . . . The child will dread in perpetuity
what frightened his ancestors." [81] If this mechanical reiteration of
fear from one generation to another seemed insufficient to account
for its endurance Boulanger fortified it with the theory of association, the regular appearance of comets, eclipses, and minor disasters keeping the original trauma alive, ever renewing the
memory of the primal event. But if as a consequence of the

triumph of philosophy the institutional stimuli were ever cut off, the malady could be healed overnight.

Throughout his writings Boulanger's sense of the persistence of mythic traditions was one of his richest intuitions, and he made use of it in many of his minor works, particularly in tracing the transformation of symbols from one religion to another. While his polemical purpose was to debunk the uniqueness of Christian symbolism and to demonstrate his old thesis that identical myths and rites could be discovered in different guises throughout the world, in the course of his unholy crusade he developed an insight into the manner in which a pagan god was converted into a Christian saint, bringing along his attributes. The demonstration also supported his underlying thesis that the myths were primordial and that they were merely dressed up anew with each major religious metamorphosis.

His dissertation on the Saint Peter image and its translation from paganism to Christianity is a brilliant early attempt to illustrate latter-day religious syncretism as a historical phenomenon. The apostle was for Boulanger a universal figure of a terrestrial religious chief with the power of opening and closing the heavens; his prototypes were pagan. "Men are really less inventive in matters of religion than one might imagine. . . . Ignorant and vulgar peoples have less often invented new legends than corrupted old ones to assimilate them to their new manner of believing and seeing things. . . . Long habit having rendered certain beings and certain ideas necessary to people, those who have undertaken to lead them along another road have preferred to present to them the ancient objects of veneration in a new guise rather than to suppress them altogether. It is true that in this the new leaders deceived themselves; but they succeeded in deceiving others too and they were not ashamed to make the new religion the dupe of the old one as long as they were considered its founders by the people. . . . When men quitted paganism for Christian religion, the gods were not the last to convert themselves and many of them left the poetic heaven to enter paradise. They did very well, no doubt; but we would do better to be informed of this after having been kept ignorant for so many centuries. It remains to be seen whether we shall be for long." [82] In his comparative mythology

Boulanger was by no means breaking completely new ground. What he did was to stand on its head the old orthodox theory which derived pagan myths from Scripture corruptions and revert to the ideas of the pagan polemicists of the first Christian centuries, who had documented similarities between their heroes and the major Christian figures.

Boulanger, like Vico, expressed adherence to what appears at first sight an anomalous, contradictory philosophy of history, fundamentally at odds with itself. Both have cyclical patterns superficially reminiscent of the ancients, Vico his *ricorsi*, Boulanger his *cyclisme*, and yet both have a stadial development in which they approve the course of the progression. In Vico this might be defined as the history of reason or the overcoming of the mythic mind under divine guidance; in Boulanger it is the emancipation from the traumatic terror of the flood, its anxieties and its reverberations through time, in the name of progress. Boulanger clearly had to face the prospect of the ultimate death of his civilization and the resurgence of the ancient fears on the morrow of a new geological catastrophe, and yet he insisted upon freeing man from the psychic religious evils of the old one so that he could live in relative happiness while his world endured. Viewed from the standpoint of the rectilinear Turgot-Condorcet theory of progress, Hume's and Boulanger's and Vico's philosophies of history may appear cyclical and pessimist by contrast. In mid-eighteenth century, however, the real opposition was not between rectilinear progression and a cyclical thesis, but between the orthodox religious theory of degeneration and a new outlook that conceived of primitive mankind as originally ignorant or possessed by superstition, rising or at least capable of rising to a stage of rationality, a theory in which Boulanger and to a minor degree even Hume, as well as Turgot and Condorcet, participated.

Like many *philosophes* and Deists Boulanger was sympathetic to the doctrine of the double truth, and he even had a word of praise for the wise legislators of antiquity who in the mysteries drew a useful curtain over the realities of the deluge, because the progress of civilization, active discovery in the arts and sciences, would have been impossible for men living under the ancient cloud of universal destruction had they known the whole truth.

Mankind had to be cajoled and through the ages seduced out of its lugubrious state by heroes who lied. But now, in the eighteenth century, men had progressed in rational knowledge far enough so that the whole truth could be revealed to them for the first time, and the sad origins of religious practices which had survived through the ages could be exposed to the light without peril. In fact the multiplication of religious, political, and moral dogmas over the centuries and the bewilderment they engendered in the mind of man made it a duty finally to uncover the source of contemporary beliefs. It was the spectacle of puerile error disguised as history and of a purported science of human happiness which served only a small number of men that forced Boulanger to lift the veil.

As a result of the confusions of moralists and philosophers eighteenth-century man had become an enigma to himself; now he was treated like a corrupt, naturally ferocious animal, now like a fool unworthy of being consulted; now demeaned, now raised beyond his sphere with expectations. As a consequence man was almost in the same emotional state as the first postdiluvian survivors: though no longer dwelling in savagery, he had either relapsed or remained — Boulanger is sometimes sceptical and not presumptive — in a state of *barbarie réelle*. In the cities Boulanger was overcome with the spectacle of sad men, their fear and melancholy. In an echo of Rousseau which was in turn the echo of the sighs of humanity, Boulanger recognized that man was almost universally unhappy.

The purpose of the dramatic tableau of the vices of oriental despotism and its dominant religious spirit was to induce man to correct his present errors. The anticipations of a recurrence of catastrophe were not unfounded in fact, for the revolutions of the earth were destined to recur throughout eternity; but, as in Lucretius, the very explanation of their natural origins made it possible to accept them, to rid oneself of the melancholy fixation upon destruction, and to enjoy and contribute to the fruits of worldly progress. There was no Great Judge who had to be appeased; geological catastrophes were natural and inevitable. If reason prevailed, the commemorative and comforting ceremonials of religion would cease to be necessary in the future, even though they had served as a solace in antiquity, when the wounds inflicted upon mankind by the cataclysm were still too raw to respond to the balsam of rationality and required the false comfort of paradisiacal myth. To legislators his work was an exhortation to teach men to love one another, to alleviate their unavoidable pains. To Rousseau it was a plea that he abandon his absurd nostalgia for the state of nature. Boulanger wrote passages of pure and sober humanity, no facile utopianism, a modern Epicurean's summons to men to banish religious superstition, self-torture, and hate.

Boulanger had solved the harassing eighteenth-century problem of why man had invented religion by establishing that it was a historical psychic necessity in a given environment. The basic historic function of religion — nothing in man could be really useless — was its placating of a floating human anxiety born under conditions of extraordinary emotional disturbance. Since religion had been an integral part of the human economy in past ages nature was vindicated in one of its most aberrant and enigmatic manifestations, but the *philosophe* Boulanger, in the moral lesson of his myth, called into grave question the future utility of religion. Boulanger concluded his essay on *Esope Fabuliste,* a continuation of the *Recherches sur le despotisme oriental,* with a summons to the rationalist West to break with myth and the fanatical religious tradition of the Orient and be free. "Europe, land favored by the heavens, realize the full extent of your superiority and what is yet required of you. Continue to renounce the strange myths and to dissipate the phantasms which were not meant for your climate and which degrade your excellence. It is your destiny to be the thinking part of humanity. A day will come when reason and nature alone will lay down your laws and you will follow them with that wisdom and dignity which should characterize your mature years. Therefore hasten the approach of that happy age by new progress in the arts and sciences, by constant emulation in the search for truth, by the perfection of all your social virtues, and turn your eyes away from Asia which like a nurse has taught her charges the first elements of morality by amusing them with reveries and children's tales." [83]

6

Baron d'Holbach's *Contagion sacrée*

*T*HOUGH HOLBACH interpreted the *système de la nature,*
no one has devised a *système d'Holbach.* The mass of clandestine
anonymous and pseudonymous works on religion, of translations
from the English, and of purported translations produced by the
atheist writers who have been associated with the names of Holbach, Naigeon, and Boulanger, has not yet been completely dis-
entangled by bibliographical expertise and it may never be.[84] For
the most part the Holbachian works are a shapeless compendium of
what had been said on the origins and nature of religion since the
beginning of rationalist thought in ancient Greece. But even
though a harmonious structure is conspicuously absent, there is
discernible a common *esprit,* a central mission. The purpose of
the group was to destroy religion utterly as a social force, and any
historical, psychological, or political argument which came to hand
was enlisted in the unholy war. The sundry theoretical demonstrations of the fraudulence of religion did not require logical consistency with one another. Variant, alternative, even mutually
exclusive disproofs of the existence of the gods were gladly amalga-
mated. Unlike the English Deists upon whom they leaned heavily
for source materials, the Holbachians did not distinguish between
primitive Christianity and the other creeds. All were equally
noxious.

Holbach loosely sewed together Euhemerism, the fear-theory,
the Critias imposture doctrine, Boulanger's diluvian trauma, and
anything else which reduced the birth of religion to a mundane
event and allowed for the eventual eradication of the primeval
superstition which still weighed upon humanity. The Holbachi-

ans roamed through the great literature on priestly deception, religious psychopathology, and the politicizing of religion which had been amassed by the second half of the century — it was all in the Baron's well-stocked library, for which a sales catalogue has survived — and picked out the most deadly instruments, sharpening them on occasion with an original *bon mot*. When Holbach returned from England in the fall of 1765 he smuggled in a secret army of English subversives, Trenchard, Toland, Collins, Woolston, and Hope. Bayle and Fontenelle, Hobbes and Spinoza, and above all David Hume could be reworked with minor modifications even when they contradicted one another. After his death Boulanger was, as we have seen, published separately under his own name; but his ideas were also incorporated into the common fund, and new Holbachian manuscripts were issued as his. Abbé Galiani playfully dubbed Holbach's factory of atheist pamphlets the *Grande Boulangerie*.

From the late seventeenth and first half of the eighteenth century, scores of unpublished French manuscripts circulated about, clandestine works bearing the names of Boulainvilliers, Dumarsais, Jean Meslier, Mirabaud, Fréret, Isaac Orobio, and Lévesque de Burigny, anonymous works like *Le Militaire philosophe ou Difficultés sur la religion, proposées au P. Malbranche* and the *Traité des trois imposteurs,* waiting for adaptation and publication by some daring entrepreneur. Nicolas Fréret and Mirabaud were once considered maliciously appropriated *noms de plume;* it now seems possible that at least some putative forgeries like the *Lettre de Thrasybule* were based upon authentic manuscripts antedating the thirties which the Holbachians merely edited — though here too scholarly opinion is still far from agreement, and the use of the names of innocent learned men like Dumarsais on atheist brochures has been regarded as wicked sport *à la* Voltaire, whose *Philosophie de l'histoire* bore the imprint of pious Abbé Bazin on its title-page.[85] The apportionment of authors' rights among the writers of the initial pre-1750 manuscript, Holbach, Naigeon, and Boulanger, perhaps even Diderot, who on occasion lent his pen to the cabal, is impossible. Though a good number of habitués of the Baron's salon and dinner parties knew what was being perpetrated in this elegant ambiance, the enterprise was one of the best-kept secrets in Paris until Jean-Jacques's attack on the Holbachians in the *Confessions,* a public biting of the hand which had fed him.

Whatever his free borrowings, the Epicurean moralism of Holbach's inquiry into the nature of religion was more forthright than that of any previous eighteenth-century writer in print with the exception of Offray de la Mettrie. Behind the walls of his château at Grandval and with Marc-Michel Rey's Amsterdam presses at his disposal, Holbach published what no one on the continent had dared to before him.

If the sacred disease was indeed a malady, it was subject to clinical diagnosis, and the new doctors of religion asked and answered pertinent medical questions. When and how did this disease enter the human body? What circumstances provoked it or rendered the patient more susceptible to its ravages? There was a consensus that the disease was highly contagious; in fact it had felled virtually all of humanity. If it did not strike man in one weak member of his psychic constitution it would in another. Man was fear-ridden and his religion was born of terror. He was dissatisfied with the simple and he naturally sought the occult, the mysterious. He craved excitement for his imagination and he welcomed marvelous tales before truth. He was arrogant, demanding immediate answers to all questions in heaven and on earth, and he preferred false explanations to none at all.

There were always men about who understood the frailties of the rest of mankind and were poised to take advantage of them. In the hands of tyrants and priests, who loved power and sought to enslave their fellows, the sacred disease was an instrument of domination. Exploiting the natural weaknesses of man, they fired his sick imagination and intimidated him with visions of a dreadful future. Once ensconced in the state, religions became agents of cruelty, for the corps interests of priests and tyrants had to be defended against rivals and millions were massacred in the internecine battles of theology and in the persecution of heretics. The bulk of the Holbachian literature was devoted to a clinical description of the spread of the pestilence, a chronicle of the torments which those possessed inflicted upon themselves and upon other members of the race.

Men were "malades imaginaires," wrote Holbach in *Le Bon Sens, ou Idées naturelles opposées aux idées surnaturelles* (1772).[86] To cure humanity of the fixation would open wide the portals of happiness for future generations. No trick was beyond the Holbachians, for theirs were benign deceptions in the cause of undeluding and restoring the miserable sufferer to health. If Frenchmen respected Fréret or Mirabaud, secretaries of the august Academies, why not publish scandalous works under their names, even without leave? A delicious prank to save mankind.

Release from superstition could come only through enlightenment and a study of the origins of the religious mania discoverable in natural cataclysms, in human psychology, in fraud, or in a combination of all of them. Exposés of the mechanics of priestcraft, of the monotonous identity of religious ceremonials in all times and places, would convince man that he had been a blind victim. If behind the fears he could discover mere illusions, not realities, he would be cured. The technique is as ancient as Epicurus and as new as Freud. "If men only had the courage to climb back to the source of the opinions which are most profoundly embedded in their minds, if only they allowed themselves a precise account of the reasons which had caused them to respect these opinions as sacred; if only they examined cold-bloodedly the motives behind their hopes and fears, they would discover that the objects and ideas capable of exciting them most violently had no reality at all and were only words devoid of meaning, phantasms born of ignorance and altered by a sick imagination," Holbach expostulated in the *Système de la nature*.[87] Once the tragic religious mania had been exorcized, the power of tyranny would be dissolved and men would be free to partake of the banquet of nature. Unveil — that was the mandate of the Holbachians — unveil Christianity, antiquity, man's sacred history, liberate him from tortures which were only appeasements of a dreadful chimera god, attempts to stave off more terrible punishments by seeking out the pain even before the divine condemnation had been pronounced.

The Holbachian atheists had in common with the English Deists a generally ahistorical outlook which distinguished them from other analysts of primitive religion. Since the Holbachians had thrown caution to the winds, they did not have to conceal their attack upon Christianity behind a cover of antiquarian learning which treated of pagan gods. Holbach, like the Deists, availed himself of illustrations from superstitious heathen religion primarily to render fanatical Christianity odious by analogy. As all religious experiences, ancient and modern, barbarian and civilized, had the same etiology, the Holbachians selected at random scientific specimens of the morbus from the whole body of reports on religious behavior in the classical authors as well as among their contemporaries in the Christian and savage world. Though Holbach, under Boulanger's influence, sometimes allowed for the intrusion of geological catastrophes as elements which affected man's religious development, these occurrences were extraneous to his central thesis. While the other psychological theorists of the birth of the gods, Vico, Hume, de Brosses, and Boulanger, explained the genesis of religious emotion in a stormy historic environment, Holbach tended to ignore the *mise en scène,* dispensing with it completely in his most original conception, a subtle psychological portrayal of the inception of religious emotion in the terrors of childhood. This ahistoricism should not, however, be exaggerated, for when Holbach and the English Deists as pure psychologists examined the victims of religious fanaticism throughout time they recognized degrees of morbidity and thus slipped into historical considerations.

Holbach's various theories on the origins of religion, which sprouted in the dark closets of the "Synagogue" like mushrooms, can be accumulated, not conciliated; they are as bewildering as the ancient gods themselves. In one part of *Le Bon Sens,* the idea of a god was simply a phantasm and the multiplicity of gods natural effusions of diverse imaginations. "Tell several painters to represent a chimera. Each one of them having a different idea will paint it differently. All the theologians in the world, do they paint for us anything but one great chimera?" [88] Mere accident dictated the choice of a religion among individuals and peoples. *J. Brunus redivivus ou Traité des erreurs populaires. Ouvrage critique, historique, et philosophique imité de Pomponace* (1771), like Fréret's *Lettre de Thrasybule* before it, blamed the invention of the gods on man's frustrated curiosity, his unsatisfied search into the origins of things. "Obstinate nature for its part refused to reveal an inexplicable secret. What did man then do? To compensate, insofar as possible, for the useless efforts he had expended in attempting to penetrate the secrets of nature, he adopted the mad idea that nature was a cadaver without strength, a being that has no existence of its own and consequently is incapable of bestowing life upon any other object. Finally he pretended, in harmony with the qualities that he had given to nature, that it was pure nothingness subordinate to the all-powerful will of another Being who had animated it, communicating to it movement." [89] In the *Essai sur les préjugés, ou, de l'influence des opinions sur les moeurs & sur le bonheur des hommes. Ouvrage contenant l'Apologie de la Philosophie par M. Des Marsais* (1770), Holbach resorted to a trite eighteenth-century variant of Euhemerism to explain the birth of the gods. Early peoples, languishing in wretchedness, revered as supernatural beings the first legislators and the inventors of arts and sciences who had harnessed the forces of nature. "Everything is prodigious, everything is divine for men without experience. As a consequence in all lands we see the people on their knees before the personages who first taught them to cultivate, to sow, to reap. Osiris, Bacchus, Ceres were nothing more than skillful people who brought to savages useful knowledge; Hercules, Odin, Mars show us warriors who taught the nations the art of self-defense and of successful attack. In a word all those who distinguished themselves by their discoveries, their talents, their extraordinary qualities became the masters, the oracles, and often the gods of men." [90] The identical theme was reiterated in the *Tableau des saints ou examen de l'espirit, de la conduite, des maximes & du mérite des personnages que le Christianisme révere & propose pour modèles* (1770), except that Holbach extended the boundaries of Euhemerist interpretation, which was once restricted to paganism, to include Moses, the prophets of Israel, Jesus, Mohammed, and the Christian saints.

The *Examen impartial des principales religions du monde* was in many ways the most eclectic and superficial of Holbach's pamphleteer explanations of the naturalistic origins of religion. Among the isolated bands of antediluvians who had, he hypothesized in the Lucretian manner, been generated spontaneously from a primeval seed of some sort, there was for a long time probably no religion at all. If there was a common principle of conduct, which was doubtful, it consisted simply in seeking the good and avoiding evil. From Hume Holbach blithely lifted the standard arguments against primitive monotheism. Early man was too preoccupied with elementary needs and ordinary gratifications to contemplate first causes. How then had religion started? Perhaps idlers or unemployed old men who watched animals cure themselves with plant remedies had imitatively introduced the pharmacopoeia, whereupon they and their medicinal herbs were apotheosized. Perhaps the idea of gods as punishers was the invention of wicked despots, for how else could a vigorous young slave be constrained to obey a doddering old tyrant (the Critias theory refurbished)? Perhaps men worshiped animals which were beneficial to them or those they feared. Perhaps men divinized forces or substances which alleviated their pain, the origins of Venus and Bacchus. To these random conjectures on the birth of the gods Holbach added Boulanger's trauma of the flood and the Trenchard and Hume predilection for polytheism over monotheism, and served them up in one undigested hash.

The motivation of man's futile quest for ultimate causes was often more fear than curiosity. Passages in *Le Bon Sens* reminiscent of the introduction to Spinoza's *Tractatus Theologico-Politicus* described man, once alarmed, as grasping the first explanation for disaster that came to mind. Through habit, that favorite psychological crutch of the sensationalists, fear became an actual necessity of existence. "Man is afraid of darkness, both physical and moral. His fear becomes so habitual that it is transformed into a need. Man seems to believe that he would be lacking something if he had nothing to fear. If since childhood a man has made it a habit to tremble each time he hears certain words pronounced he needs these words, he needs trembling. For that reason . . . he is more disposed to hearken to someone who entertains him in his fears than to one who would try to reassure him." [91] *Le Bon Sens* delineated a neurotic clinging desperately to his illness. "The superstitious man wants to be afraid; his fancy demands it. One could say that he fears nothing more than to have nothing to fear." [92] Tales of ghosts and witches, of mysteries, of exciting marvels exercised a natural fascination upon the ignorant. "In the matter of religion men are only big babies." [93] Religion was a residue of infantile mentality, a hangover of the early savage stage of humanity. "These chimeras adopted without examination by the fathers were transmitted with variations to their civilized children who often reason no better than their fathers did." [94] This was precisely the situation which wily charlatans, somehow immune to the disease themselves, could best exploit. Among the mass of the people a natural susceptibility to fear, among the "legislators" a desire to dominate, the consequence religions which prohibited reason and treated mankind like infants in the nursery put to sleep with an admixture of threats and lullabies.

The image of the cruel god was presented in the *Théologie portative ou Dictionnaire abrégé de la Religion Chrétienne* (1768), printed under the name of M. l'Abbé Bernier, *licencié en Théologie,* with a whimsicality which is rare in Holbach. And if it failed to sustain the witty level of Voltaire's *Philosophical Dictionary* it could equal it in sacrilegious obscenity. The deluge which had so possessed Boulanger was defined as "paternal correction inflicted on the human race by Divine Providence who, having failed to foresee the malice of men, repented of having made them so wicked and drowned them once and for all to render them better — which was, as we know, a great success." [95] The origin and history of ritual circumcision was abbreviated: "The Eternal Father who ... sometimes has his caprices once wanted his friends to cut off their foreskins. His son himself submitted to this fine ceremony. But since then his Papa has become more gentle. He no longer has anything against the foreskins of his friends. He is content as long as they never make use of them." [96]

The first chapter of the *Contagion sacrée, ou Histoire naturelle de la superstition, ouvrage traduit de l'Anglois* (1768), in the classical tradition of the fear-theory, was entitled "Origin of superstition: terror always its foundation." The rhetorical rhythm of the opening apostrophe was imitative of Rousseau. "Man is superstitious only because he is afraid. He is afraid only because he is ignorant."[97] Holbach raised a new apparition, a two-faced god, in many ways even more horrible to contemplate than the dependable, consistently cruel god of fear. "When man has suffered great evils, he paints for himself a terrible God before whom he trembles and his cult becomes servile and senseless. When he believes that he has received benefits or when he imagines that he can expect them he discerns in his God gentler traits and his cult becomes less abject, less mad." [98] Since the real world was unstable and the moods of man were fluid, the fast-changing images of God became bewildering and man a distraught wretch torn between visions of gods of terror and gods of hope. The *Contagion sacrée* drew a portrait of an anxiety-ridden, obsessive enthusiast familiar to the Freudian. "Now it [the Being] terrifies them, afflicts them, and throws them into despair. Now it excites their admiration, their confidence and their gratitude. As a result the rites with which they worship this Being show signs of the various passions which affect men. Depending upon the manifestations of nature, God appeared to be either terrifying or amiable, either the object of their fears or of their hopes and love, either he was an awesome tyrant for slaves or a tender father who cherished his children. Since nature does not act in a consistent manner, no God can have a consistent mode of conduct which never contradicts itself. The most wicked God, the most susceptible to anger, had a few good moments. The God who was brimful of goodness inevitably had his moments of ill-humor which men believed were aimed at them. To this changeable and inconsistent conduct of the divinity, or rather to the variability of nature, we should trace the origins of the opposite, often bizarre and contradictory devices which we see employed in the various cults, often even in the same religion." [99]

In Holbach the ancient fear-theory was supplemented by two psychological postulates, a doctrine of projection and a principle of analogy. Vico, Hume, de Brosses had all subscribed to the idea that man tended to project himself into phenomena whose cause he could not fathom and that he drew analogies between the unknown and similar known circumstances. Though the Abbé Galiani, secretary of the embassy of the Kingdom of Naples in Paris, doubtless delivered long monologues in Holbach's salon on Vico, whom he had once known in the house of his uncle Celestino Galiani, the philosopher's protector, the charge of plagiarism which he directed against the *Boulangerie* in a letter to the Foreign Minister of the Kingdom of Naples, Tanucci, cannot be substantiated. For even if the Holbachians heard Vichian themes in the ebullient flood of Galiani's conversation, they surely used them in an entirely alien context. The textual parallels which the great contemporary Vico scholar Fausto Niccolini has sought to establish seem strained. During his visit to Grandval, Cesare Beccaria also praised Vico and agreed to send Holbach a copy of the *Scienza Nuova,* but there is no evidence that the promise was ever kept. It is pointless to trace to any one source *aperçus* as commonplace as the idea of projection or reasoning by analogy, which were part of the sensationalist baggage-train available to everyone. Neither is it significant to show that Holbach knew Hume's essay on the *Natural History of Religion.* Unlike the purported Vico plagiarism, Humean influence can at least be documented by references in the catalogue of Holbach's library and by correspondence between the two men on the origins of religion. (Holbach had asked for Hume's intercession to get Boulanger's manuscript published in England.)[100] But did Holbach really understand Hume's subtly nuanced dissertation? In the second half of the century, when almost everybody held to a fear-theory, similarities are easily established and are not necessarily evidence of specific influence. Plagiarism was not, moreover, mortal sin among these brothers-in-arms.

Holbach did introduce one novel element into the traditional fear-theory. The *Système de la nature ou des loix du monde physique et du monde moral* viewed religion as a consequence of man's natural susceptibility to pain. This doctrine transcended time, and its resemblance to the latter part of Freud's *Civilization and its Discontents* is striking. The first moments of any human existence were marked by needs; the new-born infant required the aid of various persons similar to himself without whom he would not be able to sustain the life which he had received. "These needs manifest themselves in his sensitive being by a disorder, a depression, a languor in his machine which makes him aware of a painful sensation; and this disturbance endures and increases until another cause, required to put an end to the trouble, re-establishes the natural order in the human mechanism." Driven by needs, the child learned to make distinctions, to compare, to recognize the harmful and the benign, the sources of the painful and the pleasurable. Without primary needs man would be an "insensitive automaton"; if all needs and desires were agreeably and quickly appeased he would live an existence of perpetual uniformity and it would never have occurred to him to make inquiry into the unknown causes of things. Holbach does not follow Rousseau's dramatic description of thought as depravity, though he was affected by it. "To meditate is a pain," but a necessary pain, for if the needs of original man had been immediately gratified, he would, like Rousseau's savage, experience only the present. "Nothing would alarm his heart. Everything would be in harmony with his being. He would experience neither fear, nor distrust, nor anxiety for the future."

Fear and uneasiness in the grown man were in large measure the remembrance of painful sensations in childhood. Unsatisfied infantile needs, causing pain, ultimately gave birth to a generalized feeling of disquietude in man, an anxious anticipation. In addition to the normal continuous denial of gratification, adult man was inevitably subject to a series of more spectacular evils: famine, plague, accident, illness. The natural state of anxiety engendered by all pain and dread of pain was heightened by the social institutionalized memory of primeval global destruction — Boulanger's diluvian catastrophism condensed for the *Système de la nature* — and the consequence was the religious fixation of mankind upon the idea of God. "Were there no pain in the world, man would never have thought of divinity." [101]

Holbach's works were faithful to the tradition of Lucretius and his master Epicurus. He wrote a *Système de la nature* as his Roman predecessor, from whom he drew his epigraph, had written a *De rerum natura*, in order to enlighten men, to emancipate them from the evils of manifold fears. Perhaps the mechanism of painful remembrance of unsatisfied need could never be completely blocked, but there were a multitude of anxieties arising in man's dread of the unknown and of the sudden and calamitous manifestations of nature which could surely be mitigated, perhaps eliminated. Primitives, children, and common people were prey to anxieties and wild imaginings to a far greater degree than the educated. If men were taught the natural causes of phenomena which frightened them they would be less afraid, they would suffer less anticipatory pain, and they would approach nearer to that tranquillity which was the ideal of the ancient as well as of the eighteenth-century Epicureans. A quotient of anxieties in life was the destiny of child and man, as long as there were necessities and pain, but the great terror of the gods and the fear of punishment in the next world could be eradicated. Science could alleviate human misery by restricting the area of the unknown. Explain the causes of events the most painful and man could cope with them; but if he did not know causes then "his uneasiness is redoubled; his imagination goes astray; it either exaggerates or paints in horrendous colors the unknown object of his terror; it makes analogies with a few of the already known beings; it suggests to him means similar to those he ordinarily employs to ward off the effects and disarm the power of the hidden cause which has given birth to his uneasiness and his fears. His ignorance and his weakness render him superstitious." [102]

The religion of a "Dieu pauvre & crucifié," [103] a symbol of anguish, had enthroned hypocrisy. Holbach assimilated the Deist psychological identification of the sufferer and the man of vengeance. Far from diminishing during the Christian centuries — the thesis which Turgot had eloquently defended in his Sorbonne apologies of 1750 — Holbach declared that human iniquity had increased under sacerdotal absolutism. Instead of checking man's perversities, organized religion had encouraged the wicked to pursue their psychological vices, to persist in their blind desire to persecute. Many passages of Le Christianisme dévoilé, ou examen des principes et des effets de la religion chrétienne (1767) anticipate Nietzschean themes on the covert psychological function of religious emotion, even the conception of ressentiment. "The bilious one early hearkens to the precepts of his priest when he orders him to hate, the vindictive one obeys him when he permits him to avenge himself under the pretext of avenging his god." [104]

Forty years later the image of this dread god of the Baron

d'Holbach was still haunting a prisoner of the Napoleonic po-
lice, a man who in his works relentlessly pursued the radical
eighteenth-century postulates to their ultimate conclusion — the
Marquis de Sade. "Chimerical and empty being," he cried out
in one of his few surviving notebooks, "your name alone has
caused more blood to flow on the face of the earth than any political war ever will. Return to the nothingness from which the mad
hope and ridiculous fright of men dared call you forth to their
misfortune. You only appeared as a torment for the human race.
What crimes would have been spared the world, if they had
choked the first imbecile who thought of speaking of you." [105]

Before Holbach many *philosophes* had accepted the ancient
proposition that religion was an indispensable instrumentality
for the policing of the state, for without the threat of eternal punishment the stupid masses would abandon themselves to crime
and vice. Revealed religion taught falsehood and enslaved mankind to corrupt priests, but without this "noble lie" no civilization could endure. The idea that religion was a mechanism which
inspired terror, but terror useful for the preservation of society,
was a widespread conviction even among sceptics and atheists.
The *philosophes* could tolerate the truth that Christianity was
nothing but an inchoate mass of superstitions spewed up by oriental fanaticism and continue to live in accord with the moral
law, but the common people could not face this historical reality
without subverting the state. In this variant on Critias the naturalistic basis of religion in man's anxiety and fear was taken for
granted; the fear, however, was assimilated into the order of
things as a utilitarian passion capable of serving civility.

In the preface to *Le Christianisme dévoilé* Holbach countered
this Voltairean apology for religion and refuted the argument
that his own atheistic works, his publicizing of the truth about
Christianity, might endanger the security of society. Who reads?
was his first rhetorical defense. Surely not the common people,
and the philosophers who might contemplate his ideas were born
lovers of tranquillity, for everyone knew that only priests and
fanatics made revolutions. He proclaimed the absolute utility of
any truth and the absolute evil of prejudice, error, deception.
There was no noble lie. The history of man was a mournful

chronicle of the corruption of his naturally good and sociable human relations by the religious spirit, which was itself born of images of a bloody, terrifying, destructive God. No religion of love or morality, of human benevolence, could ever bloom from this foul source. The action program for men of enlightenment was self-evident: destroy the god born of fear, substitute humanity, and society would, far from being exposed to the dangers of revolution, flourish in the universal pursuit of happiness.

Holbach proposed to exalt the real power of the secular monarchy instead of the religious power of the priests as the check-rein upon mankind. The mechanics for the creation of a good society were virtuous example, rewards and punishments in this world, and sound education. Sovereigns could easily establish this new moral order and proclaim a society of free citizens by fiat because they had the power to grant riches and to inspire actual, not illusory, terrors among malefactors. "The most devout courtier fears his king more than his God." [106] Ultimately this progressist optimism was dependent upon the prospect of his ideas penetrating to the throne-room. Holbach was the *philosophe* of atheistic enlightened despotism, a rational state power founded upon terrestrial sanctions alone, after the complete elimination of the rival spiritual arm, "the enemy of the progress of the human spirit." [107] For God the State — this was the Hobbesian theory which the Holbachians transmitted to the French Revolution.

Frederick II, at the other end of Europe, sensed the full implications of the theory, only he introduced an ominous gloss in his anonymous review of Holbach: this emancipation of the ignorant from the evils of superstition could never be achieved without the shedding of rivers of blood. The king on his throne was bound by the false beliefs of his subjects. Was the philosopher prepared to mount machines of war, he asked with fiendish scorn. Christianity had been imposed by the executioners of the Roman Empire, not by the saints. Were the *philosophes* ready to follow the Christian example in securing the triumph of their beliefs?

CHAPTER V

The New Allegorism

"The genius of a man capable of explaining religion seems to me to be of a higher order than that of a founder of religion. And this is the glory to which I aspire."
— Charles Dupuis, *Origine de tous les cultes, ou Religion Universelle.*

1

Epigoni

*T*HE TRADITIONAL allegorical interpretations of the gods had been crowded out by Euhemerism and the new psychology of religion. A comparison between the 1675 and 1768 editions of Sandrart's *Teutsche Akademie der Bau- Bildhauer- und Maler-Kunst,* a standard work on iconography in the Germanic world, sharply illustrates the dominant trend. The explanations of myth in the seventeenth-century edition are still entirely in the symbolizing spirit of the Renaissance; in the introduction to the eighteenth-century version, however, the editor Johann Jacob Volkmann announced that these explications had to be altered and he committed himself completely to Abbé Banier's factual historical method.

When remnants of allegorization are found in England and in France the virtues celebrated in the images of the gods are utilitarian, and the eighteenth-century ideals of peace, tranquillity, assiduous labor, kindness, gentleness, and obedience are recognized even in myths which appear to mirror the darker recesses of the human spirit. The allegorical moralizing mythographer projected himself right back into antiquity, and without disarranging his peruke during the quick voyage through time asked himself what he as a rational human being would have wished to communicate to his contemporaries. He then found that the myths embodied precisely those wise and sensible principles which he himself as an eighteenth-century moralist would have taught mankind. In ancient times his civil status would have been that of a priest or a poet and he would have used the allegorical techniques then available to his craft. Examples of this method are delightfully naive. In their *Descriptions des principales pierres gravées du cabinet de S.A.S. Monseigneur le Duc d'Orléans* (1780–1784) the Abbés de la Chau and Le Blond interpreted the Orpheus myth as an "allegory relative to the invention, the progress, and the perfection of the arts and sciences." Robert Clayton, Lord Bishop of Clogher, called himself an allegorist, but the Ankh sign he analyzed in a postscript to a travel book by the Prefetto of Egypt, *A Journal from Grand Cairo to Mount Sinai, and back again, to which are added Remarks on the Origin of Hieroglyphics and the Mythology of the ancient Heathens* (1753), was not a symbolic representation of the world or eternity but a useful object, a symbol of labor, a setting stick for planting roots and larger seeds in the hand of the god Osiris. This wonderful, functional object had a convenient circular handle for grasping, a perpendicular rod for pushing the seed in, and a transverse bar to prevent the seed from being driven too deeply into the ground. In the traditional Pharaonic attributes of majesty Clayton's eighteenth-century eye saw only useful agricultural instruments, reaping hooks and flails. The Ankh sign remained troublesome; Cornelius de Pauw insisted dogmatically that it was a phallic symbol and denounced a colleague who saw in it nothing but a mariner's needle.

In the eighteenth century Platonic sublimities were no longer discovered in myth, there was no ancient wisdom, no cabalistic secret, no allusion to man wrestling with evil. If one seeks for a residue of the allegorizing tendency with Neoplatonic overtones it can be found in a wild Deist like Woolston, whose *Discourse on the Miracles of our Saviour* (1727–1729) adopted the older Renaissance technique in order to interpret the Christian gospels themselves as a myth of the human soul and to repudiate them as a literal account of the life of Christ, a blasphemous inversion of the ancient symbolic method for anticlerical purposes.

A caveat: while allegorism was outmoded as a method of interpretation among western mythographers it remained firmly ensconced in one sphere of grandiose creativity, in the high baroque. Fundamental and not peripheral to this art was its ideational content. The argument and spirit of the great frescoes, the painting, and the sculpture are important expressions of the eighteenth-century confrontation with the gods in the conservative Catholic areas of Europe. In the high baroque in South Germany and the central European territories of the Hapsburg Empire, where the plastic arts were exclusively in the service of the Church and the Court, the traditional allegorical conceptions held complete sway. Symbols were developed with such profusion of detail that every figure, pose, and minor decorative conceit was an emblem, an enigma, a hieroglyph which those who knew the secret language of mythology read as an intrinsic part of the aesthetic experience. Each attribute of a god or a hero was an earthly embodiment of a transcendent ideal, and the contemplation of the figure was a means to the attainment of a supernatural reality, a spiritual exercise. In Austria the majestic frescoes were painted in accord with minute instructions set down by monks learned in the allegorical significance of myths. Painting, poetry, and moral preaching were merely different ways of raising man from the corporeal to the divine. As in the multiple interpretation of Scriptural texts, an idea in baroque art could simultaneously be expressed as history, symbol, emblem, and hieroglyph. Cesare Ripa's *Iconologia, overo Descrittione d'Imagini delle Virtù, Vitii, Affetti, Passioni humane,* a compendium of moral ideas with illustrations of the manner in which they could be simultaneously and differently represented as incidents in sacred, profane, and mythic history, remained the great source book for workers in this style. The new edition in five volumes which was published in Perugia, 1764–1767, was only the most elaborate version of a text which since the sixteenth century had appeared in numerous editions in all the major European languages.[1] For this intricate art-form the allegorical theory of the ancients was an underlying presupposition which made the Christianization of the myths acceptable to the most orthodox. The myths, translated into religious homilies, were now combined in new structural patterns and inventions to reassert the Christian virtues. The iconological canon of the Jesuit father Masen, who was in complete control of the classical literary and patristic tradition, the *Speculum imaginum veritatis occultae, exhibens Symbola, Hieroglyphica, Emblemata, Aenig-*

mata omni . . . (1650), fixed the precise moral meaning of each god and his attributes, a sort of dictionary of spiritual hieroglyphs. But no novel theories were evolved for this art in the eighteenth century; and the manuals remained either antiquated Renaissance compilations or adaptations from these earlier works.

Toward the end of the eighteenth century the allegorical interpretation of mythology, under attack in France since Bayle and Fontenelle, enjoyed a brief Indian summer in the ponderous and voluminous works of Court de Gébelin and Charles Dupuis. Not that allegorism had died out entirely even among the great historical-psychological mythographers — in Vico and Boulanger elements can easily be discovered — but the new theorists were avowed, self-conscious adherents, while their predecessors would have scornfully rejected the epithet as reminiscent of Neoplatonic vapors. Though in the building of their systems and in their personal religious convictions Court de Gébelin and Charles Dupuis differed profoundly from each other — one was a prominent and respectable French Protestant, and the other an *idéologue* materialist who published his major work under the libertine Directorate — their latter-day allegorism had common features which distinguish them from mid-eighteenth-century writers. Perhaps it is their emotional tone even more than their methodology which marks the difference from their immediate antecedents. While the mid-century theorists were still harassed by doubts, the new mythography was symptomatic of the revolutionary period when commitments on the great moral issues had become fixed. The pessimist moods of a Hume or a Boulanger never cast their long shadows in the diffuse, rambling tomes of Court de Gébelin and Charles Dupuis, buoyant optimists convinced of the imminent triumph of a natural order in society and a rational system in the beliefs of mankind. They were imbued with a reborn appreciation of antiquity and the wisdom of the ancients, remarkably absent in Bayle and Fontenelle, de Brosses and Holbach. Court de Gébelin and Charles Dupuis again studied pagan religious ritual and ancient myths of all nations as emanations of a noble, exalted, moral spirit and not as sordid reflections of blind savagery. While giving ample lip service to the eighteenth-century antagonism to the *esprit de système,* they fancied themselves "scientists" writing definitive systematic treatises on the origins of religion and the interpretation of myth. They intimidated their readers with monstrous apparatuses of erudition, Court de Gébelin with a hypothetical primitive speech derived by induction from a superficial study of the etymologies of all known languages including the American Indian, Dupuis with a comprehensive knowledge of ancient and modern astronomic records. Both drew analogies among the myths in the classical corpus and the voyage literature with facility. After they had reviewed with laborious critical detail the writings of their forerunners in mythography and ancient history they rejected them one and all. They were fixated men, intoxicated with their own discovery of the secrets of the primitive world.

In some respects Court de Gébelin and Dupuis were mere epigoni of the great eighteenth-century theorists whom they attacked. In Court de Gébelin one can find the Boulanger hypothesis of the "physical revolutions of our globe which have so mightily influenced the moral character of its inhabitants";[2] the monism of all system-builders, the search for "one principle inherent in the human species whose effects or consequences were necessarily the same for all times, all climates, all peoples";[3] the Vichian theory of myth as an actual primitive language; the de Brosses conjecture of the mechanical evolution of speech from a few original sounds; the Warburtonian concept that primitive languages were concrete and pictorial before they became abstract and ideational. "This work of de Gébelin . . . What purpose does an extract of a rehash on ancient history serve?"[4] the corrosive Abbé Galiani inquired of Madame d'Epinay from his Naples exile. Charles Dupuis incorporated the cosmographic traditions of mythographers who preceded him and was hardly emancipated from the crudities of the early eighteenth-century anticlerical imposture theory. The writings of Court de Gébelin and Dupuis lacked the fantasy and genuine passion of the mid-century analysts of religion and myth, and they are memorable more for their influence — like the revolutionary oratory which they resemble — than for their intrinsic worth, though in the mountains of chaff there is a brilliant insight here and there.

2

The Great Order of Court de Gébelin

*T*HE SON of a famous Protestant *émigré* preacher, Court de Gébelin arrived in Paris from Lausanne with the purpose of alleviating the disabilities of his co-religionists. Remarkably similar in his methods to official Jewish "protectors" of their brethren, he entertained notions about purchasing Protestant "liberties" from the crown. His mission was not a great success; Protestant communities would agree neither upon the proposals of their "delegate" nor upon his person. At the time of the Calas affair he wrote *Les Toulousaines,* a passionate defense of the persecuted, which he later withdrew because Voltaire, the absolute monarch of the condemned, found fault with it. However, Court de Gébelin had a social triumph in aristocratic Paris. A friend of Benjamin Franklin and the *philosophes,* he was received everywhere, a constant reminder of the iniquities of the Edict of Nantes. Though his religion prevented him from becoming a member of the Académie des Inscriptions he was compensated by an appointment as Royal Censor, one of those curious anomalies of the *ancien régime.* In his last years illness drove him into the arms of Mesmer, and the heroic defender of rational religion died while undergoing treatment through animal magnetism. The Countess d'Albon took his body to her estate and on his gravestone had chiseled characters from the scores of strange alphabets which he had studied in the preparation of his great masterpiece of erudition.

The nine large quarto volumes of the *Monde Primitif analysé et comparé avec le monde moderne considéré dans son génie allégorique et dans les allégories auxquelles conduisit ce génie précédé du plan général des diverses parties qui composeront ce monde primitif* appeared between 1773 and 1782. It was a costly illustrated publication supported by hundreds of subscriptions from the royal houses and scholars of Europe. Court de Gébelin's style was at once dull and dithyrambic, the absorption in his revelation passionate. As a psychological type he would have fitted in better with the Saint-Simons, the Fouriers, the Wronskis, the Azaïs of the next generation. But his learning was predominantly literary in the traditional sense and his system drew the bulk of its materials from the earlier polyhistors and etymologists.

Court de Gébelin had imposed upon himself the task of finally revealing the true nature of the primitive world by encompassing all the remains of antiquity in whatever form they had survived, as language, myth, or artifact, in a grand synthesis with one dominant idea. Such monist obsessions were becoming common at the turn of the century. His all-embracing principle, introduced with great fanfare, proved to be rather trite; it was need, *besoin*. Today his magic word would probably have to be translated as function: "In a word, there exists an eternal and immutable order which unites heaven and earth, body and soul, physical and moral life, men, societies, empires, the generations which pass, those which exist, those that are to come, and this order can be identified by one and the same word, the same language, the same type of Government, the same religion, same ritual, same conduct, beyond which both to the right and the left there is only disorder, confusion, anarchy, chaos, without which nothing can be explained, but with which all times, languages, allegories illuminate each other, explain each other with certainty and irresistible evidence worthy of the eternal need, without which there is no truth, which is itself truth made for all men, and without which there is no safety." [5] With this magical key the dark primitive world of myth and religion was suddenly illuminated and arranged in exemplary order, as he demonstrated the specific function of even the most irrational bewildering expressions of ancient humanity. Once the mist which had enshrouded the primitive world was dissipated a perfect unity in human motivation and practice emerged. This was the Great Order. The history of mankind was revealed to be a reasonable progression of needs, their appeasement, and the creation of new needs as a direct consequence of the very act of fulfilling the old ones; history became an exercise in problem-solving, a philosophical approach which still has a wide appeal to twentieth-century pragmatic historians.

The source of his ponderous theory is obvious enough. He adapted the Physiocrats' tableau of the contemporary economic-social system to the history of mankind, and Quesnay rightly esteemed him as a favorite disciple. The Physiocratic mechanism was animated with a historical soul. Court de Gébelin's intent, like theirs, was didactic and reformist, not merely scholarly and curious. The discovery that the principle of utility was basic to the true order of the primitive world, thus identifying the prevailing spirit of the historic process from its very inception, would teach men to understand the foundation of a new harmonious order of rational functions freed from the trammels of feudalism which had negated the Great Order.

Though a believer in the progressive perfectibility of the arts and sciences and hostile to cyclical theories, Court de Gébelin belonged paradoxically enough to the school which held the fundamental character of human nature to be immutable. The good fortune that only external forms and circumstances, not the quintessential psyche of man, had altered, made the comprehension of the primitive world possible, an idea encountered before in Boulanger. In order to interpret an ancient monument or historic event men had only to ask themselves: "What would we have done then? What would they be like today?" And the answer was painfully circular: "Whatever we imagine that we would have done is precisely what they did in fact, because they did what we would necessarily do." [6] The historical utilitarianism of Court de Gébelin was all-pervasive, admitted of no exceptions, and ended up as a determinist phantasmagoria which betrayed its Protestant origins.

Ancient mythology and pagan religious ceremonial were intricate labyrinths through which Court de Gébelin had to thread his way if the functionalism *à outrance* was not to meet with instant defeat. Undaunted, this hero of mythography interpreted the great cycles with a rococo profusion of detail which showed them all to be reasonable records of the progressive history of primeval humanity overcoming the obstacles of necessity with new discoveries and artifices. "The mythological variations of the diverse nations are merely the *pièces justificatives* of the same needs, the same arts, without any alteration but local variations necessitated by the physical environment of each climate." [7] The mythmakers of the *monde primitif* had not been impostors but wise moral historians and legislators teaching workmanlike virtue through their exaltation of the triumphs of mankind over need. This Court de Gébelin throwback was distinguished from the Stoic allegorical tradition by the scientific paraphernalia with which he clothed his illustrations. He adopted as his epigraph the dictum of Sallust, "The whole universe is a symbol," [8] and then made symbolism a historical "science" in nine quartos.

The modern allegorist inevitably had to face the question why the ancients had had recourse to an outlandish, even vulgar form of mythic expression instead of speaking in sensible eighteenth-century prose. Since the unconscious had not yet been formally discovered, myths could not be conceived of as spontaneous archetypal expressions of the collective psyche. The nearest an eighteenth-century man came to a conception of impersonal, mass development was the evolution of speech. Mythic talk was a functional need of primitive man in the early stages of history — that was the Court de Gébelin solution. The whole system came to rest upon a fanciful mechanistic theory of the historical growth of language, an elaborate structure illustrated in appendices with diagrams, drawings, beautiful color-plates of the vocal chords that were innovations in the art of engraving, and translations from scores of tongues. In content the system is far from original and bears more than passing resemblance to the Vichian theory of poetic speech and the de Brosses hypothesis of the gradual transformation of a few basic primitive physiological sounds into language. Fundamentally Court de Gébelin's pretentious theory is rooted in the commonplace eighteenth-century idea that primitive mentality was concrete and that the first words of the original language of mankind described only a few visible objects. As mankind progressed, in order to express complex moral ideas it was necessary to have recourse to combinations of pictorial images and to analogies. The result was allegory, the genius of the *monde primitif*. "As soon as man tried to pass beyond to depict ideas relative to moral, intellectual, spiritual, abstract subjects which were not directly comprehensible by the senses, it was necessary to employ artifice, and the sensible or physical objects came to the aid of those which were not. From then on symbolic language existed because all the words which designated the corporeal objects in their literal sense also depicted nonsensible objects by comparison and analogy." [9] The ancients had not had a choice, to allegorize or not, since they were forced by the original poverty of their sensory language to resort to emblems and metaphors.

In the course of time human forgetfulness, that bromidic but convenient mechanism of the sensationalists introduced to account for historical change, had caused men to lose track of the events which the myths had originally depicted — primarily conquests over nature — and they were plunged into a maze of images whose meaning was no longer fathomable. For the primitive the pictorial speech of myth composed of combinations of simple images was natural. Contemporary "criticism," cold and analytic, had no clue to the primitive world because it was no longer capable of "feeling" symbolic language.

Gusts of the nascent romantic spirit blew through the cracks of this pompous philosophico-linguistic structure. The Court de Gébelin primitive has grace, poetry, natural goodness, charm, a unique orderliness and harmony, and though his speech may appear fantastic to a "rationalistic" modern it is a glorious expression of truth. Court de Gébelin had adopted the concept of a primitive mentality from his predecessors, but instead of denigrating barbarous poetry he had, in the temper of the late eighteenth century, the age of Ossian, found it sublime. The ancients were not crude but naturally sage, emotional, and imaginative. Court de Gébelin thus effected a concordance between the neoclassic idealization of antiquity and the new psychology which related primitive mentality with the concrete and the pictorial. His was the French theory nearest to the German vindication of primitive wisdom, to Hamann, Winckelmann, and Herder.

Court de Gébelin harked back to pre-eighteenth-century allegorism and orthodox primitive monotheism, combatting ideas
which had gained widespread acceptance among the psychologists of religion Boulanger, de Brosses, and Hume: their rejection
of the written testimony of pagan Greeks and Romans that the
ancient myths were allegorical and that the ritual was symbolic;
their false assimilation of the religious behavior of the ancients
with contemporary savages; their presupposition that early men
not yet corrupted by "prejudices" had expressed absurd ideas
about God. Court de Gébelin insisted that only through agelong
"revolutions" had mankind gradually fallen away from primitive
truths. This pious though enlightened Protestant and admirer
of the ancients rejected the idea that wise men believed literally
in the anthropomorphic attributes of the gods.

Through volume after volume Court de Gébelin piled up an
account of the circumstantial purposes, the particular causes and
needs which brought forth the classical allegories, mostly derivative and hackneyed conjectures. Some allegories were convenient
ways of issuing social orders in connection with communal agricultural labors (the Abbé Pluche fantasy on the origins of the
zodiac). There was a natural tendency to complicate ideas and
make them subtle in order to test the human capacity for understanding. The orientals were particularly addicted to this pro-
liferation of allegory, because — shades of Montesquieu — the
heat inflamed their imaginations. Eastern peoples naturally loved
enigmas; they preferred to have ideas half-expressed so that they
could be aroused to guess the rest. Far from intending to obfus-
cate or to deceive, the ancient allegory was designed to vivify, to
move, to render passionate great moral truths by stimulating the
imagination.

In the primitive world every monument and written fable,
every painting and oral tradition was an allegory of the Great
Order, which Court de Gébelin, the new revealer, could read for
the first time since antiquity. His interpretation of the Hercules
myth in "Allégories orientales" was in striking contrast both with
the prevailing Euhemerist and the older allegorical traditions.
For Vossius Hercules was the sun and the twelve labors were the
signs of the zodiac; to Jean Le Clerc, the Huguenot, he had been

a Phoenician merchant and his exploits commercial successes; Abbé Banier had recognized in him a Theban hero apotheosized for worthy services to his country; Abbé Pluche identified him with Horus and made of him a blazon raised as a call to arms in time of war; Abbé Bergier had seen in the shield of Hercules a signpost for a dike or a canal. Each mythographer had hitherto projected his private imagination into the mythic figure of Hercules. For Court de Gébelin the Hercules cycle was an allegory of the historic clearing of the forests and the initiation of agriculture in the primitive world. The similarity of this theme with the Vico reading of the Hercules myth is so patent that it is virtual adaptation — and Vico was mentioned directly and favorably in the text, a rare acknowledgment — but Court de Gébelin stamped his own Physiocratic imprint upon the profound Vichian reading of the allegory. The Physiocratic ideal of order, of peaceful labor, preferably on the land, so possessed the new mythographer that he was able to transform the terrible exploits of Hercules, his combat with monsters of all species, into a circumstantial allegorical history of the diffusion of agriculture among mankind. The tilling of the soil had been invented by Saturn, Cronus, or Osiris, Court de Gébelin reported; the calendar by Thoth, Hermes, or Mercury; and the peoples of the world were eager to reap the fruits of these beneficent discoveries. But the earth, covered with marshes, brush, rocks, lakes, teeming with ferocious beasts, was ill-prepared for the utilization of the gifts of these men of genius. The land first had to be conquered by the united brotherly efforts of mankind. Hercules was the symbol of the heroic benefactors of humanity who organized and directed the clearing of the forests. "Such were the first exploits of men and of the chiefs of the Peoples, those whereby the earth herself was conquered. They were the most illustrious heroes, the only ones who can be pleasing to humanity, the only ones worthy of immortal glory and of being preserved in the poetic annals of Nations." [10] Hercules was the vanquisher of the lion because he had caused the ferocious animals to disappear. He was armed with a spiked club, the simplest of scepters, to mark his domination over the earth and its creatures, to show that he was the true King of the World, the civilizer of mankind.

But why was Hercules a Theban, an incredulous commentator might ask. No mythic detail however minor escaped the fine net of the Gébelinian system. Among the Orientals Hercules was adored as a sun and in Oriental languages "Thebes" meant an ark or a vessel. (In the Hebrew Bible Noah's ark is in fact called "Teva.") Hercules was called the Theban, the navigator, to indicate that it was he, the sun, who piloted the vessel (the Thebes) in which he traversed the skies. The Greeks later confused Theban with a native of Thebes. Such etymological balderdash was a characteristic residue of seventeenth-century mythography introduced into a new philosophical context.

Court de Gébelin's system found pure humanity not in the Rousseauist savage state of nature but in antiquity when mankind was civilized but yet uncorrupted. The state of civility of the primitive world, once its monuments had been read by Court de Gébelin, proved that "men only wish to learn, to be educated, to become happy." The authentic primitive was a born utilitarian, a self-conscious progressist; his religion was monotheist and his social order perfect. Modern man differed from him only in his accumulation of acquired arts and sciences.

The preservation of the true order of needs brings happiness, but when men refuse to succor one another and empires seek aggrandizement, destruction inevitably follows. Court de Gébelin is the author of odes upon benevolence, of homilies against false grandeur, of preachments on the laws of harmonious development. His cultural history of the ancient monuments became a discursive learned sermon demonstrating that whenever nations exceeded the bounds of the natural order they fell into decay, because conquest was contrary to the inventive satisfaction of progressive needs, which was the sound nature and happy destiny of man. The principle of harmonious order now required the uniform civilization of all barbarous peoples. The identification of the primitive as an ancestor and the recognition of the need for his conversion to the arts and sciences were two symbiotic ideas in Court de Gébelin as they had been in de Brosses. The even spread of culture among the various provinces of a country, preventing any single city from becoming inflated to the detriment of others, was another prerequisite of the Great Order, a conception born of a Rousseauist antagonism to Paris which later became an integral element in Condorcet's theory of equality. Court de Gébelin pleaded for "Europe an Assembly of Brothers," [11] united by the same rights and duties, rejoicing in the same pleasures, subordinate to the same Order, a restoration of the beneficent harmony of the Primitive World, the age of Saturn allegorized in mythology.

3

Charles Dupuis:
The Phallus and the Sun-God

B Y the latter half of the eighteenth century the idea that sexual orgies and the display of phallic symbols played a prominent role in pagan worship was widely diffused in the learned literature on antiquities. The basic facts had of course not been ignored in previous ages. Favorite classical authors like Herodotus and Plutarch had reported on lewd Egyptian rites. The Church Fathers had described the lascivious pagan cults in great detail in order to inveigh against them. By the 1780's these practices, which in the Renaissance had either been merely alluded to and passed over quickly as aberrations or spiritualized, began to loom in the darkness of heathen religion. Perhaps the reproduction of the wall paintings and statuary excavated at Herculaneum which graphically depicted Priapic ceremonials and licentious myths contributed significantly to the spread of a new apperception of ancient religion. When the fine art of engraving was used to illustrate in book form purported antique gems on which pagan deities were portrayed in postures shocking to Christian sensibilities a primary purpose of the publication was doubtless pornographic, but these works also served to heighten the sensual image of antiquity. Even serious scholarly studies had moved in the same direction. De la Croze's history of Christianity in India had spread abroad an account of the Hindu adoration of the *lingam* and Jablonski's *Pantheon Aegyptiorum* (1750–1752) had described, from a collation of patristic and classical sources, the orgiastic and Sodomitical rites related to the worship of the Nile.[12]

The growing interest in Indian culture toward the end of the eighteenth century which culminated in the writings of Sir William Jones further highlighted the fact that in one ancient cult which was still being practiced by millions of Hindus carnal love had been associated with, not denied by, religion. Travelers in the East who described the prevalent temple prostitution, the dancing girls and the dancing boys, focused attention upon identical practices of ancient paganism which, though mentioned in the Bible, in Lucian, and in patristic literature, had previously been squeamishly avoided as too abominable to discuss. Campbell and Phillips gave a fresh reality to the extant passages in the classical corpus on Priapic ceremonials just as the seventeenth-century "voyages to Guinea" had once nourished Bayle's despiritualized presentation of pagan idol-worship. Even pious Joseph Priestley devoted a chapter to the *Licentious Rites of the Hindoo and other ancient Religions* in a work published in 1799.

In 1786 Richard Payne Knight, a member of the Radical party in Parliament, a famous collector of antiquities, printed for the aristocratic Dilettanti Society a treatise with engraved illustrations entitled *A Discourse on the Worship of Priapus,* which aroused so grave a scandal that he called back such copies as he could. At about the same time Sir William Hamilton was collecting examples of the survival of the Priapic cult in what were ostensibly Christian festivals in the Naples area. D'Hancarville's commentaries on obscene gems were transparently pornographic in their intent, but he also made a serious attempt to interpret the significance of the Bacchic rites and the worship of the bull with some awareness of the sexual symbols in his *Recherches sur l'origine et les progrès des arts de la Grèce* (1785).

Two of the greatest aestheticians of the age, Diderot and Winckelmann, had discovered an underlying relationship between sensual love and religion and had adopted this insight as a key to their comprehension of Greek art. "Thus I cannot help believing," wrote Diderot in the *Essai sur la peinture* (1765),[13] "that when the people took pleasure in watching nude men in the baths, in the gymnasia, and in the public games there was in the tribute which they paid to beauty an admixture of the sacred and the profane, a sort of bizarre intermingling of libertinism and devotion." Since Greek art was in the service of religion and since the worship of sensual beauty was incorporated into the cult the two realms interpenetrated. Humans had been models for the gods; in turn the physical attributes of the idealized divinities, when perceived in an individual outside of the temple, rendered the passion they aroused sublime and sacred. "A woman had provided Thetis with feet, Venus with her bosom; the goddess returned them to the people sanctified and divinized. A man had provided Apollo with his shoulders, Neptune with his chest, Mars with his sinewy thighs, Jupiter with his sublime head, Ganymede with his buttocks, but Apollo, Neptune, Mars, Jupiter, and Ganymede returned them sanctified, divinized." [14] In Winckelmann's famous history of art the Greek love of the young nude figure became at once the secret of Hellenic religion and of sculpture. "The highest beauty is in God. The idea of human beauty perfects itself by reason of its conformity and its harmony with the Supreme Being," he wrote in the *Geschichte der Kunst des Alterthums* (1764). Diderot's aesthetics were of course never free from his philosophical crusade against Christianity, and he eschewed such high-flown Platonic language; his "theory" led him to write one of the most whimsical sacrilegious passages of the age, a fantasy of how delightful Christian religion and art might have been had the same Hellenic mingling of earthly love and divinity been incorporated into the major figures of Christianity. "What if the virgin Mary had been the mother of pleasure, or even the mother of god, what if it had been her beautiful eyes, her beautiful breasts, her beautiful buttocks which had attracted the Holy Spirit to her and this had been written in the book of her history. What if the angel Gabriel were extolled there for his handsome shoulders, what if the Magdalene had had some affair with Christ; what if at the marriage of Cana, Christ between two wines, a bit nonconformist, had caressed the breasts of one of the bridesmaids and the buttocks of Saint John, uncertain whether he would remain faithful or not to the apostle whose chin was hidden by a light down; what would then have happened to our poets and our sculptors. With what spirit we would have described the charms which play so great and marvelous a role in the history of our religion and our God, and with what an eye we would regard the beauty to which we owe the birth, the incarnation of the Saviour and the grace of our redemption." [15] Whether one preferred the metaphysical *Schwärmerei* of Winckelmann or the crudities of Diderot the idea was being promulgated that among ancient pagans physical love and religion were emotions inextricably intertwined with each other.

Among the scenes chosen for illustration in the twelve volumes of Sylvain Maréchal's *Antiquités d'Herculanum* (1780–1803), fauns, silenes, nymphs, bacchants, centaurs, and centauresses in amorous embrace were not the least prominent paintings reproduced. When the rubble and the lava had been laboriously dug away a voluptuous ancient world was revealed to the amazed eyes of Christian Europe, which had once piously covered the nakedness of the ancients in their more passionate expressions. In the first Musèo Ercolanése established by the King of Naples, a separate section was devoted to the *priapi* discovered in the excavations. Since the refinements of historical periodization were not yet impediments to grand perceptions, the spirit of Herculaneum in the first century after Christ, its inhabitants caught in real life poses whose authenticity nobody could deny, became the true witness to the Spirit of Antiquity viewed as one undifferentiated whole. The militant atheist and libertine Sylvain Maréchal commented upon David's engravings of the Bacchic and Priapic ceremonials on the walls of Herculaneum with feigned embarrassment. "We find it difficult to conceive how the ancients, who have left us so many monuments of wisdom, who showed such delicacy and poise in all their habits, could allow themselves to consecrate a public cult to the secret parts of the human body whose very name when pronounced aloud would to-day make people blush and would outrage all proprieties." [16] But after this expression of conventional prudery he proceeded to resurrect a natural, noble, ancient religion at once dignified and appealing to the senses. "The aristocratic young girls were present at these ceremonies clothed in their most luxurious garments and they formed a part of the procession. They wore crowns on their heads and their breasts, half-naked, were bedecked with garlands of flowers. There is nothing at once more imposing and at the same time more voluptuous than these sacred parades of the ancients. It

seems that they strove to render their religion pleasurable." [17]
When under the Directorate Sylvain Maréchal became a theoreti-
cian of the theophilanthropic cult, the frescoes of Herculaneum
were brought to life in Paris.

The treatment of the Priapic rituals by eighteenth-century
writers is not easy to interpret, since many of their publications
served an exclusively pornographic purpose. Diderot viewed them
en philosophe, reveling in the antique association of frank sensual
passion and religion as an ideal. The love-life of the ancients was
thus shown to be as natural and uninhibited as the amorous ways
of the Tahitians in the *Supplément au Voyage de Bougainville;*
the passions of the ancients were rendered more sublime by being
identified with religion. But other writers, either out of prudence
or an affectation of prudery, refrained from openly accepting
Priapic cults in a literal sense, and to explain the ceremonials
they introduced elements of the old allegorism. The phallus itself was not being worshipped, merely the generative principle, a
male manifestation of divinity. "The great characteristic attribute," Richard Payne Knight pompously explained, "was represented by the organ of generation in that state of tension and
rigidity which is necessary to the due performance of its function." [18] D'Hancarville's commentary on primitive symbols related
to the worship of Bacchus, the image of a bull attacking an egg
with its horns, was in the same spirit. "For this bull, the first
Symbol of the Act of Creation, they later substituted Bacchus.
This mythological phantom took the place of the Generator of
all or the emblem used to represent power. That is why during
the change of conceptions the egg remained in the celebrations
of Bacchus." [19] And once the idea of sexual symbolism was discovered it was soon recognized in myriad forms throughout ancient art and literature.

Viewed against this background Charles Dupuis's *Origine de
tous les cultes* was not an anomalous performance, though it was
by far the most notorious, the most voluminous, and the most
pretentious. When Dupuis's primitive made the first attempts to
comprehend the order of the universe he too projected himself
into nature, but unlike the aborigine described by eighteenth-century adherents of the fear-theory, the part of his being which

he first read into the external world was not his terror but his generative faculty. The universe teemed with sexual symbols to the primitive, the only analogy he could make, and the earliest cosmographic myths and rituals of all religions were natural spontaneous equivalents of human behavior in love. The most sophisticated religions and philosophies were further elaborations of the relations between two polar principles, and the most complex theogonies were merely reflections of a sexual analogy, the interplay of masculinity and feminity. "The sky produces, but away from himself; he is therefore the father, for he produces like the male. The earth produces in herself, she is therefore female and mother of the effects which the sky causes to come forth from her fecund womb. Submissive to the sky who covers and embraces her on all sides, she sees in him the powerful husband who unites himself with her to render her a mother and without whom she would languish in eternal sterility wrapped in the shades of chaos and night. Their union is their marriage. The beings produced by them or which are their parts are the children." [20]

After ridiculing the priggishness of the Church Fathers, who in their polemics against the pagans had collected long descriptions of the heathen worship of sexual symbols only in order to excoriate the false heathen gods, Dupuis made use of their materials to illustrate his underlying proposition that all religions were in their remotest origins fertility cults. There was a profound need inherent in man to worship nature in its wondrous reproductive processes. The hermaphroditic symbolism of pagan religions, the Priapic cults, the Proserpinine myths, were not evidences of moral corruption but natural human reverence for life itself. This was the primitive natural religion, a noble sentiment which had welled up in the breast of Dupuis's aborigine.

The Dupuis conception had a strange antecedent in an inconspicuous French abbé, Charles Le Batteux, a member of the Académie des Inscriptions, whose *Traité des causes premières* had already propounded the monist thesis that all philosophies and religions were reducible to a conflict between two principles, one active and one passive, and had assimilated sexual symbolism in myth to this universal. Le Batteux in turn had related his idea to Ocellus of Lucania, whom he translated, but the Abbé has rarely been noticed while Dupuis's revolutionary theory was propagated throughout the western world.

The Dupuis text was a long tedious compendium in which examples from the sacred rites of all peoples throughout the world were arrayed to demonstrate that the fundamental *esprit* of early religion was an adoration of life-giving forces, a worship of nature, a union of an active and a passive principle. "These images, these symbolic expressions of the two powers of Nature were very simple and were first imagined in ages when organs of generation and their natural union were not yet accursed by the ridiculous prejudice with which they have become associated among the modern theologians and by the abuses of libertinism, the former out of a spirit of mystification and the latter because of the corruption of our species. The works of Nature and all her agents were once as sacred as she was; our religious errors and our vices have profaned them.

"The union of Nature with herself is a chaste marriage which all peoples have tried to depict, and the union of a man with a woman was a natural image of this union, even as their organs were expressive emblems of the two powers which manifest themselves in heaven and on earth, united among themselves to produce all beings." [21] In Ocellus, among Greeks who knew the Egyptian mysteries, in Plutarch and in Cicero, above all in Proclus' commentary on the *Timaeus*, Dupuis found antecedent references to the symbolic union of the sexes, the attribution to the male principle of the origin of stability and identity and to the female principle of the origin of diversity and the mobility of beings.

Boulanger too had made myths fundamentally cosmographic but whereas he was dominated by a perception of destructive natural forces, Charles Dupuis saw in myths only creative beneficent power idealized. The mood had changed. The fear-theorists of mid-century had portrayed the primitive world in dark hues; Dupuis reflected the great optimist outburst of energy in the French Revolution and the Directorate. Fear was banished and nature was described as endlessly fecund, bursting with diversity, with an interplay of masculine and feminine elements. Religious practices were not melancholy diluvian dirges disguised, but joyous Priapic cults. The Hesiod myth of the castration of Uranus was not associated with the primeval desire to kill the father. Dupuis rather stressed the second half of the myth for his sexual interpretation. His eye was on Aphrodite, the symbol of the reproductive process, born from the foam surrounding the amputated member which had been cast into the sea near Cyprus. Dupuis's image of nature is not mechanistic; it already bespeaks the new romantic organicism. Writing in the free uninhibited spirit of *An* III of the Republic, a rare moment in modern history when *idéologue* savants discussed sexuality with freedom and ease, before the religious repressions of the nineteenth century were imposed, Dupuis could view the ancient myths as pulsating with fertility symbols and become honored as one of the great theoretical minds of the Directorate.

In the elaboration of his theory Dupuis departed from his phallic monism and allowed for two fundamental forms of religious and mythic symbol, one astro-physical and the other sexual. They really mirrored each other. The sun was adored as a life-giving force, an extension of the idea of fertility. In one sense this is a mere continuation of physical allegorism in Chrysippus, Zeno, and Philo of Byblus, recognized even by eighteenth-century Euhemerists as a reasonable interpretation for some myths. Later mythology and religion were for Dupuis invariably the scientific communications of the ancients, allegoric presentations by priests and sages of what men knew about the natural world, and they differed from modern science only in their peculiar and extravagant poetic form, not in their content. Charles Dupuis was an astronomer who had the approval of Lalande and he could identify the precise factual information about the heavens which a sage of Chaldea or an Orphic hymn-composer had tried to express in his most flowery odes.

Dupuis's manipulation of the details of ancient religions and myths is a tour de force; hardly an item in an Asian, Greco-Roman, or American myth or religious ritual but becomes either astronomic or sexual. Solar myths were particularly amenable to this treatment because they concentrated on the movements of the heavenly body which was the great source of life and fertility and thus combined both erotic and cosmographic symbolisms.

Christ, Apollo, Orpheus, Hercules, Buddha were allegorical
representations of the sun to which men instinctively turned
with adoration when they worshiped fertility. The "natural" character of astral worship was a common interpretation of pagan religion; it can be found in the classics, was propounded in Maimonides' tractate on idolatry, and was frequently repeated in the
eighteenth century. In the Dupuis emendation of the theory the
planets were adored not as symbols of rational intelligences who
ruled the lower spheres in the Aristotelian hierarchy of being,
but as symbols of sexual creativity. Man revered the sun and the
stars for their direct life-sustaining qualities, not as ministers of
an unknown Supreme Being.

Astronomic and sexual symbolism were always supplementary,
not contradictory, forms. The generative image was perhaps more
primitive and the scientific observation more priestly, but both
were natural worship sharply distinguishable from theology in its
bizarre contemporary form. Directorate theophilanthropy was a
kind of nature and science worship, and Dupuis provided it with
an origins-of-religion theory. The new cult could thus resume
where the ancient religions had left off. Men could again become
simple adorers of science and productive nature, and the fanatical
superstitious ages of theological Christianity could be obliterated
from the memory of mankind. Antique man and modern man
would thus be worshiping their gods in the same natural way.
Only the dismal clericalism of the intervening ages of Christian
theology would be repudiated. Dupuis, like Court de Gébelin,
made it possible to assimilate the religion of pagan antiquity into
man's consciousness as a respectworthy, natural effusion, an affirmation of life.

Like all allegorists Charles Dupuis had to face the problem of
why the ancient priestly astronomers and seers had expressed
themselves through myths. By the end of the eighteenth century
he had available a wide selection of pat theories from which to
choose: allegory was a natural primitive language of communication, it was an Oriental speech manner, or it was imposture. Dupuis's "system" was composed of bits from all these rationaliza-
tions of the mythic form, though he leaned toward the idea that
it was a conscious sacerdotal device. For the ancients there was no

division of labor among theologians, scientists, poets, and clerics. "The priests were everything, they were the repositories of all knowledge about nature, the painters and the singers about nature. To lend more dignity to their lessons they adopted the rhythmic style of poetry. The number and harmony of the verses reflected the regular movement of the celestial bodies and of their periodic revolutions. The musical chords imitated the universal harmony. They seized upon grand figures, drew grand images, to elevate themselves, so to speak, to the level of their subject. In singing of the gods, they wanted to appear inspired by them, filled with a sort of enthusiasm which would draw them out of their normal states and from the ranks of ordinary men.

"They had recourse to the marvels of fiction to pique the curiosity of man, almost always a lover of surprising tales, and to astound him with prodigies in order to win admiration and respect for their lessons. They covered the sacred body of nature with the veil of allegory which hid it from the profane, which only allowed it to be seen by the wise man who had believed nature worthy of his researches and his study. Nature only showed herself to those who loved her truly and repulsed culpable indifference; this she abandoned to the errors and prejudices of the ignorant. To these she only presented herself under a monstrous exterior and under bizarre forms more appropriate to terrify than to please." [22] Mythology was thus a physiology of nature written in a poetic-allegorical style. It contained the theories of antiquity on "causes." Pausanias and Julian the Apostate among the ancients and Bacon among the moderns were authoritative corroboration that the sages of Greece never expressed themselves directly, only enigmatically. The need to allegorize in order to make science appear more sacred was universal among the gymnosophists of India, the priests of the Druids, the hierophants of Phoenicia and Egypt. In Dupuis the Deist double-truth doctrine survived in a new guise.

There is very little that is novel in this explanation of the formal aspects of myth, for virtually all the arguments had been proposed by the great pagan apologists when they were challenged with the ridiculous and vulgar myths by the early Church Fathers. The Stoic pagans, however, had tended to discover moral homilies

in myths, while Dupuis concentrated exclusively on sexual symbolism and astro-physical scientific truths. In this new allegorism
Dupuis was directing himself primarily against the Euhemerist-
historicists who still held sway in popular eighteenth-century
works on mythology. "We shall therefore conclude that mythology
is not the history of men and does not contain the most ancient
annals of the human species disfigured by the hand of time, but
the history of nature and of causes written in an allegorical style,
in conformity with the genius and the taste of the ancient philosophers and above all of the Orientals. Consequently we shall with-
draw Uranus and Ge from the number of the first monarchs and
their reigns from the records of chronology." [23]

Christianity was the most difficult religion to integrate into his
system. While the origins of the Oriental and north European
pagan cults were lost in the dim past and hence amenable to the
broadest conjectures, Christianity had been born in historic times
when documents were available. Yet here, too, Dupuis maintained that, like the cults it overthrew, Christianity was in its
essence a formulation in allegorical terms of the truths of astronomy and physics. In many ways his theory leveled a more devastat-
ing attack on traditional Christianity than had the *philosophes*.

"We shall destroy with one and the same blow the errors of the
people and those of the new philosophers and we shall strip Christ
of his two natures at the same time. The people made of him at
once a God and a Man; the philosopher today makes of him nothing more than a Man. As for us, we shall not make of him a God
at all; still less a Man than a God, for the Sun is further from
human nature than it is from the divine nature.

"Christ will be for us what Hercules, Osiris, Adonis, and Bacchus were. He will share in common with them the worship which
all peoples of all countries and all ages have rendered to universal
nature and to its principal agents; and if he seems to assume a
mortal body, like the heroes of the ancient poems, this will be only
the fiction of a legend." [24]

Charles Dupuis's became the final French philosophical version of the eighteenth-century problem of the origins of the gods.
When in 1804 Destutt de Tracy published a one-volume *Analyse
raisonée* of Dupuis's work which he had himself prepared, the

leader of the *idéologue* school gave the theory its official accolade. In his preface he described the difficulties which he had had, characteristic for the age, in assimilating mythology into his system. "The myths, above all those of the enlightened peoples of antiquity, pained me. I found there too much intelligence for them to be devoid of meaning." [25] He had tried de Brosses's "excellent treatise" and Court de Gébelin's "ingenious researches" without achieving satisfaction. Only with the appearance of Dupuis was the mythic world suddenly illuminated. For Destutt de Tracy these volumes became the ultimate scientific disproof of religious revelation, the conclusion of the great controversy, the argument to which there could be no reply. "Citizen Dupuis has fulfilled the double purpose of deriving all religions from Sabaism and of destroying them." [26] Nothing could cause the priests, who doted on rivalry, more concern than a demonstration that all the gods were merely variant names for heavenly bodies, "because the first of their passions is the hatred of their colleagues." [27]

The *Origine de tous les cultes* was soon translated into English, German, and Spanish, and whenever in the early nineteenth century avowed atheists or unitarians needed an interpretation of religion that was naturalistic and "scientific" they turned to his volumes as authority. Dupuis even made his way across the Atlantic and became a source-book for those American intellectuals who were interested in such recondite problems.

4

John Adams and the Gods

*W*HEN the venerable ex-presidents of the United States, John Adams and Thomas Jefferson, were finally reconciled to each other in 1812, their readings on the character and provenance of the Indians, the origins of religion, and the nature of mythology were among the subjects they discussed in an exchange of tender letters. Politics were avoided. Both of these eighteenth-century Americans had been deeply immersed in French philosophy and had collected grand libraries of world knowledge during and after their embassies in Paris. Their religious views were nonconformist. Adams was probably a unitarian in the Priestley manner, though that fiery exile had narrowly escaped prosecution under the Alien and Sedition Laws in 1799 during his presidency; Jefferson was a Deist, at times even more sceptical. In the first decades of the nineteenth century they were still militant anticlericals, untouched by the new wave of romantic religiosity which was sweeping over Europe.

Throughout his life John Adams had read quantities of English Deists and their orthodox opponents. The nature of Christ and immortality, the significance of revelation, the meaning of spirit and matter, were problems about which he had an enduring curiosity, and if he often expressed vexation with the refinements of theological quibbling, he does not seem to have been able to turn his back on this vast flow of religious literature. Since in Deistic controversy the distinction between the teachings of Christianity and pagan religion was a central issue, Adams had explored the rival English views on the character of heathenism from Cudworth through Priestley. A good portion of Adams' comments on

271

the writings of the English divines, particularly those which concern the nature of God, has been printed.[28] In his declining years Adams branched out in his interests, turning from the more parochial Christian debate to an intensive reading of French and English works which raised harrowing questions about the history of early pagan cults throughout the world and touched on the very essence of religion itself. The unpublished marginalia in his books, now in the Boston Public Library, and the Letter-Books in the Massachusetts Historical Society show that during this period of his life he studied Charles Dupuis, Court de Gébelin, Hugh Farmer, Jacob Bryant, Sir John Malcolm, and Sir William Jones with assiduity. He knew a number of the French Euhemerists like Banier and Fourmont at least by name. Perhaps it was Jefferson, who in July 1813 had sent him a copy of Priestley's *The Doctrines of Heathen Philosophy Compared with those of Revelation,* who reawakened his curiosity about pagan religion. By 1814 Adams was already perusing Priestley's *Comparison of the Institutions of Moses with those of the Hindoos and other Ancient Nations* and was making annotations which suggest that he was at least thumbing his Dupuis.[29]

Adams' marginalia in the mythographers are not as impressive as his commentaries on political works. His notes in the twelve volumes of Dupuis are rather sparse, consisting for the most part of repetitions in the margin of key names from the text. Only rarely did he break loose to express his irritation with Dupuis's atheism. A footnote reference to primitive monotheism was an opportunity: "Very true. It destroys your work, de fonde en comble. Nor have you proved it to be an error." [30] A quotation from Hesiod disturbed him: "Earth created heaven, imagined many gods! True! But Men have discovered one only God." [31] Reference to Thomas Hyde's claim to have identified spiritual conceptions of God among the Persians evoked a vehement "No! No!" [32] Dupuis's confession that but for his wife he would have thrown his manuscript into the flames and a flamboyant dedication to her elicited one word: "Silly." [33]

When Adams finished Dupuis, he turned to the nine folios of Court de Gébelin. On his readings in this abstruse and turgid interpreter of the primitive world we possess a far more extensive

running commentary written in a shaky hand. The aged John
Adams, ploughing through volume after volume of learned accumulation of nonsense, reacted in a most confused manner. He
does not seem to have understood the author's central theme,
which to be sure is far from crystal-clear, but he remembered him
as a friend of the American Revolution and his observations
tended to be generous. Court de Gébelin's long-winded proclamation of an eternal order and his denial of a cyclical principle
brought forth exclamations. "Huzza! Court!. . . . How beautiful!
how sublime! how divine! is such enthusiasm! May thy kingdom
come and thy will be done on earth as it is in heaven." [34] But the
affirmation of the universal concept of Need bewildered him. "Is
the foregoing passage natural or revealed Religion or both?" [35]
Court de Gébelin's plea for civilizing world savagery touched off
Adams' old antagonism to the idea of perfectibility. "We see not
the End. We can foresee no end of the weakness, Ignor[ance]
and corruption of mankind." [36] Court's exultation in the intellectual triumphs of the Enlightenment was countered with a pessi-
mistic "The beginning of the 19th Century has been de movais
Augure." [37]

"Thou reasonest well," he praised Court de Gébelin on mythography. "Cumberland, Banier, Fourmont, Huet, Le Clerc confuse
each other." [38] But he was not convinced by the pretension that
myth had finally been explicated through the new symbolism.
"This veil is not removed by all the studies of Gébelin, Bryant,
and Dupuis. Darkness still hangs over the deep. . . . I must consent
to this in a degree, yet much remains to be done. The Allegorists
are not yet agreed in all points." [39] The total denial of the imposture theory seemed to him too sharp. "Court is too good na-
tured! He does not attribute enough to the studied and interested
duplicity of Priests Philosophers and Politicians." [40] At one point
he became so captivated by Court de Gébelin's etymologies, particularly a recondite tracing of "Khow," that he added to the
catena from his own memory. "The Milk Maids at Padington
call 'Kiow' still." [41] Adams had obviously retained something of
his reading in Dupuis on fertility cults. In the margin of Court
de Gébelin's functional explanation of the god Fricco he noted:
"Phallus, Phallus. I blush to write this word: but the meaning of

it is so important in all Ancient Religions that it cannot be omitted." [42] Yet Dupuis's materialism was against the grain. "The Unity of the Universe its Author Government and end are the sublimest conceptions of which any intellect is capable. Dupuis may call the Active Power Matter if he will. I call it spirit and I know what I mean as well as he does." [43]

Court de Gébelin's prophecy of the benefits that would be visited upon mankind by the institution of the Great Order drew dark reflections from the old man. "Will Gout Stone Fever and Old age be all cured. . . . Ancient Reveries and declamations. Fine Fancies! Preachers of Order and public Felicity are laudable and useful when they understand themselves. But the French Philosophers and even Court himself, did not. . . . But what would he say in 1817. The Age is not come. The Order is not arranged. The Reign of Saturn has not yet been born. You must have lived many years after 1800 to celebrate such Facts in your divine Numbers." [44]

Despite his antiprogressism Adams seems to have been favorably impressed: "If Court's work is a system, it is as admirable as it is extensive. It does honor to human Nature and has been useful to Mankind. No Man can read it without being richly rewarded for his Time and pains." [45] When Adams then noted that "Bryant and Dupuis and Jones all illustrate and corroborate his theory," [46] one wonders whether the profusion of learning had not overwhelmed him, for these rival mythographic systems hardly resemble one another. Adams was perhaps at his best in catching minor errors. When Court de Gébelin reported on the inscriptions on Dighton Rock near the river "Jaunston" which Professor Stephen Sewall of Harvard had sent him and identified them as Phoenician since "the peoples especially around Boston are of an oriental race," [47] Adams meticulously changed Jaunston to Taunton.

Adams had also read the mythological interpretations of Jacob Bryant and Sir William Jones more or less simultaneously. Bryant's three-volume work entitled *A new system; or an analysis of ancient mythology wherein an attempt is made to divest tradition of fable and to reduce the truth to its original purity* was first published in London, 1774–1776. It is an eclectic potpourri based on borrowings from French contemporaries, impossible of analy-

sis, though it had sufficient appeal to warrant a third edition in
1807 and W. Holwell compiled *A mythological, etymological and
historical Dictionary* by making relevant extracts from it. The
author's own words must speak for him. "My purpose is not to lay
science in ruins; but instead of desolating to build up, and to
rectify what time had impaired: to divest mythology of every
foreign ornament; and to display the truth in its native simplicity:
to shew that all the rites and mysteries of the Gentiles were only
so many memorials of their principal ancestors; and of the great
occurrences; to which they had been witnesses. Among these
memorials the chief were the ruin of mankind by a flood; and the
renewal of the world in one family. They had symbolical representations, by which these occurrences were commemorated;
and the ancient hymns in their temples were to the same purpose.
They all related to the history of the first ages; and to the same
events, which are recorded by Moses." [48] This thinly disguised
plagiarism from Boulanger was combined with a theory of primeval sun-worship, a diffusionist thesis which fixed upon the
Amonians as the original transmitters of ancient religion, and a
system of etymology which traced the names of virtually all the
gods in the world to combinations of a few basic radicals.

Adams read Bryant in 1817, and by this time he had become
something of a comparative mythologist himself. "Gebelin, Bryant & Dupuis all boast of discoveries and all agree in the Ignorance
of the Greeks and the Romans." [49] When Bryant called the expedition of Jason to Colchis a fable, he demurred. "Something
mysterious, however, under all this." [50] The Amonian theory
never quite satisfied him. "How come the Amonians to substitute
the Sun for Noah. . . . Bryant has found a key; Gebelin has found
another." [51] A note indicates that he had in the meantime also
read Sir William Jones's essay *On the Gods of Greece, Italy, and
India* which was published in the first volume of *Asiatic Researches* in 1799 and was reprinted in the third volume of his
Works in 1807; from a letter of June 23, 1817, it seems that Adams
was partial to the diffusionist thesis of this pioneer orientalist.

At this stage in his life Adams could be stirred only if something
he read associated itself in his mind with one of his perennial
idées fixes such as a hatred of priestcraft or opposition to empire-

building. When Bryant mentioned the lost authors of antiquity he was moved. "Have all these authors been destroyed by accident or design! Superstition Fanaticism Priestcraft and Despotism have been burning fiery furnaces for offensive Books in all ages, down to the Missionary who boasted that he had burned 1500 Manuscripts in India. Man! how long will you continue to put out your own eyes. To be your own wilful deceiver, tempter and tormenter?" [52] The last volume contained a warning to his countrymen. "Americans! Have a care form no schemes of universal empire. The Lord will always come down and defeat all such projects." [53]

On the flyleaf of Bryant he composed a summary of his studies in the new symbolism, not a bad conclusion in its way. "This vol. was printed in 1775. Court de Gebélin's in 1777, Dupuis in 1790, finished in 1780. Though they must have been all employed in the Research at the same time they do not appear to have had any communication with each other. Each claims the discovery. Each challenges the honour of Novelty and Original Invention though they all agree in the Allegorical System. Bryant had the Stave. Gebelin is the clearest and simplest writer."

The scant marginalia of this period, whose every word John Adams fashioned laboriously and with extreme physical difficulty, are, however, only a faint distorted reflection of his extraordinary preoccupation with the gods of paganism. The true witness is in the Letter-Books of the last decade of his life. His dictated correspondence preserved its full intellectual vigor, forthrightness, and dry humor to the very end.[54]

Adams had first raised the subject of Charles Dupuis with his learned friend in Monticello in a letter of September 30, 1816. Originally his curiosity had been piqued by remarks appended to Priestley's work on the Hindus; he wrote to Europe for information about the author and he set about devouring volume after volume of the text. From this date until his death in 1826 Dupuis's *Origine de tous les cultes* became a fixture of the Adams correspondence not only in the letters to Jefferson, where he was often parading his erudition in a self-conscious manner, but in communications with sundry other intellectual friends and acquaintances — Judge Van der Kemp, Spofford, Waterhouse,

Reverend Colman, Du Ponceau, Alexander B. Johnson. A message to Lafayette included the request that he procure for him a copy of Destutt de Tracy's summary of Dupuis. Whatever the specific subject of a letter, if it remotely bordered on philosophical or religious questions, Charles Dupuis invariably cropped up; no other author is mentioned with comparable frequency.

To guard his son, the future President, against becoming a "champion of orthodoxy," Adams pressed Dupuis upon him and then Bryant, Voltaire, Court de Gébelin, and the sacred texts of India and Persia. While extolling Dupuis's erudition Priestley had labeled him an atheist. This *ad hominem* argument was no valid refutation to the lawyer who in his younger days had defended the most unpopular causes. At issue was the truth of Dupuis's astrological theory of any religion, including Christianity, which veered away from simple monotheism.

During his last years, though Adams was still easily vexed by the recollection of bitter political memories or by "false" histories of the American Revolution, he was becoming more and more absorbed in ultimate metaphysical issues. A letter of May 16, 1816, to Jefferson revealed his constant wrestling with the problem of evil. As a solution he tried a recognizable eighteenth-century amalgam of unitarianism and Lucretian psychology: "After all, as grief is a pain, it stands in the predicament of all other evil, and the great question occurs, what is the origin, and what the final cause of evil. This, perhaps, is known only to Omniscience. We poor mortals have nothing to do with it, but to fabricate all the good we can out of all inevitable evils, and to avoid all that are avoidable; and many such there are, among which are our own unnecessary apprehensions and imaginary fears." [55] He seems to have sought answers to soul-searching questions in the labyrinth of Charles Dupuis's *Origine de tous les cultes*. Jefferson replied in a lighter vein to the announcement of this formidable task: "Your undertaking the twelve volumes of Dupuis is a degree of heroism to which I could not have aspired even in my younger days. I have been contented with the humble achievement of reading the analysis of this work by Destutt de Tracy in two hundred pages octavo." [56] By November Adams had read eight of the volumes. Dupuis's scientific treatment of Christianity on the same footing with pagan religions had not, Adams assured his friend, caused him to renounce the Christian religion. Far from it; he had become confirmed in his general unitarian position, a great admiration for the purity of Christianity, and a profound distaste for its corruption by clericalism. "The ten commandments and the sermon on the mount contain my religion." The Dupuis revelations had so troubled him, however, especially the author's thoroughgoing materialism, that he proposed a diversion of the moneys collected by the National Bible Society to convert the heathen in the dark continents to an analysis of the work. "Would it not be better to apply these pious subscriptions to purify Christendom from the corruptions of Christianity than to propagate these corruptions in Europe, Asia, Africa, and America? Suppose we should project a society to translate Dupuis into all languages, and offer a reward in medals of diamonds to any man or body of men who would produce the best answer to it," he wrote to Jefferson on November 4, 1816.[57]

Dupuis's marshaling of the varieties of pagan religious experience, ancient and modern, had shaken him morally; this was for him no mere intellectual curiosity. The mythographers had fired his loathing of priestcraft. Letters to Henry Channing inveighed against the "old black Regiment of Priests"; he challenged Jefferson to work for the abolition "of polytheism in any form and to unfrock every priest who teaches it, if you can." The violence of his letters made it abundantly clear that the polytheism which he denounced was not restricted to the contemporary Hindus and savages but included the Church of England and Roman Catholicism. The religious revival of Restoration Europe had outraged him, particularly the persistence of laws against blasphemy. While his friend Jefferson had become enmeshed in the practical problems of building the University of Virginia Adams was lashing out at Roman popery with the violence of an eighteenth-century Voltairean. The historical spectacle of the religious differences among men and the chronicle of persecutions conducted by all religions led Adams to preach sermons on absolute intellectual tolerance and to profess a Joblike humility in the face of one God. "Let the human Mind loose," he wrote to his son on November 13, 1816, "It must be loose. It will be loose.

Superstition and despotism cannot confine. And the conclusion must be that Musquito's are not competent to dogmatisse."

Adams really preferred Dupuis among the mythographers. There he found more new ideas than in all the others put together. And if he did not understand the intricacies of Dupuis's argument, he read him in the original spirit and intent of the author. "Is there any work extant so well calculated to discredit corruptions and impostures in religion as Dupuis," he asked Jefferson on December 12, 1816. Though he sometimes self-deprecatingly referred to "all his learned lumber," the mythographers continued to be his main philosophical inspiration. When Sir John Malcolm's *History of Persia* and the works of Sir William Jones were added to Bryant, Dupuis, and Court de Gébelin, he took off on flights of fancy rarely associated with his stolid patriarchal person. He envisaged a Council composed of Gébelin, Bryant, Jones, and Dupuis during which they would live together, supported by all mankind, compare notes, and perhaps reach a conclusion. In his enthusiasm he forgot that all of them were dead.

The mythographers whose works were seething within him produced strange contradictory moods which he freely expressed to Jefferson. At moments, he confessed, he was on the verge of breaking out, "This would be the best of all possible worlds if there were no religion in it! ! !. . . . The very prospect of Mankind, which these books have passed in review before me, from the most ancient records histories traditions and fables that remain to us to the present day, has sickened my very soul, almost reconciled me to Swift travels among the Yahoos." As the fundamental cause for the prevalence of superstitious religion he clung to the traditional fear-theory in its Lucretian form, like most European intellectuals. "Fears and terrors appear to have produced an universal credulity. Fears of calamities in life and punishments after death seem to have possessed the souls of all men." Though Adams used Dupuis against the orthodox religionists he drew back from French atheism and materialism. His own profession of faith had been delivered to Professor Gorham on January 28, 1817, in a quaint formula after he had sustained the full barrage of Dupuis's philosophy, "I believe with Father Abraham and Sir Isaac Newton in the existence of Spirit distinct from Matter, and resign to the Universal Spirit the Government of his Heavens and Earth."

Perhaps the most revealing testimony of the profound effect of the mythographers upon the octogenarian duke of Braintree was embodied in a fantasy which he shared with Jefferson on July 18, 1817. If he were only twenty, he mused, had a million dollars and a library with a million volumes, he would write that great work of synthesis which Turgot had contemplated all his life. And how would he do it? "I would digest Bryant, Gebelin, Dupuis, Sir William Jones and above all the Acta Sanctorum of the Boland-ists."

John Adams died a mythographer *manqué*.

CHAPTER VI

Counterattack from the East

"Now if we consider this history seriously, is
there any more foundation and philosophy in
it than in our novels! For hundreds of years
men, left to themselves, went about yelping,
then howling, then speaking. What a philosophy! For hundreds of years men were painting,
then abbreviating, then allegorizing, then,
heaven knows how, discovering letters. What a
plan!"

— Johann Gottfried Herder, *Aelteste Urkunde des Menschengeschlechts,* in
Sämmtliche Werke, VI, 393.

1

The Magus of the North and his Disciple

*I*N KÖNIGSBERG on the borderlands of the Slavic world was born the great denial of the western evolutionary conception, which from a faltering beginning in Fontenelle, through de Brosses, Boulanger, and Holbach, had gained ever greater momentum until it culminated in the Turgot-Condorcet idea of progress. The Germanic easterners took Rousseau to their bosoms, questioned the moral value of the arts and sciences, scorned the new European civilization which was being foisted upon them by enlightened despots slavishly imitative of the French in manner and style, and proclaimed the greater profundity of the natural primitive over the artificially cultivated. They turned the eighteenth-century world of the *philosophes* topsy-turvy.

For a century French *esprits forts* had been unveiling the ancient world to discover in it the heart of darkness, the source of fanatical superstition, the origin of evil. The more buoyant optimists among them triumphantly proclaimed the conquest of the wild forests of aboriginal man; the sceptical, with controlled despair, doubted human nature and feared that the *ingens sylva* might again overwhelm civility. But reason remained the common criterion both among the enthusiastic believers and the men without faith for weighing and judging the historic fortunes of humanity. Apart from a few convinced Rousseauists, adulators of the historical primitives were still rare in western European thought. The rationalist early man whom the natural rights school admired was a mere hypothesis without body, not a flesh and blood primitive. Most *philosophes* turned away from the primordial with repugnance, as they would from the foolish and the ignorant.

The Deists and the French *philosophes* had conquered large segments of German intellectual opinion in the eighteenth century; their adepts, open and covert, were ensconced in Frederick II's academy in Berlin and they ruled the University of Göttingen. Gotthold Ephraim Lessing's *Nathan der Weise* was a dramatization of Deist philosophy, and his Freemasonic addresses were manifestoes of the rationalist spirit. The relations of paganism to Christian revelation, the nature of the ancient mysteries, above all the character of the early history of mankind, its primitive language and religion, were earnestly debated among small groups of intellectuals, islands of culture in the Germanic world, who waited for one another's opinions with bated breath as confirmation or refutation of the theoretical position they had adopted. The correspondence of these men, scattered among the different duchies and kingdoms, is a profuse record of their parochial controversies, for unlike the *philosophes* of Paris they did not meet together in a few salons and cafés. The French and the English had posed the initial problems for them, and in the middle of the century most young men like Herder were still adapting and modifying western solutions. But in the last decades before the French Revolution an indigenous German countermovement was launched, and the world of primitive mankind became a strategic philosophical strong-point which the men of the east hoped to take by storm. The prize was rich — domination of the spirit of modern German culture.

The reversal of values was a reactive force of great potency. In the new Germanic gospel the primitive was the creative, the strong, the religious; the rational was the decadent, the weak, the impoverished. Johann Georg Hamann, the Magus of the North, was its prophet and its Pietist roots were deep. But while Hamann's thought, phrased in a consciously fabricated, cryptic style, full of symbols and enigmas, was not readily communicable, the transports of his disciple Herder possessed generations of Germans in rebellion against Frenchifiers and facile western philosophy. The ideas from the east reecho in Goethe and Heyne, in the romantics and Hegel. Herder's vision of the *Urvolk,* in

which God, truth, and beauty, music, religion, and poetry were
fused in a harmony has had an enduring influence in European
thought. These German writers transmitted a new conception
of culture which became the great counterpoise to the rationalist
idea of civilization as the progress of the arts and sciences.

In 1758 at the behest of a Königsberg businessman young
Hamann undertook a secret mission to the Russian Ambassador
at the Court of St. James, the winning of Hanseatic autonomy
for the Baltic cities, which at the outbreak of the Seven Years'
War the merchants expected and hoped would be overrun by
Russia. His brief diplomatic career was a fiasco, but after tasting
of the pleasures of mid-eighteenth-century London, on Palm
Sunday 1758 he experienced a religious conversion. When he returned to East Prussia he brought back not a trunkful of Deists,
the usual intellectual import, but the works of the English mil-
lenarians and the theological writings of Isaac Newton.

In *Dichtung und Wahrheit* Goethe has paid homage to the
impact of this towering leader of the antiphilosophical crusade
on the younger generation of German writers. Sneering at current mechanistic solutions to problems of the origin of speech
and writing and religious mystery the Magus of the North re-
affirmed divine creation. With bitter irony and consummate
logic he demolished the whole slew of popular hypotheses of the
Enlightenment which found the driving forces of mankind in
sensation and utility. Paradoxically, Hume became one of the
sources of this counterrevolution against philosophy, for he had
denied that reason was the original source of religious feeling.
Hamann welcomed the arguments of the English antichrist and
turned them against the rationalistic German Deists who
swarmed through intellectual society, the Meiners, the Lessings,
the Starcks. But while Hume had reduced the font of religious
emotion to a mere animal passion, for Hamann its true origins
lay in revelation alone. Operating through the vehicle of man's
animality God had bestowed religion and language and writing
upon a being who was at once divine and animal. These provi-
dential gifts which distinguished man from beast could never
have been the end products of mere accumulated experience,
physiological development, learning through pain and pleasure,

imitation, and the rest of the causal stock in trade of eighteenth-century sensationalist philosophy. In a comical excursus against Helvétius, whose *De l'esprit* was for Hamann the *reductio ad absurdum* of mechanism, he caricatured the *philosophe*'s primitive man who had laboriously acquired the habit of eating by watching and copying the animals.[1]

A fresh reading of the Bible inspired the new German vision of the primitive world, as Vico's reliving of the Homeric epic had directed him to pierce the cloud hovering over barbaric mankind. Hamann taught Herder to appreciate the poetic language of the early books of Moses not only as revelation in the traditional sense but as the most sublime act of creation, the divine made human through the word. Herder's elucidation of this "oldest document of the human species" was unlike any Scriptural commentary which had ever been composed before. It was not a reconciliation of contradictions in the manner of the rabbis; nor was it an interpretation of the cosmography of Genesis in the light of astrophysics; nor did it borrow from the textual analysis of the newborn seventeenth- and eighteenth-century higher criticism. Herder studied the Bible for its graphic portrayal of the historic primitive Hebrews; and the quality of genius which he found in their early language was, *mutatis mutandis,* to be discovered in the myths and epics of all primitive peoples.

The key to the Hamann-Herder interpretation of Genesis lies in their inversion of the common eighteenth-century appraisal of the relative merits of the concrete and the abstract. The concrete now became the natural; the pictorial was not crude and obfuscatory but more powerfully human. The abstract was incomprehensible and arid. A revulsion against abstraction in language and philosophy was the single dominant emotion which sustained the enigmatic writings of Hamann. He was forever in search of new biting epithets and images from common, even vulgar language with which to puncture abstract ideas and reveal their emptiness, their balloonlike inflation, their vapidity. In his rage he ridiculed all general terms as empty bags and wax noses, thieves and murderers. Only the concrete, the graphic, the emotion-laden word was real in the sense that it bore profound meaning for man, a creature of emotion and passion. The words of the Bible, the habit in which God chose to clothe His first revelation, were earthy, specific, sensate, natural, full of feeling, not cold, metaphysical, abstract concepts. When He spoke to man He did not express His truth in syllogisms, propositions, scientific terminology, but in the words of Everyman.

There was an easy possibility that this argument might be misunderstood, that Hamann might sound as if he were in the commonplace tradition which explained the wide usage of myths, fables, parables, allegories by the wise rational legislators of antiquity as a utilitarian mechanism necessitated by the poverty of vulgar understanding. Hamann subscribed to no such twofold philosophy. The imagery of the Bible was not a practical limitation required by benighted primitives. "All mortal creatures are able to recognize the truth and the essence of things only in parables." [2] God spoke a pictorial language because that was the only language capable of moving man. Figurative speech was not allegorical and not a disguise; it was the language closest to reality. Abstraction destroyed existence and truth. Any later rationalization of experience in abstract terminology inevitably corrupted, demeaned, and degraded it. This central insight which coursed through Hamann's thought had already been expressed in the *Tagebuch eines Christen* he wrote in London at the time of his conversion. There he heaped ridicule upon the modernist commentators on the Bible who tried to read the scientific systems of Aristotle, Descartes, and Newton into the living words of Genesis. Herder later echoed him in his mockery of the rationalist interpretations of the chapters on the creation as phantasies of atoms and comets by an angelic scientific collegium (*Physisches Kollegium*) .[3] God spoke the living language of man in all its existential fullness and emotive body, not the desiccated jargon of science and philosophy. This was the original revelation, the whole word, neither moral fable nor covert science, but the living word of God made human in passionate speech. The reason of Descartes, Newton, and Leibnitz was not a universal tongue, as the *philosophes* in their arrogance supposed, but the private speech of individuals which had to be taught to be understood. The language of Man was in the Testament.

Spinoza's *Tractatus,* the fountainhead of modern heresy, had also analyzed the Bible as an ancient historical document of the Jewish people. The crucial difference lay in the nature of the history which they saw in the Bible. Spinoza examined it as a mundane social and political compilation; Herder was awestruck by the outpourings of the inspired ancient Hebrews, the first people to voice in poetic diction the relations of man and God, of man and nature, a prototype for the mythologies of all the peoples of the earth. The vividness of the Biblical imagery, its reflection of the religious spirit in a specific oriental environment, was not a limitation of the sublime. Religious man had to express himself in concrete geographic and physical images. When a theologically minded Newtonian read the word "earth" in the Bible he thought of the abstract sphere of the physicist. In Herder's commentary earth meant the sod, the real earth out of which man's primitive hut was molded and the earth of the worms to which he was destined to return. It had color and texture. The darkness of Genesis was a thick reality, not a metaphysical concept of the void. The Bible, like all primitive creations, evoked dramatic personal experiences for Herder. "Whoever on the desolate open seas, surrounded by night and the fear of death, has hoped for the dawn, he has felt this spectacle." [4]

Vico, Turgot, and Hamann would have stood together in their conviction that the history of language contained within itself the true history of human thought. But they would come to a quick divide. Vico looked upon the Enlightenment movement toward abstract rational speech as an inevitable accompaniment of the humanization process, though he was at once appreciative of the vigorous language of early barbarism and fearful of the overrefinements of the last stages of rationality before the coming of the new barbarians. Turgot heralded the age when this movement would have reached its ultimate goal in the creation of a new universal means of communication, probably a set of mathematical symbols, from which feeling would be banished forever. Turgot and Condorcet longed to free reason from the toils of language because this primitive form was invariably passion-ridden. Hamann and Herder viewed every attempt to introduce general terms as a sign of degeneration, decadence, dehumanization. Progress for them meant restoration of the primitive sen-

sibility and the poetic forms of expression which had existed
before metaphysical abstractions had dried up the imagination
of man.

While the underlying genetic conceptions in Winckelmann's
history of ancient art did not fit neatly into the eighteenth-century
dialectic of the concrete and the abstract, the romantic Hellenism which his theory propagated was soon harmonized with the
German thought-system molded by Hamann and Herder.
Though he had strayed from the fold he was one of the few
Germans whom they recognized as an ally, while Moses Mendelssohn and "Nathan" Lessing were rationalist "metaphysicians
bound to the rotten wood of their system," [5] at least to Hamann.

Winckelmann's revolution in the canons of taste, his preference
for an idealized Hellenic image over the Rome of Augustus, was
a parallel to Herder's cult of the creative early ages of mankind.
Though Winckelmann adopted the common eighteenth-century
history of human perception as a passage from the concrete-
primitive to the abstract he was never committed to the positive
worth of the progression, which seemed so patent to English and
French thinkers — and above all he never demeaned the concrete. In *Versuch einer Allegorie besonders für die Kunst* . . .
(1766) allegory was exalted above later rationalist forms of
speech and writing because it was more *wesentlich,* afforded men
"a true picture of things," and was more "natural." [6] Through
his unorthodox appreciation of the "oldest artists of Greece"
Winckelmann independently moved in the Hamann-Herder direction. In the commentaries to the *Monumenti antichi* (1767)
the allegories of the ancients both in their poetry and in their
sculpture were recognized as responses to the same profound
human need for a bridge from immediate experience to the
exalted realm of the transcendent. And for Winckelmann as for
Hamann and Herder the symbolic was not conceived as a rational
abstraction, but as sensuous corporeal imagery; and far from
being a mere expression of rude peoples alone, though it had its
beginnings among them, the symbol was an enduring spiritual and
emotional requirement of mankind. "Nature and the essence of
divinity, being abstract and remote from matter, are above the
understanding of our limited intellects which are restricted to

concrete objects. Nature can only be grasped in the guise of symbols." [7] Winckelmann wrote the *Versuch einer Allegorie* to inspire contemporary artists to bring about a renaissance of ancient allegory.

2

The Genius of the *Urvolk*

*H*ERDER WAS DISTINGUISHED from virtually all the western theorists in one vital respect: the divine revelation took place not in an individual, all men being equal, or in an archetype of a primitive, all aborigines being identical in the state of nature, but in the *Volk*. The *Völker* were at once the same and different. While the birth of the idea of God and the genesis of myth were in form similar historic events among all nations throughout the world, each people had enacted a unique version of the drama. In the Vichian evolution of religious consciousness after the flood, historic parallels and common elements among the myths of peoples at the same stage of development were the heart of the inquiry. Though Boulanger had hypothesized a substantial number of postdiluvian bands surviving and had recognized variations in myth among the nations, he too was intent upon their similarities. Hume's primitive was in all times and places the same man, a stereotype. The orthodox Christian who abided by the Biblical tradition recognized the unvarying sameness of idolatry. By contrast Herder's theory of the *Volk* focused upon divergences. Religion and mythology were the central character-forming agents, the crucial experiences of every *Urvolk*, and each history was a separate individual manifestation of the creative organic capacity of mankind.

In Herder's *Ideen zur Philosophie der Geschichte der Menschheit* (1784–1791), by far the most influential eighteenth-century work propagating the antirationalist philosophy of history, the *Volk* was a primeval historical concept, not a biological one, a crucial distinction. A single species, man, had through time acclimatized itself to a great diversity of physical environments which had yielded myriad variations in human nature. In its native habitat, in the area where a "natural" people had lived since the beginning of time, a mystical symbiotic relationship had been fashioned between a *Volk* and its *Klima*. The normal man's attachment to his native soil was passionate because his whole biological and his psychic structure had been molded by the land. Robbed of his homeland he would lose the sustaining element of his being. From contemporary travel literature and Raynal's *Histoire philosophique* Herder excerpted pathetic accounts of the horrors of the slave trade and the sufferings of Negroes torn from their native Africa; of Greenlanders in Denmark dying of nostalgia for the forbidding North; of Indians languishing in urban exile. To allow the *Volk-Klima* relationship to unfold naturally, slowly, in the spirit of its origins was the morality of history. When outsiders intervened, they broke in upon the wedlock of a natural people and its agelong inhabited land, in violation of divine law which intended all organic forces to come to full fruition. They committed sacrilege against history.

Klima was not the creative drive of the *Volk*. The climate and geography affected innate tendencies, modified but did not determine original character, did not compel. Perhaps some day its general effects would be measurable if someone wrote a *Geist des Klima;* but the motive force of the *Volk* was found elsewhere — in *Genesis*. Herder communicated his intense sense of the organic nature of man in dithyrambic descriptions of the birth of a pulsating organism. He did not know how to define the organic power which gave life to a creature. It was not reason, that was certain, for reason was always an alien faculty in the body. I live, therefore I am, he announced in a romantic manifesto. Only a set of adjectives could conjure up the spirit of the life-giving power: "Innate, organic, genetic . . . it is the foundation of my natural strength, the inner Genius of my being." [8]

In the battle eternal between *Genesis* and *Klima*, *Genesis* was the tough, hard core, refractory to change; it was the creative essence of a people which molded its national character. *Klima* was composed of a vast number of small causes which invaded from all sides, gradually, sometimes imperceptibly, until they reached the center of being and with the aid of habit ultimately succeeded in affecting the core itself. But in the beginning there was *Genesis*. Herder's great works on Hebrew poetry and the folk-songs of the nations were attempts to penetrate the individual genius of peoples, to reveal the spirit of the *Urvolk* stripped of its fortuitous alien historical accretions.

Rapid transfers of nations from one *Klima* to another had never yielded salutary consequences. The histories of military conquests, commercial possession, and missionary conversions of primitives were tragic. Both Romes, the ancient and the modern, great organizing powers, were for Herder destructive, not creative forces. They crushed the *Volk* genius of many peoples and were themselves sterile. The modern conquerors of savage nations, full of European arrogance when they arrived, ended by being swallowed up by the illnesses of the new climate; they could not adapt their natures quickly to the environment, hence they languished and died. The conquered too, forced to bend themselves to the way of life of the conquerors, did violence to their own genius and fell into decadence. The moral lesson of his history was that European arts and sciences, for all their stormy power, would not succeed in transforming overnight the new lands of the savage world into areas of civilization. In this conflict of environment and genius changes required time; abrupt transformation led to defeat and death.

A healthy national spirit only flowered in the habitat where it had grown for centuries, during which the genius of the people and its climate became intertwined with each other in a life-producing embrace. The genius of a *Volk* and the climate were sexual partners of creativity only when they were harmonious with each other. Herder did not exclude alien influences, but when men of a folk migrated they had to fashion themselves to the character of the new climate and slowly, laboriously, with the passage of time allow their novel genius and the influences of the land to interpenetrate. An organic relationship had to be established between the foreign plant and the soil. Then genius might again blossom. But if there were an attempt to force unduly the organic processes of nature, disaster would follow and the plant would yield only corrupted, poisoned fruit.

This was a historical conception with a new texture. It did not break with the prevalent eighteenth-century idea of the unity of mankind nor with many aspects of Locke-Condillac sensationalism; but the workings of environment were different from those envisaged by most of the mechanists. *Klima* did not act upon a *tabula rasa* but upon a living *Volk* that already had a genius. To the French sensationalists time was not a vital element in the process of change because each creature was completely malleable; revolutionary metamorphoses in human nature were feasible if methods could be devised to rid men of the incrustations of custom and prejudice. A European could transform the savage world at will; an enlightened despot if vested with enough power could alter the beliefs and way of life of his people to accord with the simple rules of rational philosophy, irrespective of their primitive genius, were they Frenchmen, Russians, or Magyars. Time and the customs implanted by time had produced the lies of tradition, but these could be wiped away in one grand sweep of reason. In Herder's conception of the *Volk* genius, time occupied the central position in the social process. Man could change only at a certain tempo, and there was good and evil change. If an attempt was made to expunge an existing *Volk* way of life rooted in *Genesis* and to impose European rationalism, the end was likely to be an annihilation of the creative power of existence itself. Beings were organic, not mechanical.

In Herder's conception of plenitude the nations, to use his favorite musical analogy, were like combinations of tones played upon the harp. National entities were all the chords which had been or could be produced. In a real nation as distinguished from an artificial one the combination produced a perfect harmonic whole. Nature in its fullness at some time had to give birth to all possible variations. If a conceivable harmony did not exist, or failed of ultimate expression, there was a flaw in the perfection of nature and, what was inconceivable, a fault in nature's God. History was the necessary expression, through the creation of nations with distinctive patterns, characters, geniuses, of all possible harmonies of which Providence was capable.

And the quintessential expression of a *Volk* genius was myth.

3

Herder *Mythologicus*

*H*ERDER'S EARLY ESSAYS at a theory of primitive religion
and mythology were something of a hodgepodge. He had read
the English Deists and French *philosophes* and the major conjectures on the birth of the gods in Hume, de Brosses, Boulanger,
almost as soon as they appeared. In a fragment of the sixties he
still accepted the fear-theory in the version of the "Weltweise"
Hume. But by the seventies he was already mocking it boister-
ously in the name of a rational civil theology and a teleological
philosophy of history.

The fragment which his son entitled *Von Entstehung und
Fortpflanzung der ersten Religionsbegriffe* is transitional.[9] Herder there dealt with the earliest inchoate religious perceptions
in a dim infancy of the race. At this stage there are yet no peoples with definable national characters. While he emphasized the
differences among fashioned specimens of humanity, he clung to
the idea that in the very earliest pre-*Volk* stage, distinctions were
still insignificant. Individuation only appeared with time. The
very first religious perceptions of all peoples were thus virtually
identical. Since primitives had had no previous experiences they
were like children in a continual state of wonderment and terror
whenever a new phenomenon of nature intruded upon them.
Out of their incapacity to explain ordinary events they created
individual gods who were either the sources of terror or beings
who could allay fear. The primitive utilitarian producing the
gods out of his creative psyche was by the late sixties a hackneyed
conception in England, France, and Italy, and Herder at this
period was not completely emancipated from its influence. The

whole world of nature seemed capable of harming or helping, causing pain or pleasure, and its various parts were divinized in the pantheon.

From the age of terror man advanced to the point where he was more at rest, there was more sabbath during which he could reflect on the nature of things. Then his curiosity impelled him to seek out origins and ask about the beginnings of the world of language, of men, of his own *Volk*. During this formative period each *Volk* independently developed ideas which appeased its devouring curiosity: a cosmogony, an anthropogenesis, a philosophy of good and evil, a genealogy of ancestors. Stage one, the religion of naked fear, gave way to a religion that was a historical-physical philosophy. There had been no precipitous leap from terror into rationalistic cause-seeking. Herder the organic philosopher was profoundly conscious of the residual elements of primeval human experience. The soul of the barbaric ages was still nourished "with conceptions of a strong, crude, corporeal character." Man's theological-philosophical answers to his first queries about the nature of the world were deeply rooted in the wild emotions of the earliest period of human existence. The rationalist explanations of causes preserved their primitive religious coloration. Since men had not yet completely emerged from the epoch of placating gods of terror when they asked themselves cosmogonic questions, their answers were myths of divine intervention.

The particular type of myth which each nation invented was, however, dependent upon the climate, the environmental conditions under which they lived. Whereas in the rationalistic myths of origins of the western Europeans man who made the gods projected a psychic nature which was universal, in Herder it was the *Volk,* molded during misty ages by climate, which poured its unique character into the gods. "The Scandinavian built his world out of giants of frost, the earth out of the corpse of Ymir, the sea out of his blood, and the sky out of his head. . . . Everywhere these primeval theological-philosophical-historical national traditions were dressed in a corporeal, pictorial language which could attract the curiosity of their people, fill their imaginations . . . delight their ears. . . . These earliest sources of knowledge had to be poetic, they touched upon the most vital subjects of a nation. They were built out of the most powerful ideas of the crude times. . . . They incorporated everything that was solemn and terrifying in the religion of their fathers. These poems came out of the mouth of the pious early world. They were so drawn up that children and the common people learned them and they became the favorite songs and proverbs. Their purpose was to bind the audience together, to keep it true to its national origins. The language in which these ideas were presented was full of images, concrete expressions, empty of abstractions and scientific conceptions." [10] With the exception of the idea of the *Volk* as the vehicle for this primitive religious development we have encountered many of these conceptions before in de Brosses, in Boulanger, and in Vico. But again the Germanic world of the east, in adopting western European theories, infused them with a spirit that was completely alien to the rationalism of the *philosophes*. The primary religious expressions of the various *Völker* preserved in their myths and folk-songs and epics were the grand creative moments of the nation's existence. A *Volk*'s idea of beauty and its aesthetic inventive power were indissolubly bound up with this first primitive religious effusion. Nothing a *Volk* produced throughout the centuries of its later growth and maturity would ever equal the rugged beauty of the poetry which emerged spontaneously from the *Volk* spirit in response to religious questionings at a time when mankind was still living under the violent emotional pressure of terrible images of the nature gods. When Herder inquired into the original "thinking of the nations" he found it steeped in the religious traditions of the first fathers of the peoples, clothed in poetic rhythm and language. The mythological epics told of the beginnings of a nation's most ancient marvels. Were it possible to gather the epics and myths and songs of all primitive peoples one could constitute for barbarism a "spirit of the original traditions and mythological poems" as Montesquieu had written a Spirit of the Laws for his civil society. But perhaps the political-philosophical character of humanity was today too "genteel" to permit a "philosophical history of these poetic times" to be composed. And yet how much there would be to learn from these early years of the childhood of the race.[11] The French *philosophes* had been intent upon stamping out this primitive, not learning from him.

Once Herder had recovered completely from his flirtation with rationalist philosophy, his theory of religious origins became an admixture of theology and history, a combination which Kant could not abide in his former student. Religion was no longer a naturalistic phenomonon, but divine intervention in an even more intimate sense than Vico's birth of the gods. The revelation, however, was still made manifest in historic forms so that it was never quite divested of naturalistic elements. To the Judeo-Christian world God's revelation had been most complete. It was emotionally all-embracing because the tongue of the Hebrews chosen by Him was a perfect vehicle for the communication of religious truth and the genius of the place, the Holy Land, an ideal setting for the enactment of the drama. But this revelation to the Hebrews was not a unique occurrence in time; with variations the performance was repeated again and again in the early moments of existence whenever a *Volk* was born. Among the Hebrews the word of God was made real in the Bible; among the gentiles revelation assumed less noble forms. Hieroglyphs and religious mysteries were symbolic divine interventions of the same general order as Mosaic revelation, the local *Volk* variations depending upon the physical landscape which had originally shaped the soul of the people. "That the Egyptian hieroglyphs deal with knowledge of the gods and of nature only a Warburtonian head can deny." [12] Through sinfulness and the vice of sensuality the divine revelation to the heathens was rendered impure, but in its origins a pagan mystery was a sublime truth garbed in a national costume. When Hamann and Herder defended the religious worth of the mysteries they were aiming their polemical darts at those of their German contemporaries who interpreted pagan rituals as prefigurations of Christianity or as a stage in the progressive moral uplift of man.[13] The mysteries were not academies of natural religion *à la* Starck, the author of *De Tralatitiis ex gentilismo in religionem christianam,* whose appointment to the Faculty of Theology in Königsberg had so outraged Hamann, nor schools of rational philosophy, nor ancient Freemasonic lodges, nor a stage in Lessing's *Erzieh-*

ung des Menschengeschlechts. The mystery, like the Mosaic revelation, had originally embodied the whole of divinity. A religious
truth was not communicable in driblets and was no more amenable to rational improvement than was language. Religion in any
people was a total creation, not a partial one. It might be polluted by sensuality, as it had been among the pagans, but it was
not subject to a Lockian progression, to development through
experience.

Mythologies of nations were like geographies of their poetic
souls; there were different configurations as there were different
landscapes. These distinctive expressions of the nations were almost impossible to communicate, one to another. A European
could never really comprehend the Eskimo's idea of God, Herder
demonstrated in a long colloquy in the *Geschichte der Menschheit.* In the late sixties and seventies Herder ridiculed the French
theorists of primitive religion who interpreted myths in terms
of universal, not local, perceptions of nature, *idées fixes* like the
flood or utilitarian symbols. They were merely projecting themselves as abstractionist *philosophes* into the primitive world instead of comprehending the emotional, sensuous character of the
Urvolk. A primitive people was bound to its limited geographic
area and its poetic imagery reflected not general ideas but a particular place. Each primitive folk song was unique, with a quality
which was not repeated elsewhere. The waters of the Egyptian
religious myth were not obsessive recollections of the universal
deluge but mirrors of the Nile and its characteristics. Boulanger's
monist theory of myth was an easy butt of his irony in the *Fragmente zu einer Archäologie des Morgenlandes* (1769): "The
deluge everywhere that there is water, wherever water is poured,
wherever one washes with water." [14] The bridge builder had to
have a *Wasserphilosophie.*

Since de Brosses had raised the problem of Egyptian brute-
worship Herder had to fit these practices into his system. He
too rejected allegorical interpretations of zoolatry, but while de
Brosses could not contemplate these rites without revulsion even
when he explained them, Herder eulogized them as a natural
religion. God created man among animals; the primitive Egyptians lived in close proximity to their beasts and they compre-

hended their spirit and their feelings. The Egyptians were not alien to the animal world like modern citydwellers and there was nothing startling about their feeling divinity in these creatures. "We? What is an animal to us? In our palaces, in our *Raisonnemenskreisen,* in our piles of stone withdrawn from everything in nature, what is an animal to us? Who looks upon it except for play or pleasure or for system-making? Who can sense invisible divinity in the beast and learn brotherhood from him? But look here, my dear bookish, titillated philosopher, just ask the ordinary countryman, the shepherd, the hunter, inquire of the times of Aesop, of Homer, of the dawn of the primitive world what an animal was to man! . . . how much has been learned from animals by men according to the traditions of all nations. You want to deny all this. Not so! Lies. Pose. Your *développement des arts et des sciences* is far more philosophical and finer — good! Go see what the man who lives among animals still learns and observes from them. Now let us look deeper. In a newly settled land, in the primordial world, men and beasts are brothers who understand each other, who teach each other and live together as equals." [15] Primitive men, like shepherds and countryfolk in all ages, could communicate with beasts, learn from their ways, understand their language. They could perceive the divine in every living creature and in every organic growth. The Egyptian worship of the phallus was a natural adoration of the generative power incomprehensible to the coy "pucelles" of France. Herder declaimed with the passion of a man who knew the peasants of the Slavic world on whose borderlands he had studied and worked. The gods were symbols of nature, not rationalist allegories. They expressed the sensuous world of primitive man whose emotions were more acute than his reason, who was close to the earth and its creatures, who felt himself an integral part of the organic universe and kin to all living things. The early religions were like primitive poetry, the embodiments of what men experienced in the immediate geographic world in which they were born. Herder did not dismiss the medicine men, magicians, and shamans of the primitives as deceivers, for they were the men who gave shape to the *Volk* feeling for the external environment at an early stage in its national history. Through

religious traditions, through myths and education they perpetu-
ated this original way of perceiving the world. They were true
seers.

Early in *Vom Geist der ebräischen Poesie* (1782), Herder
wrestled again with the ancient fear-theory of the origins of the
gods and the terrible attributes of the jealous Biblical God. "The
hypothesis is old . . . but I am afraid it is as false as it is old," [16]
was the new conclusion. To be sure, there were elements of terror
in many primitive religions, especially among peoples who lived
in desolate areas, near great rocks, volcanoes, or raging seas, but
these were exceptions. The whole world was not an eternal deluge, nor was it a fiery Vesuvius. With the same categoric certainty with which he had once accepted the fear-theory he now
assured his interlocutor in the dialogue that the religion of peoples in gentle landscapes was benign and that even in the most
horrendous circumstances the existence of a good spirit was never
denied. The cruel images of the gods were blamed on later
priestly corruptions. Their multiplicity in early religions, the
universal animism of primitive man, was only a reflection of his
closeness to nature. Early mankind perceived the beauty and
goodness of God in myriad forms. The imaginative poetry of
the ancient Hebrews who recognized the existence of nature
geniuses did not lead them to polytheism. To make nature alive,
to draw parallels between heaven and earth, only rendered the
primitive adoration of order in the universe more profound.
The Humean arguments against original monotheism were reversed through a romantic pantheist interpretation of the
Psalms. "Suddenly a rustle is heard through the tree-tops; He
speaks, He lives; Divinity is present. The savage sank down and
prayed. This is the history of the feeling of all men." [17] In the
spirit of Hamann, Herder participated in the adoration of the
primitive savage. He was far from the detached Humean observer of this historic moment; he was there with the primitive
on his knees, trembling and worshiping. Herder's "direct feeling" was superficially akin to Hume's quick sensibility; only
Hume had rejected it as a source for a philosophical view of the
world and Herder in the spirit of Rousseau passionately em-
braced it.

The Herder conception of myth received its most significant scholarly application in the classical studies of Christian Gottlob Heyne. Their intellectual relationship, cemented by the friendship of Heyne's son-in-law, the explorer Johann Georg Forster, was expressed in a steady voluminous correspondence. His treatises are unlike Herder's long tirades and for the most part appeared in Latin in the staid publications of the Göttingen academy, but their central thesis was the same as his. "Mythology," he wrote in an introduction to a *Handbuch der Mythologie aus Homer und Hesiod* (1789) by one of his disciples, "is in itself the most ancient history and the most ancient philosophy. It is the conceptual world of the oldest legends of the *Volk* and the race expressed in rough speech. And in this respect it assumes a new significance as the residue of the most ancient way of imagining." [18] Had we received the myths intact in their early form we would have recognized this truth immediately, but the original myths have been so distorted by later writers that they have often become mere latter-day artistic fancies and have almost lost their worth as reflections of the primitive world. But for all that, myths still preserve the "nobility and the worth" of the early dawn of antiquity and they can inspire those who know how to fathom their meaning. Heyne established interesting distinctions between the *sermo mythicus,* the original spontaneous outburst of *Volk* feeling, and the *sermo poeticus,* the elaboration of the myth by the conscious creative artist. His scholarship was impeccable, his editing of texts in the great tradition, but for all the appurtenances of learning the spirit which animated him and generations of German *Gelehrte* was the same romantic Hellenism which possessed his literary compatriots in the eighteenth century.

In fact, the German revision of the Enlightenment view of the barbaric world culminated in an epoch-making work of philological scholarship, Friedrich August Wolf's *Prolegomena ad Homerum* (1795). His learned demonstration that the existing Homeric poems were mere compilations of the age of Pisistratus and that Homer was nothing more than a name for a cycle of rhapsodies which had been transmitted orally by bards from more ancient times before the alphabet was known among the

Greeks touched off a controversy which rocked the intellectual
world of late-eighteenth-century Germany. To destroy the unity
of Homer, the repository of civil wisdom, and to transform him
into a tradition of folk poetry was as iconoclastic as Jean Astruc's
fragmentation of the Bible. Strangely enough the *Prolegomena*
was received unfavorably by both Herder and Heyne and their
reviews called forth intemperate ripostes from Wolf, but the
mutual criticism, the pedantic in-fighting, should not obscure
the fundamental agreement on principle among these rival German revealers of the Homeric world. Even their sources of inspiration were the same. Though none of them knew Vico's
Scienza Nuova until after the publication of their major works,
they were influenced by mid-eighteenth-century English conceptions of Homer and popular poetry. Both Thomas Blackwell's
An Inquiry into the Life and Writings of Homer (1735) and
Robert Wood's *Essay on the Original Genius of Homer* (1769)
had depicted Homer as an expression of the Greek poetic spirit
at the moment of its emergence from barbarism but before the
stultifying customs of civilized society had crushed spontaneous
feeling. Macpherson's *Ossian,* published between 1760 and 1765,
aroused universal admiration in the Germanic world; and Herder
quickly established an analogy between the Caledonian folk poet
and the Greek. The equation of the mist and fog of the Ossianic
forgery with the clarity of Homer may now seem preposterous,
but when men were determined to extol nature poets, early
artists, the spontaneous rather than the sophisticated, they could
be lured into the new mood through the contemplation of fakes
as well as by authentic relics of the primitive world. Herder was
taught to appreciate the grandeur of the *Naturvolk*'s poetry by
reading Ossian, as Winckelmann was moved to enthusiasm for
Hellenic perfection by his study of late Roman copies of Greek
sculpture. Heyne, the great editor of classical texts, the meticulous philologist, was driven to affirm that the true spirit of
Homeric poetry could only be learned from contemporary
travelers and the savages themselves — an opinion in which
he was supported by Forster. Though Wolf never went quite as
far as Herder in defining the primitivism of the original Homeric
poems, he too preferred the earlier to the later elements in the

text, Homer the bard to the Homer who was the education of urban Greece. True, the English romantic passion for popular ballads and folk songs was a forerunner, but only among the Germans did this reverence for the primitive become so profoundly embedded in scholarly and literary canons that it came to dominate the very conception of culture.

4

The Encounter

*T*HOUGH BAYLE and Fontenelle mournfully conceded the persistence of the primitive and the irrational, they declared war upon it. When Vico foretold the fall of mankind into the "dregs of Romulus" it was in the spirit of an Old Testament prophecy, a warning to humanity to mend its ways. Hume viewed the spectacle of the primeval birth of the gods with the same mingling of mild scorn and compassion with which he regarded a contemporary fanatic. When de Brosses reported on the residual elements of zoolatry in higher stages of civility he did so with sadness, with a feeling that though this might be the inevitable fate of man, these monstrous fetishes should be combatted. When Boulanger and Holbach identified the effects of the trauma of the flood on mankind they hoped to cure the historic patient. The French and English *philosophes* had wanted to cast off every last remnant of primitivism. Christianity and Judaism were great evils to the rationalist radicals because they were still imbued with a primordial religious spirit; they were survivals from the mythic age of mankind. Identities and conformities among all religions proved that they had a common source in terror-stricken mankind. The meagre truths in myth were at most a low-level form of knowledge of necessitous brutish man.

In the Turgot-Condorcet conception of scientific progress the western denial of the mythopoeic and affirmation of the rational attained its ultimate expression. Turgot was led by his worship of reason to prefer the purest mathematical abstraction over any other form of knowledge and to look upon the metaphors and images in which the ancients communicated their ideas as a sort

of baby talk, expressive perhaps, but a form which had to be outgrown. Eighteenth-century French thinkers were conscious of the
death of the poetic spirit in their society and they did not regret
it. In 1800 Madame de Staël, whose ideas of progress were derivative from Turgot and Condorcet, prognosticated the total eclipse
of poetry as the spirit of philosophy and positive science came to
dominate mankind.

For Turgot the progress of knowledge was solidly safeguarded
by the new symbolic forms which had been invented since the
Renaissance. Once mathematics had become the universal language of science intellectual progress was emancipated from the
historical vicissitudes to which the ordinary spoken vernaculars
were subject. Mathematical language set up an impregnable barrier against retrogression. The social sciences alone seemed for
the moment to be standing apart; but their submission to mathematics was the inevitable next stage of the development. In the
formula no room was left for the vague, for the exaggeration of
enthusiasts, for superstition, the great vices of mankind. With
the mathematical control of the study of man moral knowledge
would find itself protected by the armor of numbers and equations, and moral problems would be removed from the disputes
of the marketplace where they provoked destructive violence.
In his last years Turgot, racked with the pains of illness, drew
consolation from the vision of humanity on the threshold of this
wondrous transmutation of knowledge, a leap comparable to the
passage of human speech from a myth-making, metaphoric, poetic
language to the relatively reasonable style of the contemporary
European world. As long as men relied upon rhetoric to express
themselves then truths would inevitably become polluted with
chimeras of the imagination. Even civilized languages, rational
instruments of communication though they were, had never succeeded in freeing themselves from their primitive origins and
remained encumbered with similes and imagery. There was always something suspect about an idea that was not mathemati-
cized.

In the past, scientific knowledge had been acquired rather
haphazardly, and as a consequence of unpropitious political and
social circumstances it had been stagnant for long periods at a

time. Only since the regeneration of the sciences through mathematics had a long succession of geniuses been steadfastly adding
to the body of knowledge and extending the dominion of science
over peoples who had once been blind victims of primitive superstitious belief or obscure theological reasoning. The new vista
opening before Turgot was the imminent application of the calculus of probabilities to human behavior, invading a whole moral
world from which mathematics had previously been excluded.[19]

When arguments in support of the inevitability of future progress were momentarily weakened by the spectacle of the real
world with its oppressive stupidity and irrationality, the triumph
of the mathematical spirit loomed as a bulwark. As long as the
knowledge of abstract relationships in the world was accumulating there was faith in the ultimate triumph of reason. The final
security lay in the existence of the equation. Princes might prove
weak and false but nothing could assail one's confidence in a
theorem.

With time, Turgot hoped, reason would occupy more and
more space in the finite area of the spirit, casting out the dis-
orderly passions and limiting severely the scope of the imagination. Emotion would be progressively blotted out until in the end
of the days there was only reason. The poverty of the spirit under
the hegemony of pure reason did not trouble the eighteenth-
century *philosophe* because in the world about him, steeped in
primitive prejudice, superstition, ignorance, and fanaticism, mankind had just begun to fight the battle of rationality. The prospect of an undernourishment of the passions and the imaginative faculties could not appear real to the men of Turgot's generation. The mathematical sciences had been pursuing appropriate analytic methods only since the end of the seventeenth
century. If measured against the background of all historic time
the reign of reason was still so young.

The Germans recoiled with horror before this "ice-cold,"
"belly-hungry" philosophy of the future. Herder reveled in the
primitive and its creations, its mystery of new birth, its character-
forming impress. For him genesis was the glorious moment, the
original eternal verity, and the later stages could at best preserve
what had once been revealed. The late in any culture was de-

cadent, rationalistic, Roman, ugly — this is the great prejudice which both Winckelmann and Herder tried to instill into western thought. Their influence was mightiest in their own Germanic world, among the romantic philosophers, in Hegel, in Nietzsche, in Spengler. As soon as a *Volk* emerged from the sheer terror and shapelessness of original mankind it achieved the sublime of which its character was capable. Few nations have been able to preserve the original spirit of the *Urvolk*, the energy-laden moment of its first existence. They have allowed themselves to be corrupted through alien imitation or they have been overwhelmed by conquerors. To lose the spirit of the *Urvolk* was to become incapable of creativity.

The later romantic ideologies of the Schlegels added little to Herder's counterattack against reason. To preserve the moment of *Volk* creation, its original religious nature, was the new ideal for humanity. To drive forth alien French rationality, so contrary to the spirit of man and above all German man, was the crusading slogan of the *Sturm und Drang*. Back to the *Volk* spirit primeval, to reinvigorate the German nation invaded by foreigners, humbled before strangers. A Prussian king speaking French was a humiliating denial of German nature. All primitives had something in common. To drink deeply of the wine of early Hellas or of primitive Hebrew poetry would strengthen the German soul; to adopt contemporary Frenchified reason would destroy the renascent creative power of the German *Volk* through the mimicry of bastard forms.

The Enlightenment of the west stood for clarity through analysis, for the precise and the mathematical, for the abstract as the most perfect expression of mankind. Hamann and Herder extolled the organic, the poetic, the passionate, the complex, even the murky if its images touched the emotions. "Poetry is the mother tongue of the human race." [20] Abstraction was an empty shell. Where was the ultimate truth to be discovered, in science or in the *aelteste Urkunde des Menschengeschlechts*, the first imprint of divine truth? That was the question. The battle was joined between those who saw in the primitive the spontaneous and the generative, and those who would resolutely banish the mythic from human consciousness forever.

And the war is far from over. Historians of the human psyche have warned that the mythic cannot be exorcised without danger to the soul of man and without his utter spiritual impoverishment. Western political society has generally refused the Germanic inversion of the evolutionary doctrine and has, at least until recent years, found its optimist ideal in the Turgot-Condorcet idea of scientific progress.

Epilogue

Since the eighteenth century the gods of Greece and Rome have died a second time. They have tended to disappear from our education, poetry, art, and fantasy. But even in death their hold is tenacious. And though most of us have forgotten their ancient attributes, we have continued to speculate about their origins and meaning.

Of the vast conglomerate of eighteenth-century theories on the nature of the gods the idea of the historical evolution of religion has since enjoyed the greatest amplification and the widest acceptance. The doctrinaires of the Age of Reason were the first to posit a unique primitive mentality and to attempt its definition. The nineteenth and twentieth centuries piled up mountains of empirical evidence confirming the older conceptions. For the eighteenth century the evolutionary theory had served a definite intellectual purpose: when the varieties of religious experience were ranged in chronological order, nature and nature's God were vindicated in what appeared to be one of the most aberrant manifestations of mankind, primitive religion. Historical reason had come to salvage Reason itself; and when historical reason was not sufficient apology, then the extreme psychological necessity of childlike humanity was introduced to sustain the new theodicy. In later systems of sociology and anthropology the law of the development of religion by stages adumbrated during the Enlightenment was expanded into a world-view of the growth of human consciousness.

The embryonic eighteenth-century idea that the character of the gods was determined by socio-economic systems has been most attractive to modern positivist historians. Without reference to Fréret, and often without a word for Marx, the various gods have been represented as expressions of sedentary or nomadic warrior

311

societies, projections not of primitive psychic torments but of
modes of production. The battles of the gods mirror primeval
conflicts among pastoral and agricultural peoples. Critias' notion
that the gods were deliberate political inventions — so appealing
to one branch of eighteenth-century thought — has given way to
interpretations which make of them spontaneous emanations of
social reality. In a variant of the same theme the pagan gods became ancestors and national heroes for the more militant new
states of modern times.

The mood of popular eighteenth-century representations of the
gods reflected in Euhemerism and in the visual arts has changed
fundamentally. The divinities who ornamented the gardens of
Cythera were symbols of pleasure and happiness; and love myths
told of playful seductions, not cruel rapes. Present-day mythographers — supported by the findings of archaeology — have accepted the bestial, cruel, brooding gods of the older fear-theorists
and have turned away completely from the more pleasant and
smiling deities, the gods with cornucopias, the pampered, pink-
fleshed gods of abundance and love, the gods who taught mankind
useful arts and sciences, the joyous gods. The depth psychologists
who are now probing the ancient myths discover in them an
eternal expression of the tragic drama of the human soul. Somehow the savage gods, at once bloodthirsty and cunning, demanding brutal sacrifices, are closer to our temper.

Plate I

HISTOIRE
DES ORACLES.

Plate II

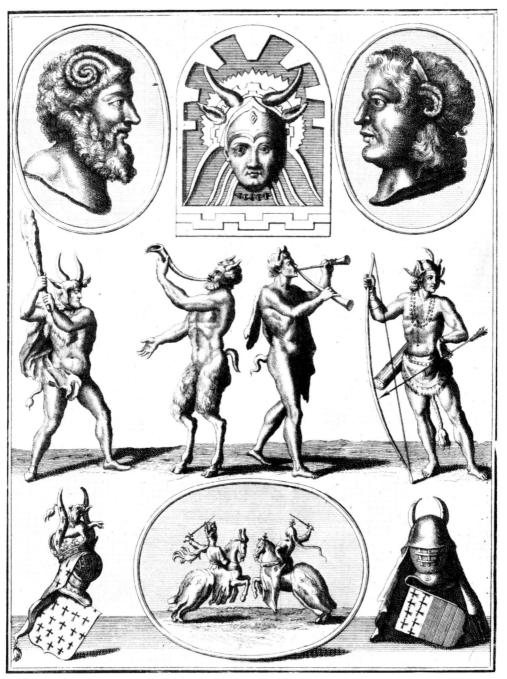

Plate III

Plate IV

Plate Va

Plate Vb

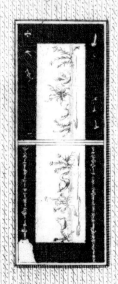

Plate VIb

Plate VIa

Plate VII

Plate VIII

Notes

INTRODUCTORY

1. Abbé Antoine Pluche, *Histoire du ciel considéré les selon les idées des poètes, des philosophes et de Moïse. . . .*, 2 vols. (Paris, 1739), was the original version. The 1740 edition was entitled *Histoire du ciel où l'on recherche l'origine de l'idolâtrie et les méprises de la philosophie sur la formation et sur les influences des corps célestes.* Other editions appeared in 1743 and 1757. The quotation is adapted from the English translation, *History of the Heavens* (London, 1740), II, 269–270.

2. Francisco Manuel de la Huerta, "Disertacion sobre si la mitologia es parte de la historia, y como deba entrar en ella," *Memorias de la Real Academia de la Historia,* I (1796), 1–34.

CHAPTER I

New Views of Pagan Religion

1. Marc Lescarbot, *Histoire de la nouvelle France,* 2nd ed. (Paris, 1612), pp. 651–877.

2. The original edition was published in Leyden, 1651; Thomas la Grue translated it into French (Amsterdam, 1670).

3. The French edition appeared in Brussels, 1704. The quotation is from the English translation, *The Agreement of the Customs of the East Indians with those of the Jews, and the other ancient peoples: being the first essay of this kind, towards the Explaining of several difficult passages in Scripture, And some of the most Ancient Writers, by the present Oriental customs . . .* (London, 1705), p. vii.

4. La Créquinière, *The Agreement of the Customs,* p. 26.

5. La Créquinière, *The Agreement of the Customs,* p. 92.

6. The Dutch original of Bekker's *De Betoverde Weereld* appeared in Leuwarden, 1691; German translation, Amsterdam, 1693; French in 4 vols., Amsterdam, 1694. Quotation is from the unpaginated preface of the English translation, London, 1695, only one volume of which was published.

314 Notes to Chapter I

7. Pierre Bayle, "Adonis," in *Dictionaire historique et critique* (Rotterdam, 1697), I, 109.

8. Bayle used the French translation (Utrecht, 1704). The original had appeared in Dutch as *Nauwkeurige beschryving van de Guinese Good-, Tand- en Slave-Kust* (Utrecht, 1704).

9. Jean Le Clerc, *Bibliothèque choisie, pour servir de suite à la Bibliothèque universelle,* VII (1705), 93.

10. Le Clerc, *Bibliothèque choisie,* VII, 97–98.

11. Matthieu Souverain, *Platonism Unveiled,* English translation (n.p., 1700), p. 71.

12. Bayle, *Réponse aux questions d'un provincial. Première partie,* in *Oeuvres Diverses* (The Hague, 1731), III, 571.

13. F. M. de Marsy, *Analyse raisonée de Bayle* (London, 1755), III, 105.

14. Bayle, *Pensées diverses sur la comète,* critical ed. by A. Prat (Paris, 1911), I, 180.

15. Pierre Jurieu, *Histoire critique des dogmes et des cultes* (Amsterdam, 1704), p. 407.

16. Bayle, *Pensées diverses,* Prat ed., I, 170.

17. Bayle, *Pensées diverses,* Prat ed., I, 169.

18. Bayle, *Réponse aux questions d'un provincial. Premiére partie,* in *Oeuvres Diverses,* III, 560–561.

19. The *Discours sur l'origine des fables* appeared as one of the addenda to the Paris, 1724, edition of the *Entretiens sur la pluralité des mondes.*

20. The *Digression sur les anciens et les modernes* was included in vol. VI of the 1715 edition of the *Oeuvres Diverses.*

21. Bernard Fontenelle, *De l'origine des fables,* critical ed. by J.-B. Carré (Paris, 1932), p. 17.

22. Fontenelle, *De l'origine des fables,* Carré ed., p. 32.

23. Georgius Moebius, *Tractatus philologico-theologicus de oraculorum ethnicorum origine, propagatione et duratione; ubi varia simul exponuntur oraculorum* (Leipzig, 1657). A third edition, 1685, had an addendum, *Cum vindiciis adversus A. van Dale.* There was a Dutch translation in 1687; it was reprinted in 1784.

24. Père Jean François Baltus, *Réponse à l'Histoire des oracles ... dans laquelle on réfute le système de M. Van D.* (Paris, 1707). There was a *Suite à la réponse ...* in 1708, which was translated into English (London, 1710).

25. Fontenelle, *Histoire des oracles,* critical ed. by Louis Maigron (Paris, 1908), pp. 1–2.

26. Fontenelle, *Histoire des oracles,* Maigron ed., p. 124.

27. Fontenelle, *De l'origine des fables,* Carré ed., p. 35.

28. Fontenelle, *De l'origine des fables,* Carré ed., p. 40.

29. Bayle, "Cainites," in *Dictionaire,* II, 721.

CHAPTER II

The English Deists

1. Ralph Cudworth, *The True Intellectual System of the Universe* (London, 1678), p. 308.

2. John Toland, *Letters to Serena* (London, 1704), p. 7.

3. The 1720 edition was in Latin. Quotation is from the English translation, London, 1751, p. 5.

4. John Toland, *Pantheisticon,* p. 56.

5. Toland, *Pantheisticon,* p. 98.

6. *La Contagion sacrée ou histoire naturelle de la superstition. Ouvrage traduit de l'Anglois* (London [Amsterdam], 1768) included a translation of *The Natural History of Superstition* in vol. II, chaps. XII and XIII.

7. John Trenchard, *The Natural History of Superstition* (London, 1709), p. 9.

8. Nicolas Fréret, *Lettre de Thrasybule à Leucippe,* in *Oeuvres* (London, 1787), I, 17–18.

9. Trenchard, *The Natural History of Superstition,* pp. 10–11.

10. Trenchard, *The Natural History of Superstition,* pp. 12–13.

11. Trenchard, *The Natural History of Superstition,* p. 13.

12. Trenchard, *The Natural History of Superstition,* p. 15.

13. Trenchard, *The Natural History of Superstition,* pp. 17–18.

14. Trenchard, *The Natural History of Superstition,* pp. 19–20.

15. Trenchard, *The Natural History of Superstition,* p. 28.

16. Anthony Ashley Cooper, First Earl of Shaftesbury, *Characteristics* (London, 1900), I, 297–298.

17. Shaftesbury, *Characteristics,* I, 24.

18. Shaftesbury, *Characteristics,* I, 12.

19. Shaftesbury, *Characteristics*, I, 13, 16.

20. *The Independent Whig*, December 31, 1720.

21. Trenchard, *The Natural History of Superstition*, p. 41.

22. Trenchard, *The Natural History of Superstition*, pp. 53–54.

CHAPTER III

The Euhemerists and Isaac Newton

1. Cambridge, King's College Library, Keynes MS. 139; London, British Museum, Landsdowne MS. 788, folios 44–56; Sloane MS. 3208, folios 49–67b.

2. Père Etienne Souciet, *Recueil de dissertations critiques*, vol. II, *Contenant un abrégé de chronologie, cinq dissertations contre la chronologie de M. Newton, une dissertation sur une médaille singulière d'Auguste* (Paris, 1726), p. 56.

3. Nicolas Fréret, *Défense de la chronologie fondée sur les monumens de l'histoire ancienne, contre le système chronologique de M. Newton* (Paris, 1758), preface, p. ix.

4. Fréret's *Réflexions* were entered in the *Registre* for 1724, folios 171 through 227. A version of this *mémoire* was published at the beginning of the one and only volume of Fréret's abortive *Oeuvres complètes . . . mises dans un nouvel ordre . . . par M. Champollion-Figeac* (Paris, 1825), pp. 1–65. Quotation is from folio 174 of the *Registre*.

5. *Registre* (1724), folio 186.

6. Abate Antonio Conti, *Réponse aux Observations sur la chronologie de M. Newton, avec une lettre de M. l'Abbé Conti au sujet de ladite réponse* (Paris, 1726), pp. 23, 26.

7. Conti, *Prose e Poesie* (Venice, II, 1756), 60.

8. Souciet, *Recueil de dissertations critiques*, II, 104–105.

9. Souciet, *Recueil de dissertations critiques*, II, 132.

10. Souciet, *Recueil de dissertations critiques*, II, 169.

11. Fontenelle, *Eloge de Monsieur le Chevalier Newton* (Paris, 1728), p. 29.

12. Clement of Alexandria, *The Stromata or Miscellanies*, in *Fathers of the Second Century* (Grand Rapids, 1951), II, 317; A. Cleveland Cox, the translator, rendered the Greek words as "figures of Olympus." In Migne's *Patrologia Graeca*, vol. 8, col. 781 (*Stromata*, Book I), "coeli figuris" is closer to Newton's interpretation.

13. Isaac Newton, *The Chronology of Ancient Kingdoms Amended* (London, 1728), p. 84.

14. Edmund Halley, "Remarks upon some Dissertations lately published at Paris, by the Rev. P. Souciet, against Sir Isaac Newton's Chronology," *Philosophical Transactions of the Royal Society,* XXXIV (1727), 205–206.

15. Halley, "Remarks upon some Dissertations," p. 207.

16. Fréret, *Défense de la chronologie,* p. 418.

17. Quoted from English translation, London, 1789–1790, I, ix–x.

18. Paris, Académie Royale des Inscriptions et Belles-Lettres, *Mémoires de littérature tirés des registres,* VII (1729). There is also a version in *Sur les fondemens historiques de la fable de Bellérophon,* in *Oeuvres complètes,* ed. by Septchènes (Paris, an IV [1796]), XVIII, 78–93.

19. Fréret, *Recherches pour servir à l'histoire des Cyclopes, des Dactyles, des Telchines, des Curètes, des Corybantes et des Cabires,* in *Oeuvres complètes,* XVIII, 39.

20. William Jones, "On the Gods of Greece, Italy and India," in *Works* (London, 1807), III, 391.

21. Cambridge, King's College Library, Keynes MS. 2.

22. Cambridge, King's College Library, Keynes MS. 2.

23. William Warburton, *The Divine Legation of Moses,* in *Works* (London, 1811), IV, 234–235.

24. M. A. Léonard des Malpeines, *Essai sur les hiéroglyphes des Egyptiens, traduit de l'Anglois par M. Warburton,* 2 vols. (Paris, 1744).

CHAPTER IV

The Birth of the Gods

1. Lescarbot, *Histoire de la nouvelle France* (Paris, 1612), p. 661.

2. Jacques Bénigne Bossuet, Bishop of Meaux, *Discours sur l'histoire universelle* (Paris, 1878), II, 227.

3. Thomas Burnet, *The Theory of the Earth,* English translation (London, 1684), preface.

4. William Whiston, *New Theory of the Earth* (London, 1696), p. 126.

5. Antonio Lazzaro Moro, *De' Crostacei e degli altri marini corpi che si truovano su' monti libri due* (Venice, 1740).

6. Georges Louis Le Clerc, Comte de Buffon, *Les époques de la nature* (Paris, 1780), II, 168–169.

7. Warburton, *The Divine Legation of Moses,* in *Works,* IV, 139–140.

8. Sextus Empiricus, *Against the Physicists,* translated by R. G. Bury (Cambridge, 1936), III, 13.

9. Cicero, *De natura deorum* and *Academica,* with an English translation by H. Rackham (London, New York, 1933), p. 137.

10. Joseph François Lafitau, *Moeurs des sauvages amériquains comparées aux moeurs des premiers temps* (Paris, 1724), I, 114.

11. *Correspondance littéraire, philosophique et critique par Grimm, Diderot, Raynal, Meister,* ed. by Maurice Tourneux (Paris, 1878), V, 363.

12. Johann Wolfgang Goethe, *Italienische Reise* (Zurich, 1949), II, 209–210.

13. Giambattista Vico, *The New Science,* translated by T. G. Bergin and M. H. Fisch (Ithaca, 1948), pp. 36–37.

14. Vico, *The New Science,* p. 5.

15. Vico, *The New Science,* p. 5.

16. The 1730 edition had still dwelt upon a gradual postdiluvian renunciation of true religion in the traditional manner. *La Scienza Nuova Secunda,* ed. by Fausto Nicolini (Bari, 1953), I, 141.

17. Vico, *The New Science,* pp. 105, 106.

18. Vico, *The New Science,* p. 106.

19. Vico, *The New Science,* p. 105.

20. Vico, *The New Science,* p. 63.

21. Vico, *The New Science,* p. 54.

22. Vico, *The New Science,* p. 107.

23. Vico, *The New Science,* p. 104.

24. Vico, *The New Science,* p. 12.

25. Vico, *The New Science,* p. 35.

26. Vico, *The New Science,* p. 65.

27. Vico, *The New Science,* p. 39.

28. Vico, *The New Science,* p. 40.

29. Vico, *The New Science*, p. 122.

30. Vico, *The New Science*, p. 52.

31. Vico, *The New Science*, p. 43.

32. Vico, *The New Science*, p. 40.

33. Giovanni Finetti, *Apologia del genera umano, accusato di essere stato una volta bestia* (Venice, 1768), p. xxiv.

34. Vico, *The New Science*, p. 56.

35. Vico, *The New Science*, p. 381.

36. David Hume, *Histoire naturelle de la Religion traduit de l'anglois avec un examen critique et philosophique de cet ouvrage*, in *Oeuvres philosophiques* (Amsterdam, 1759), III, 138.

37. Hume, *The Natural History of Religion*, in *The Philosophical Works* (Boston, 1854), IV, 419.

38. Hume, *Works*, IV, 429.

39. Hume, *Works*, IV, 422.

40. Hume, *Works*, IV, 428.

41. Hume, *Works*, IV, 428.

42. Hume, *Works*, IV, 421.

43. David Hartley, *Observations on Man* (London, 1801), I, 214.

44. Hume, *Works*, IV, 453.

45. Hume, *Works*, IV, 455.

46. Hume, *Works*, IV, 493.

47. The full title was *Du culte des dieux fétiches, ou Parallèle de l'ancienne religion de l'Egypte avec la religion actuelle de Nigritie.*

48. Charles de Brosses, *Du culte des dieux fétiches*, pp. 203–222.

49. John Hill Burton, *Letters of Eminent Persons addressed to David Hume* (Edinburgh and London, 1849), pp. 274–275.

50. Yvonne Bézard, *Le Président de Brosses et ses amis de Genève* (Paris, 1946), p. 193.

51. Hume, *New Letters*, ed. by Raymond Klibansky and Ernest C. Mossner (Oxford, 1954), p. 152: Hume to Mme. la Présidente de Meinières, July 25, 1766.

52. Bézard, *Le Président de Brosses*, p. 100.

53. Warburton, *The Divine Legation of Moses*, in *Works*, IV, 147–148.

54. Père Godefroy Loyer, *Relation du royaume d'Issyny, Côte-d'Or,*

païs de Guinée, en Afrique (Paris, 1714). There was an English translation in 1745, a German one in 1747.

55. Brosses, *Du culte des dieux fétiches,* pp. 192–193.

56. John Spencer, *De legibus Hebraeorum ritualibus et earum rationibus* (Cambridge, 1685). There was a Tübingen edition in 1732.

57. Brosses, *Du culte des dieux fétiches,* p. 267.

58. Brosses, *Du culte des dieux fétiches,* p. 187.

59. Bézard, *Le Président de Brosses,* pp. 103–104.

60. Paris, Académie des Inscriptions, *Mémoires,* XXXV (1770), 97.

61. Brosses, *Du culte des dieux fétiches,* pp. 184–185.

62. Brosses, *Traité de la formation méchanique des langues et des principes physiques de l'étymologie* (Paris, 1765), I, 220–221.

63. Brosses, *Du culte des dieux fétiches,* p. 224.

64. Brosses, *Histoire des navigations aux terres australes* (Paris, 1756), I, 44.

65. Brosses, *Du culte des dieux fétiches,* p. 285.

66. Brosses, *Du culte des dieux fétiches,* p. 200.

67. Brosses, *Du culte des dieux fétiches,* pp. 186, 228.

68. Bézard, *Le Président de Brosses,* p. 139: letter of August 20, 1757.

69. Its authenticity has been doubted by Franco Venturi, *L'antiquità svelata e l'idea del progresso in N.A. Boulanger* (Bari, 1947), and John Hampton, *Nicolas-Antoine Boulanger et la science de son temps* (Geneva-Lille, 1955), who quotes it in full (pp. 37–38).

70. Bézard, *Le Président de Brosses,* p. 238.

71. There are two editions of *Oeuvres,* one dated "en Suisse," 1791, in ten volumes, another Paris, 1792, 1793, in eight volumes. References in the text are from the Paris edition of *L'Antiquité dévoilée.*

72. The first edition of *Recherches sur le despotisme oriental* is dated Geneva, 1761; others are identified as London, 1762; Paris, 1763; Amsterdam, 1766; n.p., 1773; n.p., 1775. John Wilkes's English translation is marked Amsterdam, 1764. Quotation is from p. 22 of the 1763 French edition, which is believed to have been printed on Wilkes's private press in London.

73. N.-A. Boulanger, *L'Antiquité devoilée,* III, 184.

74. Jean-Jacques Rousseau, *Les Confessions* (Paris, 1950), pp. 201–203.

75. Boulanger, *Recherches sur le despotisme oriental,* p. 26.

76. Boulanger, *L'Antiquité dévoilée,* III, 348–349.

77. *Correspondance littéraire ... par Grimm, Diderot, Raynal, Meister,* V, 364–365.

78. Boulanger, *L'Antiquité dévoilée,* III, 3.

79. Boulanger, *L'Antiquité dévoilée,* III, 327.

80. Boulanger, *L'Antiquité dévoilée,* III, 325.

81. Boulanger, *L'Antiquité dévoilée,* III, 316.

82. *Examen critique de la vie et des ouvrages de Saint-Paul. Avec une dissertation sur Saint-Pierre, par feu M. Boulanger* (London [Amsterdam], 1770), pp. 192, 206–207.

83. Boulanger, *Esope fabuliste, ou Dissertation sur les incertitudes qui concernent les premiers écrivains de l'antiquité* (n.p., dix-huitième siècle), p. 63.

84. See J. Lough, "Essai de bibliographie critique sur des publications du baron d'Holbach," *Revue d'histoire littéraire de la France,* XLVI (1939), 215–234; XLVII (1947), 314–318.

85. See Herbert Dieckmann's introductory remarks to *Le Philosophe. Texts and Interpretation* (St. Louis, 1948), in contradiction to Ira O. Wade, *The Clandestine Organization and Diffusion of Philosophic Ideas in France from 1700 to 1750* (Princeton, 1950).

86. Paul Henri Thiry, Baron d'Holbach, *Le Bon Sens, ou Idées naturelles opposées aux idées surnaturelles* (London [Amsterdam], 1772), p. 7.

87. Holbach, *Système de la nature ou des loix du monde physique et du monde moral, par M. Mirabaud, secrétaire perpétuel, et l'un des quarante de l'Académie Françoise* (London [Amsterdam], 1770), p. 1.

88. Holbach, *Le Bon Sens,* p. 126.

89. Holbach, *J. Brunus redivivus,* pp. 52–53.

90. Holbach, *Essai sur les préjugés,* p. 367.

91. Holbach, *Le Bon Sens,* pp. 6–7.

92. Holbach, *Le Bon Sens,* p. 7.

93. Holbach, *Le Bon Sens,* p. 8.

94. Holbach, *Le Bon Sens,* p. 9.

95. Holbach, *Théologie portative,* p. 86.

96. Holbach, *Théologie portative,* pp. 69–70.

97. Holbach, *La Contagion sacrée* (Paris, an V [1797]), p. 1.

98. Holbach, *La Contagion sacrée*, pp. 2–3.

99. Holbach, *La Contagion sacrée*, p. 3.

100. Burton, *Letters addressed to David Hume*, pp. 252, 255.

101. Holbach, *Système de la nature*, II, 3, 4.

102. Holbach, *Système de la nature*, II, 6.

103. Holbach, *Le Christianisme dévoilé*, p. vi.

104. Holbach, *Le Christianisme dévoilé*, pp. vii–viii.

105. Marquis D.-A.-F. de Sade, *Cahiers personnels (1803–1804)*, ed. by Gilbert Lely (Paris, 1953), p. 42.

106. Holbach, *Le Christianisme dévoilé*, p. xii.

107. Holbach, *Le Christianisme dévoilé*, p. xvii.

CHAPTER V

The New Allegorism

1. The original edition (Rome, 1593) had been entitled *Iconologia, overo Descrittione dell' imagini universali cavate dall' antichità et da altri luoghi.*

2. Court de Gébelin, *Monde primitif*, I, *Monde primitif considéré dans son génie allégorique* (Paris, 1773), 3.

3. Court de Gébelin, *Monde primitif*, I, 4.

4. Abbé Ferdinando Galiani, *Correspondance*, ed. by Lucien Perey and Gaston Maugras (Paris, 1881), II, 201.

5. Court de Gébelin, *Monde primitif*, VIII, *Dissertations Mêlées* (Paris, 1781), xix.

6. Court de Gébelin, *Monde primitif*, I, 5.

7. Court de Gébelin, *Monde primitif*, I, 7.

8. Court de Gébelin, *Monde primitif*, I, part 3, "Du génie allégorique et symbolique de l'antiquité."

9. Court de Gébelin, *Monde primitif*, I, 13.

10. Court de Gébelin, *Monde primitif*, I, part 2, "Allégories orientales," 174.

11. Court de Gébelin, *Monde primitif*, VIII, lxi.

12. Paul Ernest Jablonski, *Pantheon Aegyptiorum sive de diis eorum commentarius* (Frankfurt, 1752), II, 172.

13. It was not published until 1795.

14. Denis Diderot, *Oeuvres complètes*, ed. by J. Assézat and M. Tourneux (Paris, 1875–1877), X, 491.

15. Diderot, *Oeuvres complètes*, X, 492–493.

16. Sylvain Maréchal, *Antiquités d'Herculanum* (Paris, 1780–1803), II, 103.

17. Maréchal, *Antiquités d'Herculanum*, II, 118.

18. Richard Payne Knight, *A Discourse on the Worship of Priapus, and its connection with the Mystic Theology of the Ancients* (London, 1786), p. 27. An edition with an introduction by Ashley Montagu was published in New York in 1957.

19. Pierre François d'Hancarville, *Recherches sur l'origine, l'esprit, et les progrès des arts de la Grèce* (London, 1785), I, 71.

20. Charles Dupuis, *Origine de tous les cultes ou Religion universelle* (Paris, An III [1795]), I, part 2, 386.

21. Dupuis, *Origine de tous les cultes*, I, part 2, 384.

22. Dupuis, *Origine de tous les cultes*, I, part 2, 412.

23. Dupuis, *Origine de tous les cultes*, I, part 2, 416.

24. Dupuis, *Origine de tous les cultes*, V, x–xi.

25. A.-L.-C. Destutt de Tracy, *Analyse raisonée de l'origine de tous les cultes, ou religion universelle, ouvrage publié en l'an III par Dupuis, citoyen français* (Paris, an XII [1804]), p. xlv.

26. Destutt de Tracy, *Analyse raisonée*, p. 15.

27. Destutt de Tracy, *Analyse raisonée*, p. xlvii.

28. Zoltán Haraszti, *John Adams and the Prophets of Progress* (Cambridge, Massachusetts, 1952).

29. Boston Public Library, Adams Collection: Joseph Priestley, *A Comparison of the Institutions of Moses with those of the Hindoos and other Ancient Nations with Remarks on Mr. Dupuis's Origins of all Religions* (Northumberland, 1799), Adams' marginalia (pp. xv, 5). The references to Dupuis, Court de Gébelin, and Bryant which follow are drawn from copies in the Adams Collection.

30. Dupuis, *Origine de tous les cultes*, I, part 1, xv.

31. Dupuis, *Origine de tous les cultes*, I, part 1, xiii.

32. Dupuis, *Origine de tous les cultes*, I, part 1, 73.

33. Dupuis, *Origine de tous les cultes*, I, part 1, x.

34. Court de Gébelin, *Monde primitif*, VIII, xvii.

35. Court de Gébelin, *Monde primitif*, VIII, xix.

36. Court de Gébelin, *Monde primitif*, VIII, lix.

37. Court de Gébelin, *Monde primitif*, VIII, lxii.

38. Court de Gébelin, *Monde primitif*, I, 107.

39. Court de Gébelin, *Monde primitif*, I, 100.

40. Court de Gébelin, *Monde primitif*, I, 104, 108.

41. Court de Gébelin, *Monde primitif*, IV, *Monde primitif considéré dans l'histoire civile religieuse et allégorique du calendrier ou Almanach* (Paris, 1776), 60.

42. Court de Gébelin, *Monde primitif*, I, 56.

43. Court de Gébelin, *Monde primitif*, I, 145.

44. Court de Gébelin, *Monde primitif*, VIII, lxvii, lxix.

45. Court de Gébelin, *Monde primitif*, I, "Vue générale du monde primitif," lxxii.

46. Court de Gébelin, *Monde primitif*, I, lxxii.

47. Court de Gébelin, *Monde primitif*, I, 59.

48. Jacob Bryant, *A new system; or, an analysis of ancient mythology wherein an attempt is made to divest tradition of fable, and to reduce the truth to its original purity* (London, 1774–1776), I, xiii–xiv.

49. Bryant, *A new system*, I, ix.

50. Bryant, *A new system*, I, x.

51. Bryant, *A new system*, I, xv.

52. Bryant, *A new system*, I, 147.

53. Bryant, *A new system*, III, 28.

54. The quotations are from a microfilm of John Adams' Letter-Books in Widener Library.

55. *Correspondence of John Adams and Thomas Jefferson, 1812–1826* (Indianapolis, 1925), p. 133.

56. *Correspondence of Adams and Jefferson*, p. 143: October 14, 1816.

57. *Correspondence of Adams and Jefferson*, pp. 146–147.

CHAPTER VI

Counterattack from the East

1. Johann Georg Hamann, *Zweifel und Einfälle über eine vermischte Nachricht der allgemeinen deutschen Bibliothek* (1776), in *Sämtliche Werke*, ed. by Josef Nadler (Vienna, 1949–1957), III, 192.

2. Quoted from James C. O. O'Flaherty, *Unity and Language: A Study in the Philosophy of Johann Georg Hamann* (Chapel Hill, 1952), p. 13.

3. Johann Gottfried Herder, *Aelteste Urkunde des Menschengeschlechts* (1774), in *Sämmtliche Werke*, ed. by Bernard Suphan (Berlin, 1877–1913), VI, 200.

4. Herder, *Aelteste Urkunde*, in *Sämmtliche Werke*, VI, 215.

5. Hamann, *Leben und Schriften*, ed. by K. H. Gildemeister (Gotha, 1857–1873), V, 684.

6. Johann Joachim Winckelmann, *Versuch einer Allegorie, besonders für die Kunst....* (Dresden, 1766), p. 3.

7. Winckelmann, *Monumenti antichi inediti spiegati ed illustrati* (Rome, 1767), II, 1.

8. Herder, *Ideen zur Philosophie der Geschichte der Menschheit* (1784–1791), in *Sämmtliche Werke*, XIII, 275–276.

9. This is the title used by Herder's son when he published it in *Johann Gottfried Herders Lebensbild* (1846); Bernard Suphan divided the fragment into two parts, heading the first *Über die verschiednen Religionen*, in *Sämmtliche Werke*, XXXII, 145–148, and the second *Von den ältesten Nationalgesängen*, in *Sämmtliche Werke*, XXXII, 148–152.

10. Herder, *Von den ältesten Nationalgesängen*, in *Sämmtliche Werke*, XXXII, 150–151.

11. Herder, *Von den ältesten Nationalgesängen*, in *Sämmtliche Werke*, XXXII, 152.

12. Herder, *Aelteste Urkunde*, in *Sämmtliche Werke*, VI, 387.

13. Hamann, *Konxompax, Fragmente einer apokryphischen Sibylle über apokolyptische Mysterien* (1779), in *Sämtliche Werke*, III, 220.

14. Herder, *Fragmente zu einer Archäologie des Morgenlandes* (1769), in *Sämmtliche Werke*, VI, 113.

15. Herder, *Aelteste Urkunde*, in *Sämmtliche Werke*, VI, 370.

16. Herder, *Vom Geist der ebräischen Poesie* (1782), in *Sämmtliche Werke*, XI, 249.

17. Herder, *Aelteste Urkunde*, in *Sämmtliche Werke*, VI, 392–393.

18. Christian Gottlob Heyne, *Martin Gottfried Hermann's Handbuch der Mythologie aus Homer und Hesiod als Grundlage zu einer richtigen Fabellehre des Alterthums* (Berlin, 1789), Vorrede.

19. Marie Jean Antoine Nicholas Caritat, Marquis de Condorcet,

Essai sur l'application de l'analyse à la probabilité des décisions rendues à la pluralité des voix (Paris, 1785).

20. Hamann, *Aesthetica in Nuce. Eine Rhapsodie in Kabbalistischer Prosa* (1761), in *Sämtliche Werke*, II, 197.

Index of Names and Titles

327

Index

329

RENEWALS: 691-4574

DATE DUE